A
PASSION
for
LEARNING

A
PASSION
for
LEARNING

The Education of
Seven Eminent Americans

PHILIP A. CUSICK

Teachers College, Columbia University
New York and London

Published by Teachers College Press, 1234 Amsterdam Avenue, New York, NY
10027

Library of Congress Cataloging-in-Publication Data

Cusick, Philip A.
  A passion for learning : the education of seven eminent Americans / Philip A.
Cusick.
     p.   cm.
  Includes bibliographical references and index.
  ISBN 0-8077-4567-7 (cloth) — ISBN 0-8077-4566-9 (pbk.)
  1. Education—United States—History. 2. United States—Biography. I. Title.
  LA230.C87   2005
  920.073—dc22   2004059829

ISBN 0-8077-4566-9 (paper)
ISBN 0-8077-4567-7 (cloth)

Printed on acid-free paper
Manufactured in the United States of America

12   11   10   09   08   07   06   05   8   7   6   5   4   3   2   1

Contents

A
PASSION
for
LEARNING

CHAPTER 1

Introduction

That education is a private and personal endeavor more than it is a public and institutional enterprise is a point that needs to be stated. America's concerns for equality and democracy have led to the establishment of a comprehensive and universal system of schools. An admirable undertaking, all agree, but one result is that the discourse about education has become largely a discourse about schools, and more particularly about the organization and running of schools. The assumption is that if the organizational issues such as curriculum, teacher preparation, standards, evaluation, authority, and finance are addressed correctly, then educational problems will be solved. In other words, America's conviction about the importance of education and subsequent creation of a comprehensive and universal school system has turned the discourse about education into a discourse about schooling.

This, it seems to me, overlooks the important point that education is an interior affair, worked for, achieved, and capitalized upon by oneself and for one's own purposes. It is independent of schools and independent of what the state or one's fellow citizens make of it. It is, as Freud argued, something one does for oneself. And so this book is about education as a private and personal rather than a public and institutional enterprise.

To illuminate this point, the book describes the education of seven eminent Americans, chosen for their distinction, diversity, and lasting contributions to American life. All had great natural gifts, but gifts notwithstanding; all had to build and then use an education to do the deeds that brought them distinction. Each chapter is about one person, tracing that person's education from early childhood into maturity. The accounts are based on the subjects' autobiographies, letters, and diaries, as well as the recollections of acquaintances and biographers. In addition, because the book's subjects extended their education in what Henry Adams (1918) called "the forces of the age," the chapters describe some of those forces and describe how the subjects continued their education inside the forces. And when appropriate, the accounts also include those life events, when "a door flew open where one had expected not anything to be and one found oneself in a landscape with its own light, where everything bore a new name, stretching further and further, to infinity" (Canetti, 1999, p. 204).

Stepladdering its way through American history, the book begins in earlier centuries with two people who had little schooling, Benjamin Franklin and Abraham Lincoln. The education of these gentlemen illustrates an autodidacticism tempered by interaction with others, and illustrates as well the benefits of early parental encouragement, early literacy, and early appreciation of the power of intelligence and the power of intelligent expression. Both Franklin and Lincoln carried on their learning with like-minded contemporaries and interested elders, the latter eager to share their learning with intelligent youth. In these first two and all of the ensuing chapters, attention is given to how the subjects extended their education in the currents of the times: how Franklin moved with his times from colonial loyalist to American revolutionary, and Lincoln, from the 1848 Wilmot Proviso, which sought to limit slavery, to the 1863 Emancipation Proclamation, which ended it.

The fourth chapter tells of the education of Jane Addams, born in 1860, founder of Chicago's first settlement house, and until she died in 1935, a lifelong advocate for social reform. Though more formally schooled than Franklin and Lincoln, Addams likewise benefited from literate and encouraging parents, early and serious reading, and association with like-minded companions. From her childhood she identified herself with large and transcendental ideas, and later she lived those ideas in association with others as she worked to make government responsible for its citizens' lives. Overcoming contemporary restrictions on her gender and class, Addams came to represent America's progressive movement and lived to see some of her efforts realized in Franklin Roosevelt's 1930s social legislation.

Both more formal schooling and a perhaps more difficult path are described in the chapter on black writer and activist W. E. B. Du Bois, who spent his long life using scholarship and advocacy to oppose institutional racism. Born just after the Civil War, enduring the worst of the Jim Crow era, and combining who he was with what he wanted to do, the Harvard-educated Du Bois decided early on that, through scholarship, he would illuminate and so reduce the irrationalities of institutional racism. But midway through life, he was forced to admit the inadequacy of study and research to attain that end, and so he turned to activism and politics. He helped to found and became the early spokesman for the NAACP's program of civil rights, advocacy, and uplift. He also pursued his private curriculum, and over the decades moved politically leftward.

The story of Jane Addams and W. E. B. Du Bois is continued in the chapter on Eleanor Roosevelt. Wealthy and well-connected by birth and marriage, Roosevelt had to develop her inner resources before embarking on the path that made her the most famous woman of her time. Her education continues the themes of early encouragement from elders and early identification with transcendental ideas, and also illustrates the importance of mentors and like-minded companions. Like Addams, Roosevelt was bound by class and gender, and well into middle age played roles established by others. But then, disappointed with her lot, she began to exercise her curiosity, intelligence, and social connections; she reeducated herself and spent the remainder of her life as a political activist.

Themes of early literacy and early attachment to serious ideas are continued in the chapter on J. Robert Oppenheimer, who during the Second World War "fathered" America's atomic bomb and whose story expands the cooperative nature of science learning, begun in the chapter on Benjamin Franklin. Oppenheimer's Jewish heritage expands the notions of ethical learning that characterizes the book's Christian subjects. A thinker and scholar like Du Bois, Oppenheimer too had to reeducate himself—in his case from research scientist to administrator and then to public man—in order to complete the atomic bomb and then deal with its political and personally devastating aftermath.

Finally, the book presents the education of Dorothy Day, pacifist, anarchist, and founder of the Catholic Worker, whose story allows further exploration of the ethical learning that underlays all of the subjects' educations. Like Eleanor Roosevelt and J. Robert Oppenheimer, Dorothy Day illustrates the power of reeducation as she turned away from her youthful and somewhat dissolute youth toward the self-abnegation and spirituality of the Catholic Church. However, she retained her socialist and anarchist ideals and came to personally illustrate, for modern times, the lives and teachings of earlier Christian saints. While all of the stories illustrate the importance of learning from others, Dorothy Day's relationship with Peter Maurin, "whose spirit and ideas [would] dominate . . . my life" (Day, 1952, p. 189) best illustrates the power of learning from others.

My goal is to present the subjects' education in their own terms, to illuminate what they said was important, and to pay attention to the instruction, readings, life events, and associations that by their own accounts contributed to their education. Franklin said he learned from Braddock's defeat at the hands of the French and Indians, so that event warrants an explanation. Eleanor Roosevelt spoke at length of what she learned from her husband, so his education and what she learned from him warrants explaining. W. E. B. Du Bois said he learned from the philosopher Hegel, and Dorothy Day from Jack London, so the chapters on Du Bois and Day include brief explanations of Hegel and London, respectively. Of course, there is infinitely more to say about each person than is said in these brief chapters. But the topic is education, and as close as possible, the text is limited to what each subject said contributed to his or her education.

Their educational experiences were unique, but the approaches the subjects took to education were similar. So the conclusion is presented, not as the sum of the subjects' learning, but as a set of pillars common to the education of all. The pillars were constructed from books, ideas, relationships, and experiences, then integrated into a dynamic whole and used to further learning and action. As an example of a pillar, each of the subjects developed—possibly stemming from early religious experiences—a sense of personal morality, a sense that he or she was to do something worthwhile, something for the common good. Another pillar was autodidacticism: When the book's subjects needed to learn something, they went and learned it, Abraham Lincoln learning law and Jane Addams learning labor legislation. All of the stories illustrate the importance of like-minded colleagues and intellectual mentors to continued learning, and illustrate as well the importance of making oneself and one's behavior topics of study. The science learning of Benjamin Franklin and J. Robert Oppenheimer illustrate the rational empiricism with which all of the subjects approached their learning; and the story of W. E. B. Du Bois, who read for 3 hours every morning and graphed his daily output of articles and letters, illustrates the importance of purpose and discipline. For each, education was a lifelong and personal enterprise rather than an early and institutional imperative. Men and women of action all, they participated in the major forces of their time. Even more, they helped to shape those forces as they continued their educations.

Finally, a word about what the book is not. It is not a statement about or a position on schools. Schooling appears, but primarily in terms that the subjects award it and when, by their own accounts, it contributed to their education. The brief and concluding discussion of institutional schooling suggests only that modern schools already offer many of the elements of the subjects' educations, but it is the responsibility of the individual to capitalize on what is offered. To go further would lead into a discussion about education as an institutional enterprise and students as sociological subsets, and would conclude with criticisms of the system and suggestions for its improvement. There is enough of that—in my opinion, too much. And so I ask the reader to abide my argument that education is a private and personal undertaking to illustrate that argument by describing the education of seven eminent Americans.

CHAPTER 2

Benjamin Franklin
1706–1789

Education is "not only formal pedagogy, but the entire process by which a culture transmits itself across generations."

(Bailyn, 1960, p. 14)

For much of American history, schooling and education were connected only loosely, schooling being where the young learned some rudimentary skills that might help them undertake an education. Only from the later twentieth century on have education and schooling been considered coterminous. It is appropriate, therefore, to begin this book with some educated people of an earlier time for whom schooling played only a minor role.

Benjamin Franklin is generally recognized by those acquainted with his life as "unsurpassed by any man in the range of his natural gifts and of the important uses he put them to" (Van Doren, 1938, p. iv). Fred Anderson (2000) called him "the smartest man in colonial America and beyond any doubt, the most ambitious" (p. 80). Franklin's accomplishments ranged from printing to publishing, to fire safety, economics, science, military matters, nation building, and personal and social behavior. Like the book's other subjects, he was an autodidact, deciding what he wanted to know and then setting about to learn it. He was also an accomplished writer and left an autobiographical sketch that "for vividness, simplicity . . . and faultless style stands among the few masterpieces of English prose" (Morse, 1917, p. 1). And like most Franklin biographies, this account of his education will rely on that autobiography for his early years and learning. Most important for our purposes is that he made himself the subject of study and left extensive accounts of his life, learning, and the place of education in his accomplishments.

Americans are fond of exaggerating the distance between their often-modest beginnings and later success, the point being that they "came up the hard way." Certainly, Benjamin Franklin could be said to have come up the hard way, the distance from his modest family and later fame being considerable. But as Edward C. Banfield (1970) has argued, social class is more a matter of perspective on the future than it is the possession of wealth, and Benjamin was born to literate and educationally minded parents who exposed him early on to good books, intelligent conversation, complex ideas, and a religion that emphasized study, hard work, and personal responsibility. Like the book's other subjects, he was, in the parlance of today, educationally advantaged.

Born in Boston in 1706, Benjamin was the 10th and youngest son and the 15th of his twice-married father's 17 children. The Franklins fit Bailyn's (1960) notion of a "patriarchal kinship community that [in colonial times] shouldered most of the burdens of education" (p. 16). On Benjamin's mother's side was a grandfather, Peter Folger, whom Cotton Mather called "a godly and learned Englishman" (Franklin, 1793/1958, p. 6). An uncle who lived with the family was an occasional poet who took a lively interest in his nephew's education. Benjamin's paternal grandfather wrote poems, and his father, a chandler, was a well-read and respected Bostonian who would invite people to dinner so that his children could hear intelligent conversation: "At [father's] table he liked to have, as often as he could, some sensible friend or neighbor to converse with, and always took care to start some ingenious or useful topic for discourse, which might tend to improve the minds of his children" (p. 8).

Massachusetts at that time required towns of 50 or more citizens to maintain schools so that all children might learn to read and write, particularly those who might enter the clergy. And Benjamin was sent to grammar school at 8 years, "my father intending to devote me . . . to the service of the church. My early readiness in learning to read . . . and the opinion of all his friends that I should certainly make a good scholar, encouraged him in this purpose" (Franklin, 1793/1958, p. 6). Benjamin proved a gifted pupil and in his second year was to be moved to his school's third level, when his father "burdened with a numerous family, was unable without inconvenience to support the expense . . . and sent me to a school for writing and arithmetic" (p. 7). Benjamin found his new teacher "a skillful master, and successful in his profession, employing the mildest and most encouraging methods. Under him I learned to write a good hand . . . but I failed in the arithmetic and made no progress in it" (p. 7).

So ended Franklin's formal schooling, around age 10. In the early eighteenth century, childhood was brief and adolescence not yet invented, and economic necessity demanded that children work. Accordingly, Benjamin was apprenticed to his father to learn the business of making candles and soap, "employed in cutting wicks for the candles, filling the molds for cask candles, attending the shop, going on errands, etc." (Franklin, 1793/1958, p. 7). Knowing how to read, write, and perhaps add and subtract but, educationally speaking, on his own, Benjamin set out on his career of lifelong learning. He was, as he says, "passionately fond of reading, and all the little money that came into my hands was laid out in the purchasing of books" (p. 10). Among his early acquisitions were John Bunyan's works, Richard Burton's historical collections, Plutarch's *Lives* (1891) and Cotton Mather's *Essays to Do Good* (1710/1808).

Benjamin was reading the eighteenth-century mixture of history, morality, and religion that reflected his family's moral strivings. The Franklins were Protestant dissenters—Puritans—who had come from England in part to practice their religion free from the Church of England. Learning was central to Puritan theology, and study was an important part of living. Of the seven subjects in this book, Franklin, Addams, Du Bois, and Roosevelt were early on inducted into Puritanism's intellectual dictum, "to open the mind to the influx of truth and to steel the character to bear the truth and testify to it in one's actions" (Copley, 1923, p. 25). And because ethical learning was important to the education of all of this book's subjects, this chapter needs to pay some attention to Franklin's Puritanism.

Puritans believed that "the light of reason is the light of God and the voice of reason is the voice of God" (Copley, 1923, p. 26), and Puritanism stressed the study of scriptures, which "are the sole means by which any could assure himself that his will was exerting itself . . . in true harmony with the will of God" (Wendell, 1882, p. 6). As well as the word of God, one was to study the works of God. To the Puritan, Perry Miller (1953) says, "knowledge of natural things . . . [led to] knowledge and admiration of God" (p. 212). He elaborates:

> In Puritan thought, piety and intellectual heritage were reconciled . . . dogma and rationality were joined . . . the concepts of man as fallen and the saints . . . regenerated by grace were made compatible with [a] passion for learning, for argumentation, and demonstration. (p. 112)

In addition to a life of the mind, Puritan beliefs included a distrust of the world and a particular distrust of the human experience, which was filled with "failure, guilt, corruptibility, the precariousness of existence, and the challenge of moral responsibility" (P. Miller, 1953, p. 28). A Puritan had to do the right thing and be known for doing the right thing. Puritan readings teach the virtues of humility, order, and self-restraint, beginning with the individual who is to be personally watchful, self-examining, and internally disciplined. Puritans who had been elected by God for salvation would be known by outward piety, austerity, self-control, and humility. They would remain humble in the knowledge of their insignificance in the sight of God, avoid fleshly temptations, ecclesiastical error, pride, conceit, hubris, and worldly sins.

Puritanism is a uniquely American religion that connects learning and diligence with humility. In practical terms, one is to study, honor contractual obligations, work hard, discipline the self, and remain humble. Max Weber (1946) termed the Puritan set of beliefs "the Protestant ethic" and connected its doctrine of hard work and modest living to the emergence of American capitalism.

By his mid-teens, Benjamin Franklin gave up Puritanism and came to define himself as a deist. Like Thomas Jefferson, he believed in God and the moral teachings of Christ because they helped to distinguish between vice and virtue, but he attributed knowledge, not to revelation, but to sense experience aided by reason, and he saved his Sundays for reading. But he retained the Puritan combination of study, modesty, belief in being known as "a doer of good [over] any other kind of reputation" (Franklin, 1793/1958, p. 52), and a sense of duty toward community. Franklin's early Puritanism was combined with his later experiences with Quakerism, a religion that also stresses modest living and hard work, which will be discussed in more detail in the chapter on Jane Addams. For now, one may say that Franklin's education was early on influenced by his parents' religion.

Puritans took seriously the education of the young, and a child's early lessons were designed to promote, along with literacy, a sense of duty, self-awareness, and spiritual uplift. Consider Plutarch's *Lives* (1891), the stories of 40 ancient and notable Greeks and Romans that Franklin read "abundantly" as a child, and consider too the moral and social lessons contained in this passage from the life of Themistocles, an Athenian admiral, who suffered from too high an opinion of himself:

> At last the Athenians, unable any longer to bear the high distinction in which he—Themistocles—stood, banished him by the ostracism, and this was nothing more than they had done to others whose power was become a burden to them, and who had risen above the equality which a commonwealth requires; for the ostracism of ten years banishment was not so much intended to punish this or that great man, as to pacify and mitigate the fury of envy, who delights in the disgrace of superior characters. (p. 247)

Franklin reports also being taken with Bunyan's *The Pilgrim's Progress* (1678/1932), a widely read, fast-moving, and loosely connected set of allegorical and inspirational episodes about a pilgrim named Christian making his way toward heavenly salvation while overcoming a host of earthly difficulties. One of the stories tells of Christian and his friend, Faithful, in the town of Vanity, which was having a fair, called—what else—Vanity Fair. Christian and Faithful refuse to participate in the buying and selling of "honors, preferments, titles, countries, kingdomes, lusts, pleasures and delights of all sorts as whores, bawds, wives, husbands, children, . . . precious stones and what nots" (p. 108). For this offence, they were brought before the judge, Lord Hategood, and tried by a jury consisting of Mr. Hate-Light, Mr. Lyar, Mr. No-Good, and so on, which found friend Faithful guilty, whereupon he was burned at the stake and after which a shining angel "carried [him to] . . . the Celestial Gate" (p. 121). Then Christian left town with a new friend, Hopeful, to go on to further morally inspiring adventures. Like Plutarch's *Lives*, *Pilgrim's Progress* was an eighteenth-century favorite, an exemplar of moral heroism, and in Christian homes might be among the first books a child from a literate family read. Whatever else may be said about his education, Franklin was, early on, exposed to language, literacy, serious and transcendental ideas, and a "system of thought and imagery which underlay the culture's values and aims" (Bailyn, 1960, p. 18).

Benjamin's propensity for reading encouraged his father to apprentice him at age 12 to his oldest brother, James, a printer, and so he had access to more books. And he found a like-minded companion, John Collins, with whom he initiated a correspondence about books and ideas. An early fan of *The Spectator*, Benjamin endeavored to emulate that journal's writing. He would think about the events recounted, take notes, and see if he could improve on the writing. But "I found I wanted a stock of words, or a readiness in recollecting and using them, which I thought I should have acquired before that time" (Franklin, 1793/ 1958, p. 13). He set about to remedy this lack and found himself in time "lucky enough to improve the method or the language [of *The Spectator*'s story] and this encouraged me to think that I might possibly in time come to be a tolerable English writer, of which I was extremely ambitious" (p. 13).

Franklin also followed the practice of copying into a commonplace book passages from what he had read, sometimes putting the passages and ideas into his own words, and adding personal comments. Coming down from the Middle Ages, this practice had spread through England and America, and "involved a special way of taking in the written word . . . early modern Englishmen read in fits and starts . . . they broke texts into fragments and assembled them into new patterns while adding more excerpts. Reading and writing were therefore inseparable activities" (Darnton, 2000, p. 82).

Like his later colleague and fellow revolutionary, Alexander Hamilton—who went to work at age 12, read on the run, and was always jotting down facts in his pay book—Franklin kept a running account of his learning (Brookhiser, 2000). He gives us an idea of his continuing progress at age 16 when he was apprenticed to his brother's shop: "When I lodged in Little Britain [a rooming house] I made an acquaintance with . . . a bookseller, whose shop was next door. He had an immense collection of second-hand books. . . . we agreed [that] I might take, read, and return any of his books" (Franklin, 1793/1958, p. 39).

He was also picking up what he needed of arithmetic and studying John Locke's *An Essay Concerning Human Understanding* (1690/1975). Locke was among the mid-seventeenth-century philosopher-statesmen who, among others, proposed that all ideas and subsequent knowledge come from sensation and reflection. Locke rejected the then more common idea that truth was revealed in the Bible and that the function of education was the proper interpretation of scripture. According to Locke, there existed no revealed truth, nor any innate ideas, and even if our sensations are incomplete and reflections misguided, they are still our only source of knowledge. Locke extended his empiricism into civil society and argued that the social contract is not between ruler and ruled, but between men and women who, according to experience and reason, work out a way to handle civil affairs. Accordingly, kings have no "divine rights" and revolution—even against kings—is a legitimate reordering of civil society. Locke's ideas profoundly affected Franklin and all of the framers of the American republic.

Franklin was also taken with Xenophon's account of Socrates. Fascinated with the Socratic method of questioning, he began to use it to argue with his friends, but found that he was becoming a burdensome companion. Reflecting on the embarrassment he was causing by "obtaining victories that neither myself nor my cause deserved," he left off this method of disputation and retained

> only the habit of expressing myself in terms of modest diffidence, never using . . . the words "certainly," [or] "undoubtedly" or any other that give the air of positive-ness to an opinion. . . . This has been of great advantage to me when I have had occasion to . . . persuade men into measures that I have been . . . promoting. (Franklin, 1793/1958, p. 15)

Franklin was both learner and learning theorist. He learned from books that tell one not so much what to think as what to think about. He learned from people, observations, and reflection. His theory included the value of knowing a large stock of referential material and knowing too, that while learning is individual, understanding is social and best cultivated in fellowship and conversation. The latter requires the cooperation of others, and in order to achieve that cooperation, one needs to study and govern one's own behavior.

For example, when Franklin, a religious skeptic, found that his questioning of religious doctrine "began to make me pointed at with horror by good people as an infidel or atheist" (Franklin, 1793/1958, p. 18), he began to keep his skepticism to himself. In addition, he became careful to appear modest and to be aware that "disputing, contradicting, and confuting people are generally unfortunate in their affairs. They get victory sometimes but they never get good will, which would be of more use to them" (p. 122). All of which could be simply stated in some advice that Franklin later passed to Thomas Jefferson: "Never contradict anyone" (Wright, 1986, p. 3).

In his 16th or 17th year, Benjamin's brother James, to whom he had been apprenticed, publicly criticized Boston's religious authorities and, as a result, was locked up. Benjamin took over the running of the printing shop, but the apprentice was too much his own person and some trouble arose between James—by then out of jail—and Benjamin. No longer willing to submit to his brother's authority, Benjamin determined to strike out on his own. At that time, parents exercised proprietary rights over their children until their 21st year, and Benjamin's father was unwilling to allow his son to exercise his first choice, to go to sea. However, he approved of Benjamin's career in printing, and allowed him to seek a position in New York. Finding none there, Benjamin turned to Philadelphia. There he found a place in a printing shop, did some further apprenticing in London, returned to Philadelphia, started his own shop, and became a successful printer and publisher, general businessman, and in time, a pillar of the Pennsylvania colony.

Franklin had had earlier ambitions about higher education, which was then reserved for those who went to England or to Harvard or William and Mary to become ministers. He had wanted to attend Harvard, but later dismissed that institution with the autodidact's disdain, referring to it as a "Temple of Learning, where, they learn little more than how to carry themselves handsomely and enter a room genteelly and from whence they return . . . as great blockheads as ever only more proud and self-conceited" (Van Doren, 1938, p. 23).

Rather than formal schooling, Franklin read and studied on his own and then availed himself of a network of friendships with other young men also interested in learning. Until the later twentieth century, entertainment was conversation—among many it still is—and groups of educationally minded young people would gather for readings, discussions, and debates. To pursue his learning and his desire for stimulating companionship, Franklin initiated the Junto Club for apprentices like himself, desirous of learning and wanting to discuss books and ideas. Such associations were common in eighteenth- and nineteenth-century America, and they served as graduate seminars for unschooled but eager-to-learn young people. Abraham Lincoln made his first speech before such a group in 1830. Later nineteenth-century author, Hamlin Garland (1899) found them in the Nebraska territory in the 1880s.

Always the organizer, Franklin suggested that each member should bring discussion questions on matters of morals, politics, or philosophy, and each would take his turn producing an essay for a topical issue: "Had members encountered a citizen failing in his business and if so, what was the cause? . . . Were certain citizens thriving and why? Had any citizen accomplished a praiseworthy feat? How might it be emulated?" (Brands, 2000, p. 92).

Combining the functions of book clubs and junior chambers of commerce, these social units were made up of doers and learners, curious and civic-minded young people, anxious to improve themselves and their community. Members were encouraged to recruit additional members and to form their own chapters. Franklin later used this network to promote such projects as a paid police force, circulating library, volunteer fire company, fire insurance company, and public hospital. The members' minds grew as their world grew and, along with Franklin, they were changing themselves and their community.

Franklin was advantaged by an educationally minded family, by immersion in a religion that stressed learning and connected learning to virtue, by his own studies, and by association with other people intent on improving themselves. An additional link in this educational chain is the wisdom and encouragement of elders. Today, promising young people find—it is hoped—their wise elders in school. But in eighteenth-century America, unschooled and ambitious young people had to create their own opportunities, and elders had to find promising young people wherever they could. Accordingly, Franklin's knowledge and ability to converse gained him notice by people who cared about books and ideas and who were on the lookout for talented youth. George Washington, who had slightly more schooling than Franklin—there is a record of his studying geometry—had his career advanced by the wealthy and influential Fairfax family, who were impressed by his mature demeanor and excellent horsemanship. Franklin had no influential neighbors, but he was acquainted with books and ideas, and was noticed by older and learned people who encouraged him. As he says, "a merchant, an ingenious, sensible man . . . who had a pretty collection of books and who frequented our printing house, took notice of me, invited me to see his library, and very kindly proposed to lend me such books as I chose to read" (Franklin, 1793/1958, p. 11).

Later, he was on a sea passage from Boston to New York, and another passenger, William Burnet, governor of New York and New Jersey (1720–1728), had heard from "the captain that a young man, one of his passengers, had a great many books, [and] desired [the Captain] to bring me to see him. . . . The Governor received me with great civility, showed me his library . . . and we had a good deal of conversation about books and authors" (Franklin, 1793/1958, p. 29).

Reading Franklin, one has the impression that mid-eighteenth-century America was a land of educational opportunity; open, fluid, and accessible to those serious about and willing to avail themselves of learning. That it was mostly limited to white men is true and a point I will address in later chapters; but limits of race and gender notwithstanding, as presented by Franklin, this system appears natural and has the advantage of being based more on merit than class. Of course, social distinctions were as prevalent in Franklin's time as they are today. But learning is a great equalizer and inside that larger and class-conscious society was a smaller world where people were judged on their knowledge and their facility with language and ideas. Franklin found further connections when contracted to print some paper money for New Jersey. Fulfilling the contract meant living for a time in Burlington, New Jersey, where he "made an acquaintance with many principal people of the province . . . my mind having been much more improved by reading . . . my conversation seemed to be . . . valued. They had me to their houses, introduced me to their friends and showed me much civility" (Franklin, 1793/1958, p. 51).

Thus in the absence of formal schooling, there existed in early eighteenth-century America, a system of transferring knowledge and culture across generations. In addition to family, church, and vocation, the system included groups of young people whetting their minds on topics of interest, and elders on the lookout for and willing to assist ambitious youth. Within this system, the young improved themselves, their elders found successors, and culture and learning were transferred across generations and spread throughout young America.

Along with fluidity and equality, the system was communal. While my topic is education and my unit of analysis the individual, Franklin's story shows that education's more solitary and early-acquired aspects— reading, writing, study—are not sufficient to explain later learning and accomplishments. As well as study, one needs discourse, criticism, and challenge. The three spiral back upon one another and so demonstrate Karl Popper's (1965) notion that the way to reduce error is "by criticizing the theories or guesses of others and—if we can train ourselves to do so—by criticizing our own theories or guesses" (p. 26). Popper quotes Erasmus: "Know thyself and thus admit to thyself how little thou knowest" (p. 16).

Franklin voiced similar beliefs about the importance of openness, criticism, and community. Speaking of how learning accumulates through multiple efforts, he states: "Even short hints and imperfect experiments in any new branch of science, being communicated, have often times a good effect of exciting the attention of the ingenious to the subject and so become the occasion of more exact disquisition, and more compleat [*sic*] discoveries" (Cohen, 1990, p. 38).

Following the notions of learning as a self- and community-improving activity came Franklin's first attempt at creating a lending library made up of books donated by Junto members. That effort failed, but fomented a second and more successful effort, a subscription society, with the members paying 40 shillings each and 10 shillings per year for the purpose of circulating books. Reflecting on his venture, Franklin offers his thinking about the place of learning in a free society. In his words, the subscription libraries had "improved the general conversation of the Americans, made the common traders and farmers as intelligent as most gentlemen from other countries, and perhaps have contributed to some degree to the stand so generally made throughout the colonies in defense of their privileges" (Franklin, 1793/1958, p. 64).

Each of this book's subjects has a theory of education, and Franklin's theory was that learning adds to knowledge, knowledge makes one more intelligent, and intelligence improves society. That argument formed the basis of Franklin's later advocacy of a country free of kings such as George III and proprietary heirs such as the English descendants of Pennsylvania founder, William Penn (discussed later in this chapter).

In addition to improving the self and improving society—according to Franklin—learning is the path to virtue; a learned person is a self-reflective person, a self-reflective person is a disciplined person, a disciplined person is a better person. Franklin may have left off the outward professing of Puritanism, but he retained its zeal for a disciplined approach to moral improvement and, like John Calvin, practiced the systematic reduction of his faults. He reasoned that such efforts would lead to personal happiness: "I knew . . . what was right and wrong. I did not see why I might always do one and avoid the other. But . . . while my attention and care was taken up in guarding against one fault, I was often surprised by another" (Franklin, 1793/1958, p. 75). "On the whole . . . I was by the endeavor a better and happier man" (p. 83).

Later, he worked out a scheme of virtues, among them temperance, silence, order, resolution, frugality, industry, sincerity, moderation, cleanliness, tranquility, chastity, and—at the urging of a Quaker friend— humility. He added that one should "rarely use venery but for health or offspring" (Franklin, 1793/1958, p. 12). This combination of learning, discipline, virtue, and internal satisfaction would suit a Benedictine monk. But Franklin was no monk: He associated freely with women; he was politically and financially ambitious; and he took care to behave in a way that would publicly enhance his reputation for hard work and virtue, which was good for business in Quaker Philadelphia. He explained his reasoning and subsequent behavior in his own writings:

> I dressed plain. . . . I never went out a fishing or shooting; . . . and to show that I was not above my business, I sometimes brought home the paper I purchased at the stores thro' the streets on a wheelbarrow. Thus being es-teemed an industrious, thriving, young man and paying duly for what I bought . . . I went on swimmingly. (Franklin, 1793/1958, p. 60)

Not everyone is taken with Franklin. To some, his hyperrational ap-proach indicates contrivance and a lack of passion. Nathaniel Hawthorne complained that Franklin's advice was "all about getting money and sav-ing it" (Wright, 1986, p. 2). Herman Melville saw Franklin as full of platitudes, obtrusive advice, and mock friendliness, "possessed of a book-keeper's mind, and altogether of that race of men who were keen observ-ers of the main chance" (Wright, 1986, p. 2). Loyalists—his son William among them—thought him a traitor, and his Quaker enemies considered him a "crafty and lecherous old hypocrite" (Wright, 1986, p. 2). The latter accusation stemmed from his fathering a child—William—out of wedlock, his lifelong passion for women—and, as he aged, younger women—and his virtual abandonment of his wife. Wright (1986) praises Franklin for his "moral arithmetic" approach, but points out that in all of Franklin's descriptions of his travel, even in Scotland, he left no de-scription of scenery. Franklin's critics say that his writings, particularly the *Autobiography*, are calculated mainly to leave a false impression of virtue.

Some of the criticisms may be true. But there is no indication that Franklin's search for knowledge and personal improvement was anything less than an attempt to make himself into a person he could admire. And his critics ignore his Puritan background that instilled in him the ideas of self-scrutiny, outward humility, and importance of community. His critics ignore too his scientific work, contributions to public education, accomplishments on behalf of Pennsylvania, and later efforts in the American Revolution.

A successful printer and book seller, Franklin became also the publisher of the popular *Pennsylvania Gazette*, which he filled with the comings and goings of ships, items lost and found, advertisements, legal matters, and whatever news could be gotten in those word-of-mouth days. Franklin was also the public printer for Pennsylvania as well as for the colonies of Delaware, New Jersey, and Maryland. He augmented his publishing ventures by running the post office in Pennsylvania, which he organized so that the mail—carrying his own *Gazette*—would travel more often and dependably. He was also an enterprising capitalist, setting up his former and trusted apprentices in their own shops.

Benjamin Franklin wrote many of the things he printed, often using fictitious names, a practice that he began when he was with his brother James and publishing pieces under the name of Widow Silence DoGood. At one time, he had Widow DoGood suggesting that, since the British Parliament sent convicts to the American colonies, the colonies should return the favor by sending rattlesnakes to England where they could be let loose in the gardens of the nobles. It was more than a fair exchange as Widow DoGood reasoned: At least rattlesnakes give warning before they strike. And from 1732 to 1758, he wrote annual editions of what proved to be one of the most famous books of the eighteenth century, *Poor Richard's Almanac.*

Almanacs were a profitable and competitive enterprise and Franklin explained his entry into the field by predicting that Titan Leeds, a rival almanac publisher, was about to die. Somewhat put out by the news of his impending demise, Leeds protested in his own gazette that Franklin was wrong—in addition to being a "false predicter, an ignorant and presumptuous predicter, a conceited scribbler, a liar, a fool"—and that he, Leeds, was neither dead nor about to die (Brands, 2000, p. 127). Poor Richard took the rebuttal as proof that Leeds—in asserting that he was alive—was mistaken. Leeds had to be dead because he "was too civil a man to use an old friend so shamefully; because the stars had predicted his death and they were not to be disappointed [and] that he should die [and] because he should die punctually at the hour named" (McMaster, 1970, p. 105).

After Leeds actually died, Franklin had him coming back from the grave to spread gossip about other almanac makers, such as when he reported that one—a good and loyal Protestant—had gone to Rome, met the Pope, and turned Catholic. Franklin also predicted the weather, plus or minus 2 days, and if the prediction failed, he would in the next issue blame it on the printer's error. *Poor Richard's* was—in addition to an outlet for his humor—an opportunity for promulgating Franklin's beliefs about living. And in that spirit of advice giving, in 1758, he published one of his most famous pieces, Father Abraham's speech entitled "The Way to Wealth." Speaking of pride, Father Abraham says that it

> breakfasted with Plenty, dined with Poverty, and supped with Infamy. And after all, what use is this pride of appearance, for which so much is risked, so much is suffered? It cannot promote health, nor ease pain; it makes no increase of merits in the person; it creates envy; it hastens misfortune. (McMaster, 1970, p. 123)

While engaged in these business pursuits, Franklin continued his education. Just as today people desiring to expand their knowledge would learn to access the Internet, so in the eighteenth century, they might learn foreign languages, which they needed to access journals. In languages as in learning everything else—including swimming, which he learned by first reading a book, then teaching himself—Franklin did his solitary study, practiced what he learned, then used his newly acquired knowledge to leverage more learning. For instance, after he had learned French, some Italian, and Spanish, he "was surprised to find that I understood so much more of [Latin]" (Franklin, 1793/1958, p. 92).

Franklin's mind grew as his world grew, and by the late 1740s he had become one of the more respected citizens in Pennsylvania. He had his subscription library for reading and his Junto for debate, discussion, and public projects. He was the postmaster of Pennsylvania, a position that enabled him to propagate his varied enterprises as well as distribute his publications. And in 1749 he published in his *Gazette* an invitation to the citizenry to contribute to what would become the first public academy in America, which later became the College of Philadelphia and later still the University of Pennsylvania.

Like his views on slavery—that blacks lacked only education and that slavery was stimulated by greed and supported by ignorance—Franklin's views on curriculum were decidedly progressive, even Deweyan. His ideas for his academy included reading, writing, arithmetic, and penmanship. He proposed a plain but distinctive attire for the students, as well as frugal and modest living habits, and suggested that students "learn those things that are likely to be most useful and most ornamental" (McMaster, 1970, p. 151). Included in the curriculum were the practical arts of gardening, grafting, planting, and inoculating, with field trips to the better farms so that students might see how things are done. Further, he suggested that teachers should generate curiosity prior to instruction:

> There should be no oratory till the study of history had filled [the students] with admiration of great things done by the masters of oratory. There should be no geography until a knowledge of past events awakened a longing to the bounds, the situations, the exact extent of the countries wherein such events took place. (McMaster, 1970, p. 151)

Franklin promulgated the view that education was both the path to individual improvement and a communal treasure. The latter was a revolutionary idea at a time when the divine right of kings was taken seriously. We may credit Franklin for being among the first to think of offering to all children through age 17 a publicly paid-for education.

To further promote the country's supply of knowledge, Franklin founded in 1743 the American Philosophical Society in order to put scholars living across the colonies into contact with one another. The idea was to create a "network of kindred spirits that spurred [each scholar] to better and more original work than he knew he had in him" (Brands, 2000, p. 171). The society was open to those interested in books, ideas, natural science, and general social advancement. Mutual contact would increase not only the individual scholar's knowledge but the general knowledge about "planting, gardening and clearing land; and all philosophical experiments that let light into the nature of things, tend to increase the power of man over matter, and multiply the conveniences or pleasures of life" (Van Doren, 1938, p. 139). Appointing himself secretary of the organization, he encouraged discourse and correspondence; organized meetings—not as many as he would have liked—at which papers were presented; and sometimes, at his own expense, published members' works in his *Gazette* and distributed them through his post office. Like his postal roads, the Philosophical Society was an important link in the communication system that, in time, would assist the isolated colonies in becoming united.

Franklin had decided by 1747 that he had insufficient time for his interests and so left off the publishing and printing business to devote his time to his studies, reflecting perhaps the Quaker idea that to chase after wealth is an unworthy way to spend one's life. Time to study was the dream of a man who observed everything and for whom everything he saw incurred the questions of how and why: "I too am taking the proper measures for obtaining leisure to enjoy life and my friends, more than heretofore, having put my printing house under the care of my partner, David Hall, absolutely left off book-selling and removed to a more quiet part of town" (Van Doren, 1938, p. 123).

Modern Americans—at least the 65 percent who do not believe in alien abduction—believe that physical matters can be demonstrated empirically, explained in cause-effect terms, and understood by those of normal intelligence. These beliefs are the basis of what public schools teach and the basis of contemporary educators' resistance to theories such as those proposed by creationists. Independent of those beliefs, however, most people go through life only dimly aware of the way the world works. Changes in the seasons, the working of the internal combustion engine, what DNA is and how it works, the function of the Federal Reserve, or the internal workings of a computer remain mysterious. Despite the success of the public schools in creating a literate and numerate society and despite the best efforts of science teachers to awaken our minds, a high level of ignorance—perhaps due to a lack of curiosity—persists as to the workings of things.

Not so for Franklin. Curious, observant, and methodical, he was a born empiricist for whom the world presented an endless array of interesting questions that could be subject to investigation. He pursued science in the tradition of Isaac Newton, who advanced his ideas by questions, observations, experiments, evidence, inference to a larger class of events, and then into discussion where the ideas would be articulated, criticized, and sharpened. Imbued with a commonsense approach to the world, Franklin did not interest himself in philosophical questions about cause and effect or about the nature of ideas, as did his more philosophically inclined contemporaries and admirers David Hume and Immanuel Kant. Physical, not philosophical, observations were the subject of his inquiries. His solitary and mental weight lifting was accompanied by reflection and, simultaneously, by discussion with people engaged in similar efforts. To Franklin, education was not only knowledge, it was also freedom and society.

And it was endlessly interesting. Among the topics Franklin studied and wrote about were tides, shooting stars, salt in sea water, ocean currents, population projections (his work encouraged the economic theories of Thomas Malthus), navigating the North Atlantic, the common cold, whirlwinds, storms, inertia of matter, earth strata, the transit of Mercury, swimming, home heating, and the behavior of American Indians, whose culture he considered in many ways superior. He advised on how to sail the Gulf Stream, and developed a theory of geology that suggested the surface of the earth moved about on a liquid core. He wrote about numerology, northern lights, northeast storms, meteors, shooting stars, comets, free trade (Adam Smith was also an admirer), and—as early as 1750—the dangers of lead poisoning. He was equally comfortable with experts in electricity, chess, meteorology, geology, linguistics, mathematics, literature, philosophy, and politics.

Bernard Cohen (1990) reports that, as early as 1729, Franklin had determined that the caloric effects of the sun's rays are absorbed in varying degrees by the same kind of cloth dyed in different colors, and suggested that "soldiers and seamen who must march and labor in the sun . . . should have an uniform of white" (p. 32). He played the violin, guitar, and harp and invented an *armonica*, a set of globular glasses of differing size and capable of different tones. To his scientific studies, Franklin added mathematics and foreign languages so that he might better access progress made in other countries. When listening to speeches of the Pennsylvania Assembly, he would do mathematical puzzles, and he used the mathematics of heredity to ridicule England's notion of inherited aristocracy and projected population increases to argue that England could never defeat America in war. And he always maintained his system for learning, which included study, practice, discussion with like-minded friends, and, most important, openness to criticism.

Among his more famous efforts was home heating, then done by wood-burning fireplaces, which were expensive, dangerous, inefficient, and environmentally ruinous. After studying the matter, he created a stove—variations of which one may purchase today—that used less fuel and sent more heat into the room and less heat up the chimney. Franklin's description of the stove is a model of clear writing:

> The smoke proceeds in the passage that leads it under and beyond the false back and so rises into the chimney. The air of the room warmed behind the backplate, and by the sides, front, and top plates, becoming specifically lighter than the other air in the room, is obliged to rise. (Franklin, 1904, p. 93)

Franklin's major scientific contribution was knowledge about electricity, including his discovery that lightning is electricity. Before his time, lightning and the fires that accompanied it in towns of closely packed wooden houses were serious and ill-understood dangers. A then-common defense was ringing church bells in the hope that the bells would drive away the "stroke of lightning, the harm of thunder, the disaster of storms, and all the spirits of the tempest" (Cohen, 1990, p. 118). The skeptical Franklin had little use for such theories. He knew by observation and reading of others' ideas that lightning behaved similarly to electricity, and he had been studying other scientists who worked on magnetism, electricity, fluids, and elasticity. Through his experiments, he created a battery, invented the idea of positive and negative charges, discovered the function of insulation and grounding, and was the first to advance the notion that electricity can be stored. By 1750, his *Experiments and Observations in Electricity* was published in 10 editions and four languages, gaining him an international audience and membership in the Royal Academies of France and England.

Summarizing Franklin's education is impossible—he knew too much. But summarizing his approach to education, characterized as it is by blazing simplicity, is within reach. Some themes emerge: curiosity; early encouragement from the family; a religion that stresses knowing God's works as well as God's words; wide and early reading of books that introduce transcendental ideas; an early appreciation for the power of intelligence and the power of intelligent expression. Added is his habit of discussion wherein one opens one's ideas to scrutiny, debate, and correction, and his additional interest and efforts in business and public affairs that made him one of the most respected persons in the colonies.

All of the book's subjects continued their education in the social and intellectual currents of their time. Therefore, each chapter must pay attention to the confluence of those events and to the learning that its subject took from participating in them. In Franklin's case, the events are those that led to the American Revolution. Franklin did not start out as a revolutionary. He was loyal to English kings and denied any democratic leaning. "We are not so absurd as to deign a democracy," he wrote, but he also pointed out that insensitive behavior on the part of England's rulers might "make people inclined to a democracy who would never think of it" (Brands, 2000, p. 257). But as Pennsylvania's— and later, America's—representative to England, he was unable to convince the king or Parliament that their perspective on America was outdated and their actions harmful. Franklin's several-year transition from colonial loyalist to American revolutionary was a central part of his education.

The Seven Years War, called the French and Indian War in America, began in 1754 when a French and Canadian force moving down into the Ohio Valley took over Fort Necessity in western Pennsylvania, then under the command of young George Washington. The war went back and forth across western Pennsylvania, the eastern Great Lakes, upper New England, and New York for 6 years, ending in 1759/60 with English victories at Quebec and Montreal and on Lakes Champlain and Ontario. England's land victories were assisted by their naval victories, enabling them to supply their soldiers and allies while denying the French the right to do the same. The Treaty of Paris in 1763 stopped the shooting, but did nothing for Native Americans left without French allies, French goods, and French protection from England's colonists moving across the Appalachians on roads built for passing armies.

Prior to and throughout that war, Franklin had been among those advocating that the colonies adopt some common way to deal with Indians, Indian traders, land disputes, and defense; and in 1759 his ideas were presented at a meeting in Albany where "Franklin's reasonableness, his understated style, his willingness to work through others . . . and his ability to accommodate varying viewpoints made his arguments [for union] almost irresistible" (Brands, 2000, p. 238).

But England's Parliament resisted any American action that might promote self-reliance or self-government, and regarded the notion of colonies uniting for mutual protection as subversive. However, the need for common action continued. When the war ended, the Indians failed to understand that papers signed across the ocean gave Americans the right to their trans-Appalachian homeland. From South Carolina to the Great Lakes there erupted a series of Indian attacks on frontier settlements. Loosely called Pontiac's Rebellion, the attacks on settlers came as close as 80 miles from Philadelphia. Franklin, long an apostle of cooperative action and a member of the Pennsylvania Assembly, took charge of the local militia and supervised some fort building west of the city. As a result, he established himself as a proponent of vigorous defense, and so was named a colonel in the militia.

As his reputation as good citizen spiraled into military rank, so his citizen-soldier work spiraled into diplomacy when questions arose about who would pay for the defense of the then-western frontier. Franklin was among the Pennsylvanians who wanted the descendants of William Penn, still the colony's major landlords, to pay their share. The Penns thought that the colonists owed them rents, but as absentees, they—the Penns—had no obligation for defense. To settle the dispute, the Assembly sent Franklin to petition England's Parliament to turn Pennsylvania from a proprietary into a royal colony, with the possibility—unstated—that Franklin himself might serve as governor. He had partial success: Pennsylvania received some money, but the Penns—whom Franklin came to detest—would not submit to the Assembly's right to impose taxes.

The larger issue for the Parliament was how to protect the colonists from Indians, the Indians from colonists, and make sure that their French-Canadian subjects kept their newly sworn allegiance to England. All of this cost money, a matter complicated by England's debt, which during the French and Indian War had grown to 137 million pounds. To pay down the debt and to pay for what was essentially a military occupation of North America, Parliament in the late 1760s passed a series of money generating schemes, among them the infamous Stamp Act, which imposed a government fee on every piece of legal paper.

The colonists—at least the more vociferous among them—reacted with outrage to these impositions, as well as to the notion that Indian lands should be off-limits. Colonists had done as much or more of the fighting and had paid as much or more of the war costs. American merchants, among them John Hancock, neither wanted English agents peering into their ships nor having their goods seized for legal infractions. Lawyers—like Patrick Henry—and real estate speculators—like George Washington—resented the Stamp Act in particular; and Americans, in the midst of their own postwar depression, did not want to pay more for English goods, house British soldiers, or have their manufacturing restricted. They reasoned that they were loyal to the king, had the rights of English citizens, and did not like being taxed by aristocrats and merchants in Parliament. The results were riots; a boycott on British goods; burning of houses of Britain's representatives; and open defiance of sheriffs, governors, and English soldiers sent to restore order. The more thoughtful reasoned that the dispute was not only ostensibly about money and defense, it was about the fundamental relationship between the two countries.

And so Franklin, internationally respected and among the least anti-British, was sent to explain to England's leaders that their actions were setting them on a collision course with America. He reasoned from his studies of America's size, resources, and population growth that if conflict came, America would win: "America, an immense territory, favored by nature with all the advantages of climate, soil, great navigable rivers, and lakes, etc. . . . and will in a less time than is generally conceived, be able to shake off the shackles that may be imposed on her and perhaps place them on the imposers" (Van Doren, 1938, p. 363).

Initially, Franklin was a supporter of the notion that Americans could pay for their defense, but he saw the fragility of the English position relative to America's growing population and thought that Parliament's actions would alienate Americans. Moreover, he had been suspicious of the power of British arms since an encounter with General Braddock in 1756, when the general was setting out to western Pennsylvania. After procuring supplies for Braddock, Franklin had questioned him on whether it was wise to march 1,100 troops on a narrow road with his flanks exposed. Braddock had dismissed Franklin's concerns, and Franklin "was conscious of an impropriety in my disputing with a military man . . . and said no more" (Franklin, 1793/1958, p. 131). Late in the march, 400 Indians and French ambushed Braddock's army, killing that general and 800 of his soldiers. Always studying situations and inferring conclusions, Franklin remarked, "The whole transaction gave us Americans the first suspicion that our exalted ideas of the prowess of British regulars had not been well founded" (p. 132).

The situation deteriorated. British manufacturers supported the repeal of the Stamp Act, but threatened by America's manufacturing potential, they continued their mercantilist thinking. Americans boycotted British goods, resisted the military occupation, and threw the tea into Boston Harbor. Although Franklin proclaimed his loyalty and attempted to argue America's case with the more reasonable among England's leaders, he was unable to prevent the coming conflict. He had assisted in some victories, the repeal of the Stamp Act among them, but in the end he was himself hauled before the Parliament's Privy Council and blamed for the problems: "When I see that all petitions and complaints of grievances are so odious to governments that even the mere pipe which conveys them becomes obnoxious, I am at a loss to know how peace and union are to be maintained" (Van Doren, 1938, p. 475).

And so Franklin, by then an agent for Massachusetts as well as Pennsylvania, gave up trying to convince king and Parliament that their actions were as misguided as their thinking. In 1775, after 10 years in England, he went home to be the oldest member of the Continental Congress. For the next 2 years, he worked on every aspect of the Revolution except the fighting. He selected officers and obtained arms, powder, and trade, the latter being most important because the Americans had been cut off from their source of manufactured goods. He undertook a commission to Canada to see if some American-Canadian alliance could be worked out. He encouraged Thomas Paine to write *Common Sense* and printed and distributed that essay through his post offices. He edited the Declaration of Independence and was part of group appointed to devise the great seal of the United States. He worked on establishing a national post office and wrote the "Articles of Confederation and Perpetual Union," the first agreement of the then-separate colonies to join together. In 1777 he, along with John Adams, was sent by Congress—desperate for money and supplies—to France to try to work out an alliance. Aided by the 1777 victory at Saratoga, he negotiated the alliance of arms between France and America that 2 years later at Yorktown defeated Cornwallis's army and so ended the war.

After the fighting, Franklin helped negotiate a complicated settlement between America and England, France, and Spain, all of whom were distrustful of one another as well as of America's expanding power. In 1781, in his 77th year and after he had helped negotiate the full recognition by European monarchies of the American republic, he went home. Old and suffering from gout and kidney stones, he still applied his inquiring mind. During the Atlantic crossing, he kept daily records of the temperature, the air, and the water. He lowered a keg into the ocean to take the temperature at 20 fathoms. He studied the ship's rigging, suggested the use of watertight compartments to prevent sinking, and wrote about the management of lifeboats and how to escape from shipwrecks.

He came home to be elected president of Pennsylvania and representative of that state to, and later chair of, the Constitutional Convention of 1787, which drafted the Articles of Confederation. In the deliberations, he maintained a commonsense idealism about the civic virtue of plain people. He died in 1790. His last public act, a letter to Congress written in his capacity as president of the Abolition Society, asked that slavery—that "atrocious debasement of human nature"—be removed (Jorgenson & Mott, 1962, p. 505).

CONCLUSION

Benjamin Franklin was smarter than most of us, but he too had to construct an education in order to do the things he did. His approach was plain and he followed it relentlessly. Literate parents exposed him to language and ideas, taught him that learning was a way to live and a way to live better, and gave him as much schooling as he needed to begin his working life. Thereafter, he followed his habits of reading, writing, asking questions, reflecting, and conversing, all the time connecting what he learned to his own, later society's, development. At each level, he continued his observations and reflections, kept personal behavior among the list of topics studied, and through associations extended his learning and his influence. So he progressed from apprentice, to printer and businessman, to scientist, educator, revolutionary, and diplomat. Because he established, at each stage, a reputation for competence and dependability, he was often invited to take a larger role in events, where he continued his learning. That he did so by taking personal responsibility for his learning and then acting upon that learning makes him a fitting model for the book's argument that education is primarily an individual, not an institutional, responsibility.

CHAPTER 3

Abraham Lincoln
1809–1865

I was born and have ever remained in the most humble walks of life.
(A. Lincoln in Thomas, 1952/1993, p. 29)

Abraham Lincoln, unlike Benjamin Franklin, did not make his inner life a subject of discourse. He spoke almost nothing of his personal life, his parents, his marriage, or even his many friendships. Lacking the modern penchant for endlessly explaining oneself, he was, in the words of a long-time acquaintance, "the most reticent and secretive man I ever saw or expect to see" (Herndon & Weik, 1889/1930, p. 356). He was himself content to refer to his early life with a phrase from Gray's "Elegy Written in a Country Church-Yard" as "the short and simple annals of the poor" (D. D. Anderson, 1970, p. 17).

Some of what is known about Lincoln's youth comes from a brief autobiography that he wrote when running for president in 1859. More comes from his longtime law partner, William Herndon who, after Lincoln died and along with Jesse Weik, collected stories from people who knew him. Some of Herndon and Weik's (1889/1930) work—about Lincoln's personal life and marriage—is disputed, but much of what they said of Lincoln's knowledge and habits of study, particularly in his early years and later when he and Herndon were partners, is consistent with what others have said. All Lincoln students rely on Herndon and Weik. They rely as well as on John Nicolay, Lincoln's secretary in Illinois, and John Hay, who joined Nicolay in working for Lincoln in Washington (Nicolay & Hay, 1917), who wrote an extensive account of Lincoln's life and work. Of the many biographies available, this chapter will rely on Luthin (1960), Stern (1940), Tarbell (1900), Thomas (1952/1993), and an account of Lincoln's education by Houser (1957). The direct evidence of his learning will come from his letters and speeches.

The background is familiar. The Lincolns were among early Puritans who came from England to Massachusetts around 1635. Being people of some ability, they prospered there, as they did later in Pennsylvania where, by Lincoln's account, they became Quakers and then in Virginia where Abraham's grandfather served in the Revolution. In 1779 this grandfather crossed the Appalachians and went into Kentucky with Daniel Boone. Ambitious and hardworking, he was on his way to some prosperity, but in 1788 while at work in the field, he was killed by Indians. His son Thomas—10 years old and later Abraham's father—was with him at that time. According to Tarbell (1900), the family then languished and Thomas drifted down in the world. However, Nicolay and Hay (1917) refer to Thomas as a man "without ambition but not without self respect" (p. 23). He was a farmer, hunter, sometime carpenter, and a "very quiet sort of man . . . a moral man and in the crude way of the pioneer, religious" (Tarbell, 1900, p. 7). Thomas paid taxes, held minor political offices, served on juries, and married a woman named Nancy Hanks from another pioneer family. The pair had three children: Sarah, Abraham, and a younger son who died in infancy. Thomas continued his parents' westward proclivities. When Abraham was 7, the family went from Kentucky to Indiana; when Abraham was in his teens, to southern Illinois. Having wrested the land from the Indians, the pioneers commenced to fight with one another about who owned what and questions of land ownership fomented some of the family's moving.

The issue of Thomas's learning is disputed. According to his son, he "was a wandering laboring boy who never did more than bunglingly write his own name" (Lincoln, 1940a, p. 600). Herndon and Weik (1889/1930) report that Thomas's wife Nancy taught him to write and he could "in his later years, spell his way slowly through the Bible" (p. 12). But Stern (1940) says that Thomas "was uneducated and inclined to look down upon book learning as useless in the hard battle for existence" (p. 8). Whatever his literary level, he was a dutiful father. After Nancy died, he married a widow named Sally Bush Johnson. Herndon and Weik's account of their courtship is perhaps illustrative of the matter-of-fact way frontier people handled personal affairs. Probably lonely, certainly needing help with his children, and knowing Mr. Johnson had recently died, Thomas went to the widow and approached the matter directly: "Miss Johnson . . . I have no wife and you no husband. I came a-purpose to marry you. I knowed you from a gal and you knowed me from a boy. I've no time to lose and if you're willin' let it be done straight off" (Herndon & Weik, 1889/1930, p. 28). Sufficiently wooed, Ms. Johnson agreed to marry if Thomas would pay her debts. He did and they married the next morning. She took over and, according to all accounts, improved vastly the running of the Lincoln household and the education of her new stepson, Abraham.

With Tom and Sally, Abraham and his sister Sarah, Sally's three children, and Denis and John Hanks—the latter being relatives of Abraham's mother—the Lincoln house was full and busy, and the children worked from their earliest years. There was not much of a money economy, and whatever the family had, they got by growing, shooting, catching, or trading Thomas's carpentry skills. Abraham was expected from his earliest years to do what work it took to care for the family: "He drove the team, cut the elm and linn brush with which the stock was often fed, learned to handle an old shovel plough, to wield the sickle, to thresh the wheat with a flail, to fan and clean it with a sheet, to go to mill and turn the hard-earned grist into flour" (Tarbell, 1900, p. 21).

From the recollections gathered by Herndon and Weik, Abraham was good-humored and liked. If there was anything noteworthy, it was his interest in study and the way he connected ideas and language. Lincoln himself offered this recollection:

> I can remember going to my little bedroom, after hearing the neighbors talk . . . and trying to make out what was the exact meaning of some of their, to me, dark sayings. I could not sleep, when I got on such a hunt after an idea, until I had caught it; and when I thought I had got it, I was not satisfied until I had put it in language plain . . . for any boy I knew to comprehend. (Luthin, 1960, p. 11)

Occasionally, when Thomas thought he could both spare his children from work and afford the $1 or $2 per term subscription fee—and often at his wife's insistence—he enrolled them in so-called "blab schools because the pupils studied aloud in order that the master might measure their diligence from the volume of the babel" (Thomas, 1952/ 1993, p. 12). Nicolay and Hay (1917) describe the instruction taking place in "deserted cabins of round logs with earthen floors, and small holes for windows, sometimes illuminated by as much light as could penetrate through panes of paper greased with lard" (p. 34). Students learned their ABCs and the rudiments of reading, writing, and arithmetic from teachers who may have been themselves barely literate. Lincoln said that "no qualification was required of the teacher save readin', writin', and cipherin'" (Luthin, 1960, p. 10); and another early Illinois resident, Ulysses S. Grant (1885) said that his teachers were "incapable of teaching much even if they imparted all they knew" (p. 19). Herndon and Weik (1889/1930) report that "if a straggler supposed to understand

Latin happened to sojourn in the neighborhood, he was looked upon as something of a wizard" (p. 34) and one of Abraham's classmates describes a teacher as able to "teach spelling and reading and indifferent writing and possibly could cipher to the rule of three, but he had no other qualifications of a teacher unless we accept large size and bodily strength" (Herndon & Weik, 1889/1930, p. 18). Whatever the instructional circumstances, Abraham attended school for brief periods during his 7th, 10th, 14th, and 17th years. The total was less than 12 months, and of the experience he later said that he "went to school by littles . . . was never in a college or an academy as a student and never inside a college or an academy building 'till he had a law license" (Lincoln, 1940a, p. 601).

The popular image of Lincoln as an undereducated youth, schooled primarily in the use of an axe is partly true, the true part being about the axe which he referred to as "that most useful instrument which [I] was almost constantly handling until [my] 23rd year" (Lincoln, 1940a, p. 601). It is also true that his early world was a rough place, and besides the lack of knowledgeable teachers, contained several elements that might hinder an education. Superstitions, many of them having to do with the moon, supplanted knowledge, for example, "fences built when there was no moon would give way" (Nicolay & Hay, 1917, p. 42). Unlike more spiritually disciplined Puritans, those frontier people took religion as a means of entertainment as well as spiritual uplift. The citizenry "attended church, heard the sermon, wept and prayed, shouted, got up and fought an hour, and then went back to prayer just as the spirit moved them" (Nicolay & Hay, 1917, p. 54). There was also among the citizenry a general sadness, which Herndon and Weik (1889/1930) say showed up in Lincoln as "habitual melancholy" (p. 331). Nicolay and Hay, however, attribute that mood to the frontier's unexplained child-death, exposure to the elements, and threat of starvation should one fall sick and be unable to do the hard work it took to live. Lincoln, according to those authors, was no more melancholy than others who grew up in that place and time. In sum, during Lincoln's early years, there were several barriers to obtaining an education. Lincoln said as much, telling Herndon later that when he was young "there was absolutely nothing to excite ambition for education" (Herndon & Weik, 1889/1930, p. 34).

Houser (1957), however, regards that assertion as understatement, reflecting Lincoln's innate reticence, as well as the political benefits he gained by presenting himself without advantages. He had worked for the election of President William Henry Harrison (1841), a wealthy Virginian, who won the presidency partly on the basis of his manufactured image as a hard cider–drinking and corncob pipe–smoking frontiersman. Lincoln gained similar capital from his own later image as a log cabin–born rail-splitter. The rails symbolized his frontier background, and in 1860 those rails—some of which his cousin John Hanks brought out and displayed during Lincoln's presidential campaign—helped portray Lincoln as a champion of working men fearful of a slave system that would undercut wages.

A laborer and rail-splitter Lincoln had indeed been. Because children were bound to their parents until their 21st year, Thomas could rent Abraham out to neighbors who had the 25 cents to pay for his day's work. And so our future president worked by the day, clearing land, farming, splitting rails, and doing whatever it took to tame a wilderness. And in the process, he was enlarging his network of friends and finding his own way through a rough but egalitarian society where one was measured on one's wit and physical strength.

At the same time, he was an inveterate reader and avid learner who was encouraged in his mental pursuits first by his mother, later his stepmother, and father, and others who took an interest in a curious, intelligent, and lively boy with a propensity toward learning. Those who knew him attested to his extraordinary interest in acquiring knowledge. Not only did he write poems, a former classmate recalled, but

> He was always at school early, attending to his studies . . . at the head of his class, and passed us rapidly . . . when he was not at work, he was at his books. He kept up his studies on Sunday and carried his books with him to work so that he might read when he rested from labor. (Herndon & Weik, 1889/1930, p. 32)

Abraham's father had hoped his son would become a carpenter, but as his stepmother explained, "Abe manifested such a striking want of interest that the effort to make a carpenter out of him was soon abandoned" (Herndon & Weik, 1889/1930, p. 33). He was also, according to her, "the best boy I ever saw or expect to see" (Tarbell, 1900, p. 46), and she assisted his interest in study:

> I induced my husband to permit Abe to read and study at home as well as at school. . . . At first he was not easily reconciled to it, but finally he too seemed willing to encourage him to a certain extent . . . we took particular care when he was reading not to disturb him. (Herndon & Weik, 1889/1930, p. 32)

Sally Lincoln recalled further that in the absence of paper, Abraham would write with a turkey-quill pen and briar-root ink on a board, plank, hewn side of a log, or coal shovel. Later, he would copy onto paper and read her what he had written. Even then he was keeping his own commonplace book. And when he was somewhat older and doing farm-work with his cousin John Hanks, the latter recalled that

> when Abe and I returned to the house from work, he would go to the cupboard to snatch a piece of cornbread, take a book, sit down, cock his legs up as high as his head and read. He would ask my opinion of what he had read and often explained things to me in plain and simple language. (Herndon & Weik, 1889/1930, p. 39)

That Abraham carried habits of study, reflection, and conversation into work occasionally dismayed his employers. One of them, John Romaine, recalled:

> He worked for me, but he was always reading and thinking. I used to get mad at him for it. I say he was awful lazy. He would laugh and talk, crack his jokes and tell stories all the time; didn't love his work half as much as his pay. He told me one day, "his father taught him to work, but didn't learn him to love it." (Herndon & Weik, 1889/1930, p. 38)

That view of Lincoln as a somewhat rough and irresponsible youth was seconded by one of his cousins who, in the election of 1860, de-scribed young Abraham as "gadding about the country barefoot, with his toes outrageously spraddled out in the mud, and instead of reading his books as brother John [Hanks] so poetically tells us . . . . would be rowdying around with a pack of wild young men" ("Lincoln On-line," 2002). But that young Abraham was a child of his time does not detract from the accumulated evidence that he was also a serious learner. Mini-mally schooled in institutions that kept no records, it is difficult to docu-ment his curriculum. But he had told a friend that "while he was a boy in Indiana, he borrowed and read every book he could hear of for fifty miles around" (Houser, 1957, p. 18). Houser, a professor at Southern Illinois University who was distantly related to Lincoln, took that state-ment seriously and spent 20 years looking into the matter. He began by asking what books were available to Lincoln and what he might have read if he had indeed availed himself of every book he could find. Houser concluded that there was no dearth of reading material, and indeed, he makes frontier Illinois sound like a land of educational opportunity.

First there was the Bible, which Lincoln read at home. Then there were the schoolbooks commonly used at the time, among them Web-ster's *Spelling Book*, the *American Speller*, Pikes's *Arithmetic*, and Mur-ray's *English Reader*, which Lincoln told Herndon "was the best school-book ever put in the hands of American youth" (Houser, 1957, p. 34).

Working around as he did, Lincoln became acquainted with people who had books they would lend him. William Weems, whom Lincoln referred to as "Uncle," gave him books and newspapers and encouraged him to write essays. Houser (1957) reports that Weems also secured helpful friends for his protégé "by showing Abraham's compositions to prominent people at the county seat" (p. 17). And if Lincoln read what he could find, then he could access an increasing number of the area's private libraries. The local constable lent him Scott's *Lessons in Elocution*, which contained passages from Shakespeare, *The Arabian Nights*, and the *Revised Statutes of Indiana*, which contained the Declaration of Independence, the Constitution, and the Northwest Ordinance. And from a friendly merchant, he obtained and read William Grimshaw's *History of the United States* and a biography of George Washington. He also read *Robinson Crusoe, Pilgrim's Progress*, and *Aesop's Fables*. In his early years in Illinois, he was acquainted with Major William Warnick and from him obtained and read the *Revised Code of Laws of Illinois* and a life of Napoleon. With the local postmaster, a graduate of Dartmouth, he read the poetry of Shakespeare and Burns, and throughout his life, he would recite long passages from both. Moreover, Houser argues that some of Lincoln's early teachers, far from being illiterate, were good grammarians and penmen as well as serious about their profession. His last teacher, a Mr. Dorsey, never forgot his favorite pupil and predicted, in 1829, that if he lived, Abraham would become a great man.

Houser (1957) argues further that the newer settlers were more schooled than the early pioneers and Lincoln benefited from the area's intellectual elevation. Several academies and colleges were springing up. Among them were Transylvania University in Lexington and Vincennes University in Vincennes, Indiana—both attended by later Confederate president, Jefferson Davis—as well as the Salem Academy in Bardstown, Hampton Sidney College in Western Virginia, Jefferson Seminary in Louisville, and Owensboro College. Houser argues that those who went to schools passed their texts around and so Lincoln most likely had access to books such as *The Kentucky Preceptor*, a commonly used text, filled with selections from English literature. As well, he had access to books on moral philosophy, political economy, astronomy, geography, algebra, and surveying.

In addition, Lincoln was a frequent visitor to the home of the area's leading attorney, John Pitcher, and had access to that gentleman's 450-volume library. At his invitation, Lincoln also attended court and listened to the legal arguments. Most important, according to Houser, was the presence in southern Indiana of the New Harmony Social Experiment and the English Colony, assemblies of people who had purchased large tracts of land for communal and religious living. New Harmony was established by the Rappites, a religious sect from Pennsylvania, so called after their founder George Rapp. Their goal was to make the colony the "center of American education" (Houser, 1957, p. 39). New Harmony attracted several noted scientists, educators, and women's rights advocates, and its activities were well known and widely discussed in Abraham's neighborhood. Abraham's cousin, Denis Hanks, said that "for a time scarcely anything else was talked about" (Houser, 1957, p. 3). Lincoln certainly read the colony's newspapers and accounts of the experiment in other papers. He may well have borrowed books at both of those colonies.

In sum, as Houser argues, Lincoln did not go directly from a poor child scratching out letters by firelight on a coal shovel to a knowledgeable and sophisticated lawyer-politician with world-class speaking and writing abilities. In his early years, he availed himself of a wide range of opportunities for learning and acquired knowledge of worlds far beyond his own. By the time he was in his early 20s, he had read his way through a respectable undergraduate degree in humanities, had a newspaper habit, and was acquainted with issues and events far beyond his locale. He was a practiced essayist, had acquired serviceable and attractive handwriting, could spell down anyone he knew, discuss a wide range of topics, and following the habits of the age, kept a commonplace book wherein he wrote his ideas. Capitalizing on his opportunities for reading and reflection, he had connected his inner self to worlds beyond his own, and he was then creating an intelligible and usable version of that wider world in which he would live (Nagel, 2002). He was on his way to becoming educated.

In 1831 Lincoln declared his independence from his father—although he continued to help the family—and moved to the town of New Salem, Illinois. He was, in his own words, "a friendless, uneducated, penniless boy, working on a flat boat—at ten dollars a month . . . a piece of floating driftwood" (Luthin, 1960, p. 19). I have attended to the matter of his being uneducated, and concluded that he was merely unschooled. As for friendless, he was perhaps unacquainted, but for only a brief time. He had great natural attractiveness and all his life people would go out of their way to do things for him. Wherever he went, he was well liked for his modesty, tact, humor, intelligence, and kindness. And he was also respected among males for his prodigious physical strength. He could "out-lift and out-wrestle, any man he came into contact with" (Tarbell, 1900, p. 50).

He did not like physical labor and never spoke with fondness about his early years of clearing land, but the work left him terrifically strong.

He had regularly lifted loads of 400 pounds and was once seen to lift a chicken coop that the farmer said weighed 600. He could hold an axe out straight and steady with one arm and an early acquaintance recalled that Lincoln "could sink an axe deeper into wood than any man I ever saw" (Nicolay & Hay, 1917, p. 43). He was respected as well as popular with the community's boisterous young men and when he began to run for political office, he had their active and reliable support. He did not have to tolerate hecklers.

While clerking, and gaining a reputation as a popular conversationalist, he was advised that he needed to improve his speaking ability. Taking a characteristically direct approach, he borrowed a copy of Kirkam's *Grammar*, and "for weeks he gave every moment to mastering its contents. 'Well,' Lincoln said to his fellow clerk Greene, 'if that's what they call a science, I think I'll go at another'" (Tarbell, 1900, p. 67). His assessment of his learning remained modest. In his preelection biography, he wrote this about himself:

> After he was twenty-three, and had separated from his father, he studied English grammar, imperfectly of course, but so as to speak and write as well as he does now. He studied and nearly mastered the six books of Euclid . . . He regrets his want of education and does what he can to supply the want. (Lincoln, 1940a, p. 601)

Unschooled does not mean uneducated. Mr. Lincoln, like the other subjects of this book, was an autodidact who never allowed his education to be stalled by want of instruction. When he wanted to learn something, he went to the source, and in his case, the source for mathematics was Euclid. Consider some text of that gentleman's fifth and sixth books that, with the help of the local schoolmaster, Lincoln was studying.

Art. 113 CORRELARY TO PROPOSITION 38
Part I. If three straight lines are proportionals, the rectangle contained by the extremes is equal to the square of the means.
Part II. Let there be three straight lines, which taken in a definite order are K, L, and P; and let it be taken that the rectangle contained by the first and third K and P, is equal to the square on the second L, then it will follow that:
K:L == L:P (Euclid, 1908, p. 84)

Lincoln had a theory of education that was reflected in his efforts. If he wanted to learn something—grammar, mathematics, and later law—he simply borrowed or bought the books and went at it. For instance, when he needed employment and the opportunity to do some surveying arose, he "accepted [the job], procured a compass and chain, studied Flint and Gibson a little and went at it" (Lincoln, 1940a, p. 604). And later, when he was an attorney, he advised a young aspiring lawyer to "get the books and read them and study them until you understand their principle features . . . the books and your capacity for understanding them are just the same for all places . . . always bear in mind that your own resolution to succeed is more important than any other one thing" (Thomas, 1952/1993, p. 49).

Continuing his self-study habits, Lincoln, like Franklin, recognized the importance of elocution and in his 23rd year, joined the New Salem Debating Society where, from the beginning, he demonstrated a grasp of ideas and an engaging manner of speaking. At the same time, he needed an occupation, something more than the part-time laboring and flat-boat work. He thought of learning the blacksmith trade, rejected that, tried a store, but between his partner's drinking and his own reading, the store failed. There then occurred the Blackhawk War for which he volunteered and was elected captain. Blackhawk was a chief of the Sac Indians who had sold their land on the east side of the Mississippi, moved across the river, and promised not to return. But Blackhawk—an earlier ally of the British—regretted the sale and resented too the capitalistic penchant for turning everything into a commodity. He decided that "land cannot be sold. The Great Spirit gave it to his children to live upon and cultivate as far as it is necessary. . . . Nothing can be sold but such things as can be carried away" (Tarbell, 1900, p. 74). Whereupon he and some warriors came east of the river to reclaim their land, and after some brief fighting—none of which included Lincoln—Blackhawk went into captivity under the supervision of Jefferson Davis.

Lincoln went back to Sagamon, and continued running for office. And in a speech that presages his later and more eloquent efforts, he demonstrated an easy and appealing way with words and an openness to larger matters. At the time, canals were being superceded by railroads, and Lincoln was on the side of progress: "Upon the railroad, the regular progress of regular intercourse is not interrupted by either high or low water, or freezing weather, which are the principal difficulties that render our future hopes of water communication precarious and uncertain" (Lincoln, quoted in Houser, 1957, p. 92).

Lincoln lost the election but, as an indication of his popularity, received 227 of the 300 votes cast in his home town (Tarbell, 1900, p. 91). Returning to New Salem and working in the store, he met a man named Jack Kelso with whom he would read Shakespeare and Burns. He also studied law, as he had been interested in court proceedings from earlier years. At an auction in Springfield, he bought a copy of Blackstone's *Commentaries on the Laws of England*. He also studied a standard law book, Chitty's *Pleadings*: "The more I read [of the law], the more intensely interested I became. Never in my whole life was my mind so thoroughly absorbed. I read until I devoured them" (Tarbell, 1900, p. 94).

So Lincoln had gone through his early 20s, a period when the young look for something productive to do. He had decided on politics and set about learning the process, and won election to the legislature the second time he ran. The appointment had brought him into contact with older men, one of whom, John Stuart, encouraged him to pursue his law studies. As he had done with grammar and surveying, Lincoln took a direct approach:

> He borrowed books of Stuart, took them home with him and went at it in good earnest. He studied with nobody. He still mixed in the surveying to pay board and clothing bills. When the legislature met, the law books were dropped, but were taken up again at the end of the session. (Lincoln, 1940a, p. 605)

Again and without instruction, he was learning what he needed to know. And although he valued school where the young would learn to "duly appreciate the value of our free institutions [and derive] satisfaction from being able to read the scriptures" (Thomas, 1952/1993, p. 29), he did not allow his own lack of schooling to impede his education.

During his 20s, Lincoln's transition to law and politics was assisted by self-study, older mentors on the lookout for talented youth, and like Benjamin Franklin, involvement in wider issues. Illinois was becoming a populous and important state, and as a lawyer and sometimes legislator, he involved himself in the issues of the age. He expanded his acquaintance with people and issues by being a circuit rider, who along with other lawyers and a judge would travel around the territory, the judge hearing cases, the lawyers picking up business among litigants and arguing the cases before the judge and sometimes a jury. Lincoln preferred circuit riding to a position that he was offered in a Chicago firm. He told a friend that "if he went to Chicago he would have to sit down and study hard and that would kill him, and he would rather go round the circuit than sit down and die in Chicago" (Luthin, 1960, p. 146).

As to the matter of Lincoln's adult reading, there is a disconnect between the boy who read every book for 50 miles around and the adult whose associates said was neither a wide nor deep reader. Albert T. Bledsoe, who knew him well in his early Springfield years, said, "all that is said about his having been a great reader is sheer fiction . . . he possessed the power of patient thought; he could distinguish, analyze and meditate, and these things alone made him a formidable antagonist, both at the bar and on the hustings" (Luthin, 1960, p. 113).

One of Lincoln's early law partners, Stephen T. Douglas (not the Stephen Douglas of the later debates), responding to a question about Lincoln's reading reported, "I don't think he studied very much . . . he was not much of a reader" (Stern, 1940, p. 32), and law partner Herndon said that "Mr. Lincoln seldom bought a new book and seldom read one. Mr. Lincoln's education was almost entirely a newspaper one" (Luthin, 1960, p. 22). Indeed, he did love his newspapers. When he was appointed Salem's postmaster in 1826, a friend recalled, "Never saw a man happier. Said he could now read all the newspapers he wanted" (Luthin, 1960, p. 22).

But he also enjoyed poetry and plays. He read Shakespeare, Byron, and Burns, and was fond of reciting a melancholic poem by William Knox, "Oh Why Should The Spirit of Man Be Proud?" and Gray's (equally) melancholic "Elegy Written in a Country Church-Yard." His favorite Shakespearean play was *Macbeth*, passages of which he could recite, and he later enjoyed the poetry of Walt Whitman, whom he considered a great man. He did not read novels, and he distrusted histories and biographies, considering the latter too one-sided. But he enjoyed lectures and public readings, which were major forms of social entertainment. And what he read, he remembered. He had, according to those who knew him, amazing powers of concentration as well as "a blank, unapproachable habit of inner meditation; at times a somber, black, melancholy . . . at those times it was best to leave him severely alone" (Rankin, 1924, p. 149).

And so he continued his education in the law, which demands study, clarity of thought, and carefulness of expression. Regarding his absence of formal training, one of his partners commented:

> He learned his law more in the study of cases. He would work hard and study all there was for a case he had in hand. He got to be a pretty good lawyer, though his general knowledge of law was never very formidable. But he would study out his case and make as much of it as anybody. (Luthin, 1960, p. 67)

And another partner commented, "If there is one indisputable fact about Lincoln's work in the courts, it is that from the moment of his retainer, he played for keeps . . . [he] left no stone unturned in invoking every defense available to a client. . . . Every faculty . . . was focused upon the fact or problem before him" (Luthin, 1960, p. 148).

The salient events in Lincoln's early education were his disciplined approach, self-study, eagerness to learn, wide reading, and desire to articulate what he had read. His later education was characterized by all of those traits and an engagement in public affairs. As Heidegger (1949/1976) explains, being unfolds in time; and the argument of this book is that one's education, rather than something imposed by or obtained in youth, develops as one's being, one's life, unfolds. So just as in the previous chapter it was necessary to explain the events among which Benjamin Franklin moved from England loyalist to American revolutionary, so it is necessary here to explain the events that brought a one-term congressman and prairie lawyer of obscure origins into the presidency and the country into the Civil War.

Illinois entered the union in 1818 and by the 1840s was becoming a populous and important state. The frontier had moved beyond the Mississippi; there was a capital to build; towns, roads, canals, and schools to lay out; issues of governance and politics to be addressed. Inside this world, Lincoln had became a respected public man. He was ambitious, well acquainted and well liked, a veteran, and a lawyer who had a way with words. He was involved in the development of his town, and through circuit riding, had become familiar with the southern part of the state. He had been elected to the state legislature, was a member of the Whig party, and in 1846 had been rewarded by that party with a term in the United States Congress, where he was exposed to broad issues of westward expansion, states rights, and that most dominant issue, slavery.

Ostensibly, the important issue was westward expansion, but within expansion was always the question of whether the western territories and the states to be carved out from them would be slave or free. In Lincoln's time, slavery was supported by the South, the Democratic Party, southern planters, the United States Senate (where southern states held the majority), and Presidents Polk, Pierce, and Buchanan. It was supported passively by those who bought, used, or traded in the products of slave labor, and by northern workers who feared that freed slaves might compete for their jobs. It was opposed by the North in general and by Whigs, abolitionists, Free-Soilers, and others who found it—to varying degrees—repugnant, un-American, un-Christian, unconstitutional, economically ruinous, and a threat to free labor. Moreover, its opponents considered it absurd that while slaves were denied all basic human rights, each one could be counted as two thirds of a vote, a rule that kept the South—barely—in command of the House of Representatives. Whigs had opposed the Mexican War, which they regarded as an effort to extend the slave system, and in the 1840s they, including Lincoln, supported various versions of the Wilmot Proviso designed to limit slavery and keep it away from western territories and new states. The majority of Whigs were not intent on abolishing slavery as much as they thought it an outdated institution, which in time would fall of its own weight as it had done in England. To distinguish them from abolitionists, these Whigs were called unionists; they did not like slavery, did not want it extended, and hoped it would go away or remain confined. But unlike abolitionists who would have left a country where slavery existed—"If thy right hand offend thee, cut it off" (Menand, 2001, p. 4)—unionists did not want the country rent by the issue. Lincoln was a Whig and a unionist.

The problem was the hand-in-hand relation between cotton growing and slavery. America was growing more cotton, England's mills were purchasing more cotton, everyone in the known world was wearing more cotton, and American planters were selling more cotton. But cotton was dependent on slavery, and the success of cotton killed the hope that slavery would go away by itself as Thomas Jefferson had predicted, or at least be confined to the South, as the Missouri Compromise of 1820 had confined it. Determined to both preserve and extend their system, cotton growers wanted lands in new states where this relation of cotton and slavery could thrive. At the same time, the growers saw that northern industrial states were becoming more populous and richer, and if new states came in free, they would strengthen the North in Congress; thus slavery might not be allowed to expand, and it might be outlawed, even in the old South. For a time in the late 1840s, the issue subsided under Mexican War fever, but in the 1850s, there were a series of events that brought slavery back into prominence and opened the question of whether the Union would survive.

In 1850 the southern-dominated Congress passed the Fugitive Slave Law, which empowered federal marshals not only to pursue slaves into nonslave states, but to call any able-bodied person to assist in pursuit. In 1852 Harriet Beecher Stowe published her sentimental *Uncle Tom's Cabin* and increased the popularity of the abolitionist cause. Also widely read were the 1852–1854 newspaper accounts by then journalist and later landscape architect Frederick Law Olmstead, who traveled south to study the issue and presented slavery as a trap that had engulfed the whole region. Olmstead (1861) argued that slavery was inefficient and inferior to a system of freely engaged skilled labor; it benefited only the richest 2 percent of the population, and even they had their minds closed by the prohibition on talking about it.

On the political side, in 1854 Democratic senator Stephen Douglas—head of the Senate Committee on Territories—introduced the Kansas-

Nebraska Act, which repealed the Missouri Compromise's federal prohibition of slavery north of Missouri and opened the area of what is now North and South Dakota, Montana, Colorado, and Wyoming to slavery, should the voters of those areas decide they wanted it. Why Douglas, who was from the free state of Illinois, supported an act that nullified the Missouri Compromise is unclear, but it seems to have been what he had to do to get congressional support for his favorite causes, namely, railroads and western expansion. With federal prohibitions repealed and slavery open to popular vote, Kansas—which was going to be the next territory to enter the Union as a state—had a civil war over whether it would enter the Union as slave or nonslave. Should Kansas enter free, southern control over the Senate could end.

Further fueling the matter was the Dred Scott Decision. Scott had been a Missouri slave who, in 1834, was taken by his then owner from a slave state to army posts in Minnesota, then federal territory, and later taken by the same owner back into Missouri. Scott argued that because federal law prohibited slavery in the federal territory, the act of taking him into that territory had made him a free man. The leading point in the controversy came down to whether Congress had the power to prohibit slavery in federal territory, as it had done in the Missouri Compromise. The United States Supreme Court opined that slavery is a state, not a federal, issue; that the Constitution of the United States does not include Negroes; and that they cannot become citizens nor can they sue in federal courts. The Court had decided that slavery is moral and legal, and that the "all men are created equal" provision of the Declaration of Independence was not to be interpreted as prohibiting it.

The Supreme Court and Presidents Polk, Pierce, and Buchanan supported slavery. Congress was almost evenly divided between slave and nonslave representatives, but the Senate was controlled by slave states, and slavery's opponents were at their wits' end. There was open violence in the capital with South Carolina congressman Preston Brooks attacking and almost killing Massachusetts senator Charles Sumner. And with Jefferson Davis as secretary of war and busy transporting ordinance to the South, even the military was complicit. Seccession was discussed openly in the North and South.

On October 14, 1859, John Brown, a religious fanatic and a veteran of the Kansas Wars who believed that "a few men in the right and knowing they are right can overturn a king" (Nicolay & Hay, 1917, p. 199), took his 18 followers into Harpers Ferry, Virginia. Brown's goal was to arouse and arm the slaves and then—since he had no clear plan—see how things worked out. Things did not. The slaves did not join, the townspeople attacked, and Colonel Robert E. Lee with two companies of marines put an end to the matter. Brown's followers were killed or, along with him, tried and hanged. Jefferson Davis held the whole Republican Party responsible and Henry David Thoreau compared Brown to Christ-crucified.

Lincoln was a unionist. He did not like slavery, thought it unconstitutional, immoral, and socially and politically ruinous. While in Congress he had supported the Wilmot Proviso that sought to restrict slavery, had introduced a bill to outlaw slavery in the District of Columbia, and on behalf of the party had traveled in New England where he met William Seward, a leading abolitionist, later presidential hopeful, and even later the most trusted member of Lincoln's war cabinet. Lincoln did not adopt Seward's abolitionist views, but he studied that man's polished manner of speaking.

However, Lincoln's active political career ended in 1849 when his term in Congress was up and the seat went to another party loyalist. Lincoln went home to his law practice, and with his experience as well as his political and personal connections, the years between 1849 and 1854 were busy and profitable. He continued his study of Euclid and kept his interest in politics, but he declined to stand for the state legislature and the governorship of Illinois. He did compete for the U. S. Senate nomination in 1854—senators were then elected by state legislatures—and although he failed, the running kept up his interest and involvement in national affairs.

Throughout, he remained a loyal Whig and he supported the party and the party's candidates. For those efforts and because of the general respect in which he was held, he was asked in 1854 by his party to respond to Senator Stephen Douglas who was then touring the state defending his Kansas–Nebraska Act. With customary thoroughness, Lincoln, who "had been nosing for weeks in the State Library pumping his brain and imagination for points and arguments" (Luthin, 1960, p. 176), gave a highly regarded but unrecorded speech, which he enlarged upon in Peoria 12 days later. The latter was recorded; it was one of his most famous speeches, the one in which he framed many of the arguments he would use in later debates. That speech shows Lincoln's historical knowledge, the moral basis for his opposition to slavery, and his ability to put complex ideas into ordinary language: "Nearly eighty years ago we began by declaring that all men are created equal; but now from that beginning, we have run down to the other declaration, that for some men to enslave others is a 'sacred right of self-government.' These principles cannot stand together" (Lincoln, 1940d, p. 374).

He enlarged this point of the incompatibility of slavery with a free society with reference to Douglas's act of repealing the Missouri Compromise: "Repeal the Missouri Compromise—repeal all compromises—repeal the Declaration of Independence—repeal all past history, you still cannot repeal human nature. It still will be the abundance of man's heart that slavery extension is wrong, and out of the abundance of his heart, his mouth will speak" (Lincoln, 1940d, p. 369).

Lincoln opposed Douglas again in 1858 and the Lincoln-Douglas debates, which centered on the important issues of the day, drew national attention. Douglas won the election by a narrow margin, but Lincoln had become the spokesman for the new Republican Party, which combined unionists, Whigs, Free-Soilers, abolitionists, and others opposed to slavery and to the South's determination to spread it. The logic and clarity of his arguments had given a reasonable voice to slavery's opponents:

> When the white man governs himself, that is self government; but when he governs himself and also governs another man, that is more than self government—that is despotism. If the Negro is a man, why then my ancient faith teaches me that "all men are created equal" and that there can be no moral right in connection with one man's making a slave of another. (Lincoln, 1940d, p. 362)

Later in that same speech, he demonstrates his skill in argument. When responding to Douglas's assertion that repealing the Missouri Compromise was a demonstration of a desire for liberty, Lincoln replied:

> Some men live in dread of absolute suffocation if they should be restricted in their sacred right of taking slaves into Nebraska. That perfect liberty they sigh for—the liberty of making slaves of other people—Jefferson never thought of, their fathers never thought of, and they never thought of themselves a year ago. (Lincoln, 1940d, p. 341)

As to Douglas's and the Kansas-Nebraska Act's indifference to the matter of slavery:

> this declared indifference . . . I hate because it deprives our republican example of its just influence in the world; enables the enemies of free institutions . . . to taunt us as hypocrites; causes the real friends of freedom to doubt our sincerity . . . and forces so many good men among ourselves into an open war with the very fundamental principles of civil liberty. (Lincoln, 1940d, p. 348)

He extended his reputation in a speech at Cooper Union in New York, where northerners got their first look at him, and in a subsequent tour of New England, and became, although initially a dark horse, the

Republican nominee for the presidency in 1859. Lincoln was back in public life. As much as he hated slavery and argued against it, he hated more what it did to the country and so he came to represent a middle ground between unionists and abolitionists. He was opposed to extending slavery into the territories, as the Kansas-Nebraska Act would permit; was willing to take a strong stand while not alienating western democrats; and was opposed to the Anti-Immigration Party. His background made him appealing to working people, and he did not hesitate to use his life as a poor man's son as an argument for equality. In a New Haven speech, he combined the right of workers to strike with racial equality: "I am not ashamed to confess that twenty-five years ago I was a hired laborer, mauling rails, at work on a flatboat, just as what happens to any poor man's son. I want every man to have a chance, and I believe that a Black man is entitled to it" (Lincoln, 1940c, p. 592).

As much as Lincoln opposed slavery, he and his wife were born in a slave state, Kentucky; he had strong sympathies with local customs. A politician and obligated to work within the limits of the possible, he admitted right up until 1863 when he signed the Emancipation Proclamation that he did not know how to get rid of slavery except to let it expire of its own weight. But while he was sympathetic to those caught in a slave system, he ridiculed the two-thirds rule. Pointing out that South Carolina and Maine had the same number of Congressional representatives although the former contained half the number of free people, and that therefore not only slaves, but those like himself living in non-slave states, were denied equal representation: "I should like for some gentleman, deeply skilled in the mysteries of sacred rights to provide himself with a microscope, and peep about and find out if he can, what has become of my sacred rights" (Lincoln, 1940d, p. 367).

Always the logician, Lincoln drew out the logical conclusions of his opponents' argument:

> What will satisfy them? Simply this . . . cease to call slavery wrong and join them in calling it right. And this must be done thoroughly—done in acts as well as in words. Silence will not be tolerated. Senator Douglas's new sedition act must be enacted and enforced, suppressing all declarations that slavery is wrong. (Lincoln, 1940d, p. 369)

So Lincoln orated his way to the presidential nomination. Along the way in the presidential debates of 1859, he lured Douglas into saying that slavery, according to the Kansas–Nebraska Act, could be outlawed by state and local government, admitting, in effect, that should the local residents decide, slavery could be outlawed even in slave states. The slave owners' interests, arguing their moral and constitutional right to maintain their system, derided Douglas's suggestion as "squatter sovereignty" and regarded his assertion as betrayal. Subsequently, in 1860 they left the Democratic Party and put up their own candidate for president, John Breckinridge of Kentucky. Breckinridge drew the southern Democratic vote away from Douglas, thus ensuring the election of Republican Lincoln who—not even on the ballot in 10 of the slave states—won with 40 percent of the popular vote and 173 of the electoral votes. Whereupon—and through no fault of Lincoln, who was trying to preserve the Union and contain, not abolish, slavery—the southern states, arguing that it was they, not the Republicans, who were the true inheritors of America's Constitution, and it was they who were honoring the "all men are created equal" phrase of the Declaration of Independence, left the Union. Further, they argued that the Declaration was being translated from a statement about the body politic to an issue of racial equality, and northern interpretations were an attack on southern social institutions.

Our topic is the education of Mr. Lincoln who, when he became president, had a lot to learn. Not a military man, he became a student of military tactics, a student of his cabinet, and a student of his generals. He studied texts on military strategy and, before he appointed General Halleck, read every book that strategist-general wrote. When he was unable to make General McCellan attack, he considered placing himself in charge of the army. A practical politician, he had learned how to win elections, cultivate voters, compromise on issues, and negotiate the line between the free-the-slaves-at-any-cost abolitionists and the no-extension-of-slavery westerners. He learned that an antislavery platform would not get him the presidency; and after he was president, he learned to go slowly, try to re-create the Union without war, and later maintain a balancing act among northern abolitionists, and the border states—notably Tennessee, Kentucky, and Missouri—which while allowing slavery, had stayed in the Union, and where if the war were just about slavery, might leave the Union.

The issue of what stance to take on the matter of slavery was at the center of the war. Lincoln believed most northerners supported the Union but opposed emancipation. Before hostilities, he had promised representatives from the South "that the utmost care will be observed . . . to avoid any devastation, any destruction of, or interference with property" (Klingaman, 2001, p. 47). Later during the war, he insisted that the issue was not slavery but "whether a minority have a right to break up a free government whenever they choose" (Klingaman, 2001, p. 52). No one knew what would happen after the slaves were freed. Would they form an internal rebellion? Would they slaughter their former masters? Should they be drafted into the Union army and would they fight? (They were, did, and, by the war's end, 177,000 served.) Would they flood northern cities and compete for jobs at lower wages? Even worse for the North, the first two war years were marked by defeat, bloody draws, or simple inaction. Only after the Union loss at Antietam in later 1862 was Lincoln willing to turn the cause toward freeing the slaves.

> Things had gone from bad to worse . . . until I felt we had reached the end of our rope on the plan of operations we had been pursuing; that we had about played our last card and must change our tactics or lose the game; and without consultation or knowledge of the cabinet, I prepared the original draft of the proclamation. (Klingaman, 2001, p. 139)

Throughout his deliberations over the matter of freeing the slaves, Lincoln kept his habit of turning the sentences over and over in his mind, seeking advice from friends, cabinet members, until the document was, on January 1, 1863, ready. Accordingly, "All persons held as slaves within any state, or designated part of a state, the people whereof shall be in rebellion against the United States shall be then, thenceforward, and forever free" (Klingaman, 2001, p. 192).

Two years and a few months later and the war over, Lincoln was gone without having the time to leave us a record of his thoughts. But he left his second inaugural address, which illustrates his public prose at its poetic best and which Walt Whitman referred to as "the American poem":

> With malice toward none; with charity for all; with firmness in the right, as God gives us to see the right, let us strive on to finish the work we are in; to bind up the nation's wounds, to care for him who shall have borne the battle, and for his widow and his orphan to do all which may achieve and cherish a just and lasting peace among ourselves, and with all nations. (Lincoln, 1940b, p. 842)

CONCLUSION

Among the more appealing aspects of Lincoln's story is the way he overcame educational disadvantages, modest birth, barely literate father, early-departing mother, poor neighbors, and negligible schooling. But there were offsetting advantages: a religious mind-set that valued learning and connected learning to virtue, early-encouraging mother and step-mother, tolerant father, and adults—some of them teachers—eager to share their learning with interested youth. Like Benjamin Franklin, Lincoln had an active and curious mind and lived in an open and information-rich society. As well, he had a pioneer's self-reliance. He looked upon learning as a necessity that, like food and shelter, one had to personally go and get. And again like Franklin, he elected to live his life in the currents of time, and so was obligated to continue his education, which he did for all of his 56 years. If there is a problem with our portrayal of Mr. Lincoln's education, it is that it appears too natural, too unaccompanied by the stress induced by having to push one's mind into unfamiliar territory. But Lincoln shows us that the sticking point is not the material or its level of difficulty, but the act of choosing to be a person for whom learning and life are coterminous.

CHAPTER 4

Jane Addams
1860–1935

There is no education as that which comes from participation in the constant stream of events.

(Addams, 1902, p. 93)

Jane Addams's early fame was based on her work at Chicago's Hull House, which sheltered, fed, organized, and educated slum-dwelling immigrants who flooded the country in the late nineteenth century. Needing a "wider and more efficient instrument" to carry on her efforts (Farrell, 1967, p. 133), Jane, whom Faderman (1999) describes as "the virtual mother of social work" (p. 115), became active in city, state, and national politics where her combination of morality, idealism, and organizing ability made her a leader of the Progressive Era. That era emerged in the later nineteenth century when it became apparent that America's beliefs in universal equality had not resulted in the society of small farms and virtuous farmers envisioned by Thomas Jefferson. Rather, assisted by the Civil War and the country's emerging industrialism, a number of more inventive, lucky, energetic—perhaps rapacious—citizens had gotten very rich and influential. As it moved into its Industrial Age, America had become an aristocracy, with vast inequalities of wealth, opportunity, and influence. I will discuss this wealthy group further in the chapter on Eleanor Roosevelt who, along with her husband, Franklin, came from such people. For now, the point is that America's liberal and left-alone-by-government society had turned into a highly unequal society. And that situation forced a different—"progressive"—way of thinking about government and its obligations. As that thinking emerged from a combination of evangelical Christianity and economic liberalism, it evolved toward the belief that one's situation was a product of circumstance, not personal worth, and government should act in ways that countered capitalism's natural tendency toward accumulation and influence by the few.

Thus a movement that began with personal efforts by the more well-off to assist the less well-off turned into an effort to put social justice on the government's agenda. In America, Jane Addams was one of the effort's leaders.

Among the conditions that Jane Addams pressured government to alleviate were child labor, the unlimited workweek, the buying and selling of political office, public sanitation, and working conditions in factories. She started one of America's early kindergartens and Chicago's first public playground. Later, she joined the crusade for women's suffrage and women's rights in general, and was one of the founders of the American Women's Peace Party, which opposed America's entry into the First World War. Later, she became lifetime president of the Women's International League for Peace and Freedom, and worked to support the League of Nations. During the European famines that followed the war, she worked to lift the naval blockades and get food to the starving. Fighting off the 1920s accusation that she was a Bolshevik or socialist, she spent her latter years working for international peace and, among other things, working with Herbert Hoover to relieve famine in Russia. In 1931, she received the Nobel Peace Prize and saw her efforts reflected in President Franklin Roosevelt's New Deal legislation.

We will consider her education, like the educations of our other subjects, from her parents to her early reading, formal schooling, and her life's work and accomplishments. But the story of Jane's education is different from that of Franklin's and Lincoln's, a point that bears some brief attention. Franklin left a record of his approach to the task, as did Lincoln. And from the lives of both, it may be inferred that what they wanted to learn they went about learning, and when they wanted to apply that learning, they set about applying it. Both saw the world as open, knowable, and approachable for men with energy and intelligence. To be sure, each encountered limits of place and resources, but from their earliest years, both benefited from the openness by which men regard and judge, accept or reject, one another. Franklin's status as a poor and unknown printer's apprentice was overcome by his intelligence, learning, energy, and abilities. Similarly, Lincoln overcame his rough background with intelligence, personal appeal, learning, facility with language, and—important in the male world of all ages—size and strength. Neither Franklin nor Lincoln ever acknowledged that the barriers they faced were anything less than the natural order of things, and both benefited from participation in that male world, where merit and ambition find their reward.

Not so Jane Addams. Before she could go about the deeds that made her the most famous woman of her age, she had to overcome the restrictions placed on her gender, and in her case, its upper-class members. It was only a few years prior to her birth that feminists held the first meeting of the Women's Rights Movement and it was not until she was almost 60 that the Nineteenth Amendment gave American women the right to vote. When Jane was a child, Paulina Davis, the chair of the Women's Suffrage Convention in 1870, affirmed that, for women, the road to the ballot, to owning property, and to equality of education remained long: "Women . . . the slaves of prejudice, passion, folly, fashion and petty ambitions, and so they will remain till the shackles, both social and political, are broken, and they are held responsible beings" (Diliberto, 1999, p. 7). In accounting for Jane Addams's education, one has to pay attention to the part devoted to working through the restrictions placed on her as a woman.

Jane Addams was born in 1860 in the small Illinois town of Cedarville. Her father was a prosperous miller, farm owner, state legislator, and influential citizen who, with the backing of his family, had moved from Philadelphia—their earliest American ancestor had purchased land from William Penn—to Illinois. John was a friend and supporter of Abraham Lincoln; they had served in the state legislature together, and during the war, John had raised a regiment for Mr. Lincoln's army. Jane's mother died when Jane was 2; her father did not remarry for several years, and Jane and he were very close. She speaks of her "great veneration and pride . . . [and of her] adoring affection [for him]" and refers to her feelings for him as "so emotional . . . so irrational" (Addams, 1910/1998, p. 11). Later, while advocating passage of some factory legislation, she recalled being offered a bribe of $50,000 if she would "drop this nonsense about a sweatshop bill" (p. 27). She refused, but admits to being ashamed that she was even offered the bribe, her father being the one man in the Illinois legislature whose reputation was such that he was never offered a bribe because "bad men were instinctively afraid of him" (p. 27). John Addams, as Mr. Lincoln noted, "would vote according to his conscience" (p. 26). Inscribed in John's diary, the commonplace book that he carried all his life, are the words "Integrity above all else" (Diliberto, 1999, p. 25). The issue of integrity—adherence to moral and ethical principles—was central to John's and, subsequently, his daughter's life.

Jane attributes to her father her own ideas about ethical living and moral consistency. And because morality is reflected in religion, and because ethical learning is an important part of the education of all the subjects in this book, attention must be given to John's—subsequently Jane's—religious learning. Jane Addams's father was religious, her stepmother more religious, and early on, she was formally subject to what

Bailyn (1960) refers to as religion's integrating functions, its "thought and imagery which underlay the culture's values and aims [and which] provides the highest sanctions for thought and behavior and [brings] the child into a close relationship with the intangible loyalties, ethos, and principles of society" (p. 18).

In regard to her father's religion, Jane recalled an early outing with him in the woods: "We were in high spirits as we emerged . . . into the clear light of day and as we came back into the road, I categorically asked him: 'What are you? What do you say when people ask you?' His eyes twinkled a little as he soberly replied: 'I am a Quaker'" (Addams, 1910/1998, p. 16).

The Quakers, as the Society of Friends were called, were begun in 1651 by George Fox, an English minister and religious enthusiast who went about in a Jeremiah-like way: "Woe to the bloody city of Lichfield . . . the man in leathren britches has come" (Raban, 2002, p. 34). Fox, who knew how to read and to write as much as would serve to "signify his meaning to others" (Raistrick, 1950, p. 15), advocated separation from England's established Church because that church—with its rituals, doctrines, and hierarchy—too much resembled the Roman Catholic Church that earlier Protestants had rejected. Fox went further down the Reformation road, preaching that man did not need a church or even a congregation. What was good and true could be ascertained by an individual in contact with God, and his or her personal relationship would create a divine light within the individual, a light that would guide the person's life. Quaker practices consisted of silent worship (they were called Quietists), prayer, meditation (listening to the light of God from within), community, equality, peaceful living, simplicity, faith in human nature, and the absence of show. Both men and women knew the light, and women could preach, prophesy, and work alongside men.

The Quakers' outward passivity was offset by their fierce objection to civil and religious hierarchy. Individualistic, anarchic, and pacifistic, they were regarded as odd, isolated, and threatening to the established order. Particularly galling was their refusal to doff their hats to those in authority and to take public oaths, as well as their active proselytizing among non-Quakers. These practices brought them into conflict with both civil and church authorities. Tens of thousands were imprisoned in England, and Quaker missionaries were sometime banished. Four—among them a woman—who refused to abide by a Massachusetts banishment were hanged.

But in America and by the late eighteenth century, the Quakers' sobriety, hard work, mutual support, simplicity of living, and habits of combining the religious life with business practices had given them a reputation for stability and soundness. Also by that time and continuing on into the nineteenth century, many were respected and wealthy businessmen, among them the frugal owners of Nantucket whaling ships whom Herman Melville (1851/1996) referred to as "Quakers with a vengeance." Quakers were valued also for their opposition to slavery, work with prisoners, and missionary efforts among the Indians.

As to the matter of education, there were Quakers who believed education would produce the moral citizenry necessary for the functioning of society. Among the opponents of education, however, was Elias Hicks (1748–1830), a Long Island Quaker fundamentalist, who feared that education would draw his followers' (called Hicksites) attention outward rather than inward and would lead to the establishment of a hierarchy, which would be antithetical to equality. All of which would be irrelevant to this story except that, after John Addams had told his daughter that he was a Quaker, she replied: "'But that isn't enough to say.' 'Very well,' he added, 'I am a Hicksite Quaker.' And not another word on that weighty subject could I induce him to utter" (Addams, 1910/1998, p. 16).

Religion teaches that actions have moral consequences and Jane Addams learned about moral consequences early on. Among her first remembrances is having told a lie and subsequently being unable to sleep until she confessed her father. And he, with perhaps characteristically Quaker restraint, allowed that, "If he had a little girl who told lies, he was very glad she felt too bad to go to sleep afterwards" (Addams, 1910/1998, p. 8). Another early lesson was when she presented herself to her father in a new cloak that she was to wear to Sunday service. He admitted that "it was a very pretty cloak, in fact so much prettier than any cloak the other little girls in the Sunday School had, that he would advise me to wear my old cloak, which would keep me quite as warm . . . [and would] not make the other little girls feel badly" (p. 15). Upon reflection, she admitted that "it was very stupid to wear the sort of clothes that made it harder to have equality" (p. 15).

Jane Addams was a serious child, the daughter of a serious man. On one occasion, she speaks of asking her father about why God foreordains some for salvation, even before their birth and independent of their actions. He told her that it did not matter if she understood theological matters, the important thing was that "you must always be honest with yourself, whatever happens" (Addams, 1910/1998, p. 16). Later, in college, when pressured to accept—against her inclinations—a religious calling, Jane consulted her father who reminded her, "mental integrity above everything else" (p. 16). We may say that Jane Addams early on developed a sense of personal morality, social equality, and an internal drive to do the right thing.

She exhibited also a sense of her relationship with the less well-off. She wrote that, when she was 7 years old and saw for the first time a poor neighborhood, "I remember launching at my father the pertinent inquiry why people lived in such horrid little houses. . . . I declared . . . when I grew up I should of course have a large house . . . right in the midst of horrid little houses like these" (Addams, 1910/1998, p. 8).

There is more to Jane's early education than accumulated moral lessons and a desire to translate ethics into action. There is a seriousness about the mysteries of life and a desire to take part in great events. She was born into a time of what Fogel (2000) calls "a great a moral awakening" that accompanied the Civil War. "Thousands of children of the [eighteen] sixties and seventies . . . caught a notion of the imperishable heroism when they were told that brave men had lost their lives that the slaves might be free" (Addams, 1910/1998, p. 26). Jane speaks of her pride when showing visitors the picture of the colonel of the Addams Regiment, his sleeve pinned up where he had lost an arm. And she describes a family trip to visit Wisconsin's capital in Madison where war veterans kept Old Abe, the eagle that the state's regiments had carried through 36 Civil War battles. As she later recalled: "The entire journey to the veteran war eagle had itself symbolized the search for the heroic and perfect which so persistently haunts the young" (p. 25).

Jane also had a sense of the spiritual that perhaps came with her familiarity with death, so much more immediate in the nineteenth century than today. Her mother died when she was 2, President Lincoln when she was 4 (she recalled her father's grief), and many of the Addams regiment never came back from the war or came back for only a brief time before their funereal banners were hung. She recalled a farm always surrounded by sadness, the family having lost four of its five sons in the war and the fifth to a hunting accident. "When we were driven past this forlorn little farm, our childish voices always dropped into speculative whisperings as to how the accident could have happened to this remaining son out of all the men in the world" (Addams, 1910/1998, p. 24). Reflecting on the way death was distributed so mysteriously, Jane says: "We were overwhelmingly oppressed by that grief of things as they are, so much more mysterious and intolerable than those griefs, which we . . . trace to man's own wrongdoing" (p. 25).

Finally, there is Jane Addams's mysticism, her communion with the human spirit. She describes a time when she was 15 and called to attend the deathwatch of her mother's old nurse: "Suddenly the great change came . . . the dying eyes were turned upon me . . . and there lay upon the pillow strange, august features, stern and withdrawn . . . The sense of solitude, of being unsheltered in a wide world of relentless and elemental forces . . . seized me irresistibly" (Addams, 1910/1998, p. 18).

Jane emerged from her childhood with a Quaker's sense of duty and morality and of spiritual and moral independence, a citizen's sense of civic responsibility and heroism, a democratic sense of equality, a mid-nineteenth-century awareness of death, and a devotion to duty. She had also a Stoic's resiliency and understood that one's inner moral compass, not the opinion of others, is life's important guide.

Besides the moral and spiritual aspects, Jane's more conventional education, her readings, and exposure to ideas must be considered. The importance of literate and encouraging forebears cannot be overstated, and all of this book's subjects benefited from family situations where they were talked to, included in discussions, and made aware of the subjective nature of their thoughts. Such experiences teach the young to distinguish between their internal and external worlds. As Piaget (1929) puts it, our subjects had little difficulty "in realizing what their own thoughts are" (p. 203). And without entering into his explanation of how the child's sense of morality arises from a sense of animism—that is, things doing naturally what they are intended to do—each developed early on a sense that things should be a certain way.

Moreover, all came from families whose members understood the connection between education and accomplishment. Jane's maternal grandfather had been a colonel in the American Revolution, helped found Lafayette College, and was a successful miller-landowner. John Addams's father was also successful and financed John's purchase of two mills and several hundred acres in Illinois. When he was a young man apprenticing in the milling trade, John had read "through the entire village library, book after book, beginning with the lives of the signers of the Declaration of Independence" (Addams, 1910/1998, p. 14). Although a Hicksite Quaker, he believed in the education of women, and as Cedarville's leading citizen, he built a school, hired a qualified teacher, started the county's first subscription library, and ran it out of his house. He encouraged his children to read, offering them, among other inducements, 5 cents for each of Plutarch's *Lives* that they read (Farrell, 1967).

Like Franklin and Lincoln, Jane Addams makes no mention of having learned to read, presaging perhaps a comment by the 1930s art critic, Clement Greenberg (1939) that "reading is a minor skill, like driving a car" (p. 39). She just picked it up and, early on, set about a reading program that emulated her father's:

> Copies of the [same books he had read] were to be found in the library
> below, and . . . I began a course of reading in the early morning hours.
> [But] Pope's translation of the Iliad [and] Dryden's Virgil did not leave
> behind the residuum of wisdom for which I longed and I finally gave them
> up for a thick book entitled "This History of the World." (Addams, 1910/
> 1998, p. 14)

When Jane was 8, her father married an educated widow, Anna Hal-
deman, who also cared about books, ideas, and music. Anna "thought
of herself as an aesthetic, and subscribed to the *Atlantic Monthly*" (Diliberto, 1999, p. 27). She encouraged her own and her stepchildren to
read novels, and she would have the family read from the works of Byron, Scott, Shakespeare, and Goethe. On occasion, she would take the
children to Chicago for concerts or plays. Anna also inducted her step-
daughters in the arts of cooking, sewing, crocheting, baking, and knit-
ting. But Jane was bored by domestic chores and had little interest in
pretty things. "Her chief interests were nature, books, and science" (Diliberto, 1999, p. 53), and from Anna's son, who was studying medicine,
she asked for and received a collection of chemicals.

In her teens, Jane Addams mentions reading Dickens, and her favorite author, Louisa May Alcott. She was also reading Homer, Shakespeare,
Dante, Milton, and the Bible, and as Jean Elshtain (2002) says, "drank
up literature as a thirsty creature drains a pool of rain-water" (p. 45).
From her reading, one may infer that she learned how words should
sound when they are put together and had developed an ear for narra-
tive. Indeed, like Franklin and Lincoln, her later writing is clear, graceful,
and lucid. In the style of the day, her sentences flow easily and one never
wonders what she is talking about. Let us attribute her writing, at least
in part, to her familiarity with good literature; and let us suggest from
our survey of the three individuals thus far discussed, exposure to books
helped them develop a wide vocabulary, follow a line of thought, and
learn about matters beyond their experience.

There is the question of whether reading serious books will make
one a good, or at least better, person. Harold Bloom (1994) argues that
reading good books—those included in the Western Canon—is more a
private and aesthetic than it is a public and practical undertaking: "Reading deeply in the Canon will not make one a better or a worse person, a
more useful or more harmful citizen. All the Western Canon can bring
one is the proper use of . . . solitude whose final form is one's confronta-
tion with one's own mortality" (p. 28).

However, Mr. Bloom is a professional scholar, and Jane Addams was
not. And his limiting of the uses of literature to personal ends overlooks

the practical accomplishments of Jane Addams who was both well read and responsible for early laws restricting child labor. The argument to be illustrated here is that, at least for this book's subjects, serious books do more than help one confront one's mortality; they open the way to serious ideas, and serious ideas open the way to serious accomplishments. While there is no way to trace what Jane Addams learned from Shakespeare, Cervantes, or Homer to what she learned from studying labor legislation, my argument is that the former presaged—indeed was a necessary condition of—the latter. Serious books are not merely a way to help one deal with one's mortality. They provide, along with language and an expanded sense of the world, a perspective that suggests that one is responsible for and can alter the human condition. Moreover, it will be argued further on that serious reading helps one articulate serious ideas, and so is central to one's later selection into positions of leadership.

Jane Addams was aware of the limits of literature. In her mid-20s on the second of her European culture tours with a visit to the slums of East London, she feared that she was becoming like Walter DeQuincey, whose mind was so befogged by literature that he found himself unable to shout a warning to someone about to be run down by a coach until he had recalled a similar warning from the *Iliad*: "This is what we were all doing, lumbering our minds with literature that only served to cloud the really vital situation spread before our eyes. Conduct and not culture is three fourths of human life" (Addams, 1910/1998, p. 51).

At 17, having attended the village school, Jane was sent to nearby Rockford Seminary for Women, which an older sister had attended and where her father was a trustee. The curriculum was liberal, but the emphasis was religious. Miss Sill, the school's founder and headmistress, wanted "to teach girls to elevate, purify, and adorn the home and to teach the great Christian lesson that the true end of life is not to acquire the most good . . . but to give oneself fully and heartedly to others" (Farrell, 1967, pp. 30–31). Rockford required daily chapel, weekly prayer meeting, Sunday worship and Bible recitation, regular monthly fast days, an annual prayer week, informal evening devotions, and frequent missionary and temperance society meetings. Jane had wanted to go to Smith, then one of the few degree-granting women's colleges, and considered Rockford, with its "weak academic program, emphasis on religion, [and] rigid code of conduct" (Diliberto, 1999, p. 61) unsuitable. But still Rockford was ahead of its time, a time when the nation's premier authority on female nervous disease argued that it was dangerous for college-aged women to study when they needed to develop their sex organs. Another "leading authority" believed that brain activity "diverted to [women's] heads vital blood they needed for menstruation" (Diliberto, 1999, pp. 60–61).

Jane was impatient with the school's restrictions, ascetic atmosphere, limited food, surfeit of rules, mandatory exercise, small library, low respect for science, and the constant scrutiny by Headmistress Sill. But like both Franklin and Lincoln, she found a set of serious and like-minded colleagues with whom she expanded her education and with whom she studied Latin, natural science, oratory, music, Greek, Bible history, and mathematics. She mentions reading Boswell's *Life of Johnson*, Gibbons, DeQuincey, and Browning. She debated, was class president and valedictorian, and worked her way through the school's newly instituted Bachelor of Arts. Her courses included "Tacitus, two years of Greek, history and literature—Chaucer to Tennyson—algebra, plane and solid geometry, and trigonometry, geology, chemistry, mineralogy and astronomy" (Farrell, 1967, pp. 32–33).

Jane was also attracted to then-popular writers such as Thomas Carlyle, John Ruskin, and Ralph Waldo Emerson, with their romantic and transcendental doctrines of humanism, personal responsibility, and self-reliance. Like Jane, those gentlemen had grown up in religious homes, but were later influenced by nineteenth-century thinking, which puts the emphasis on the individual rather than on institutions, and emphasized human good, not human depravity. They may have regarded the Bible as God's word and salvation as man's destiny, but they saw churches as human institutions, and therefore questions such as how to lead a good life and attain salvation had to be asked and answered personally and without guidance by established churches. Emerson had turned religion into morals and personal responsibility. He believed that "genuine insight arises spontaneously from the individual soul" (Menand, 2001, p. 58) and that one's principle obligation was to attain self-knowledge and to involve oneself in the world's affairs: "Life is our dictionary. . . . Colleges and books only copy the language which the field and the work yard made . . . years are well spent in country labors; in towns; in the insight into trades and manufactures; in frank intercourse with many men and women; in science" (Emerson, 1965, pp. 56–57).

Ruskin, a wealthy nineteenth-century critic, combined idealistic reflections on nature and beauty with practical interests in social legislation and educational reform. Thomas Carlyle (1984), one of the most influential thinkers of the late nineteenth century, opposed the emerging capitalism on the grounds that it honored self-interest over community and left masses of people living in squalor and poverty. This popular critic and historian of the French Revolution was concerned with the excesses of industrialization and, along with Ruskin, preached a doctrine of individual and moral responsibility, which he hoped would offset the materialism of the age.

These authors helped Jane think about moral and religious questions such as these: In the absence of church authority, can one enforce morality? How—without following institutional doctrine—can one attain salvation? How—with the advent of capitalistic-driven industrialism—can society maintain equality? And particularly, how—without a guiding religious hierarchy—can one exercise moral responsibility? Jane Addams's early religious inclinations had been influenced by her father and what Elshtain (2002) calls the "generic liberal Protestantism of the day" (p. 35). In her youth and at Rockford, she wrestled with the matter of Christ's divinity, but decided that she needed religion "only in the practical sense" (p. 35), and turned her attention to what Himmelfarb (1991) calls a "secularized evangelicalism," characterized by a desire to do good without religious doctrine, and to maintain Christianity's ideals and good works without hierarchy and hellfire. To Jane Addams, Emerson, Carlyle, and Ruskin, Jesus was a moral force and spiritual exemplar rather than a personal deity. At Rockford, Jane expanded her ideas, explored her intellect and was finding her own way, which was, as she says, "the best moral training I received at Rockford College" (Addams, 1910/1998, p. 42).

There was also the issue posed by her social class. To do good was not only personal and humanitarian, it was her duty as the child of a wealthy father. In this regard, she reports being influenced by Leo Tolstoy's *What Is to Be Done? Life* (1899), in which that Russian landowner and author articulated his distaste for the life of the idle rich—"a life given to amusements"—and his belief that the greatest happiness was giving: "No one has any rights or privileges and there is no end of duties and no limits to them and . . . the first and unquestionable duty of man is to take part in the struggle with nature for his own life and the lives of other men" (p. 246).

Tolstoy (1899) recounts his disgust with the wealthy who give money but keep their distance, and describes his own decision to "become more intimately acquainted" (p. 27) with the poor. As he recounts, his attempt to cross that barrier failed. He found that the lives and society of the poor were more intelligent, diverse, and complex than he had imagined, and he had no idea how to behave in their presence. His efforts were ill-received and embarrassing to both parties, and he "became persuaded that between us rich men and the poor there stood, erected by ourselves, a barrier . . . and that in order to help them we have to first break down this barrier" (p. 72). Moreover, he discovered that, to the degree that one could eliminate such distinctions, one would become "livelier, healthier, sounder, kinder; and . . . learn the real life which . . . [theretofore] was hidden" (p. 263). Tolstoy's ultimate solution was to live as did the peasants, to work with them in the fields, to dress as they dressed, eat what they ate, and try—as much as he could—to eliminate the distance between him and them.

Later on, in the spring of 1896, when Jane was running Hull House, she visited Tolstoy and told him about the conditions of working girls in Chicago: "[He] listened gravely but glancing distrustfully at the sleeves of my traveling gown which unfortunately at that season was monstrous in size . . . took hold of an edge and pulling out one sleeve . . . said quite simply that 'there was enough stuff on one arm to made a frock for a little girl'" (Addams, 1910/1998, p. 176). Upon learning that Jane's own living came from an inherited farm, Tolstoy—who while serving his guests a European dinner ate only porridge, black bread, and homemade beer—replied, "So you are an absentee landlord" (p. 176). After that visit, Jane was determined to emulate this man who had "put himself in the humblest relations with the humblest people, with the men who tilled his soil, blacked his boots, cleaned his stables" (p. 177).

Like Tolstoy, Jane Addams struggled with the issue of how, as a person of wealth, she could relate to those less well-off. She may not have lived like the poor, but like Tolstoy and later at Hull House, she lived as she had earlier predicted, "in a large house . . . right in the midst of . . . little houses" (Addams, 1910/1998, p. 8). And like Tolstoy, she came to respect and honor as equals the people she came to assist.

A greater barrier than class was gender. A liberal thinker for his time, John Addams believed in education for women because it would help them in their inside-the-home duties, but he and his family were not willing to admit that it would lead outside to male-dominated endeavors. So Jane Addams was caught in a time when women like herself—upper-class, educated, unmarried and without children—could be exposed to broad and interesting ideas, but discouraged from doing anything useful. Alluding to her situation in a later lecture, she recounted that her family "permitted and promoted her going to college, traveling in Europe or any other means of self-improvement. . . . When however she responded to her impulse to fulfill the social or democratic claim, she violated every tradition" (Diliberto, 1999, pp. 74–75).

With a desire to do, but with nothing to do that needed doing, the years between her graduation from Rockford in 1881 and the opening of Hull House in 1888 were most unhappy. Financially independent with the $3,000 per year from father's estate—he died in 1881—Jane attempted medical school but found it boring, traveled to Europe with her stepmother, Anna, where she attended operas, studied languages, and toured museums, palaces, and castles. She came home and, to correct a curvature of the spine, went to see a noted authority on the matter who prescribed his "rest cure," which consisted of lying in bed for a year and doing nothing. When the year ended, she felt worse. She seemed to suffer from what was then called *neurasthenia*, characterized by weakness, lack of energy, listlessness, nervousness, depression, and various physical ailments, in Jane's case, a bad back. She made a renewed attempt at religion, got baptized, moved with her stepmother to Baltimore where Anna's son was in medical school, and where Anna tried to arrange a marriage between her son and Jane.

Not much interested in marriage or her stepbrother, Jane took a second tour of Europe with a group of women, but was depressed by her companions' lives of "manufactured busyness" and the trip left her with a moral revulsion and desperate emptiness. Her companions' ambitions were limited to marrying well and continuing their pampered lives, and she feared that she was becoming like them: "I am simply smothered and sickened with advantages. It is like eating a sweet dessert the first thing in the morning" (Addams, 1910/1998, p. 52). Her desire was "to live in a really living world," but she was caught in what she called an "elaborate preparation with no work provided" (p. 82).

But Jane sometimes behaved in ways that portended her future. One of those moments occurred in Germany when she watched a line of women brewery workers who were carrying heavy wooden tanks of the hot brew and then lifting the tanks shoulder-high to pour the contents into larger containers, often burning their hands with the spill: "Stung into action by one of those sudden indignations against cruel conditions which at times fill the young with unexpected energy, I found myself across the square . . . interviewing the phlegmatic owner of the brewery who received us with exasperating indifference" (Addams, 1910/1998, p. 53).

More important, it was on this trip that she visited London's East End, which in the late nineteenth century had a large number of people who were poor, ill-housed, out of work or marginally employed, often hungry. Some were immigrants, some newly industrial workers, some displaced by laws that favored large landowners over small farmers and tenants. Many worked in factories with long hours, low pay, and life-and-limb-threatening conditions. England's industrialization had created a situation where the poor may or may not have been more numerous, but crowded into growing industrial cities, they were more visible. Instinctively drawn to the poorer quarters of whatever city she visited, she noted that "nothing carried with it the same conviction of human wretchedness which was conveyed by the momentary glimpse of an East London street" (Addams, 1910/1998, p. 50).

In East London, Jane and her friend, Ellen Star, met Arnold Toynbee and a group of people like themselves, well born, well educated, religiously inspired, who saw "side by side with a great increase in wealth . . . an enormous increase in pauperism" (Himmelfarb, 1991, p. 276). Toynbee and his associates combined a Victorian sense of morality with a personal sense of responsibility, and had come to London's East End to preach and practice a social, rather than a religious, gospel. The problem was not inequality; there would always be rich and poor. The problem was not even poverty. The problem was that poverty did not lead to Christ-like virtue, but to economic dependence, alcoholism, abuse of self and family, disrespect for law, neglect of children, corruption, and despair. Connecting their beliefs to action, the reformers began by instructing the poor in the virtues of "thrift, prudence, diligence, self discipline, self dependence" (Himmelfarb, 1991, p. 7).

Contrary to the government's perspective that social problems were caused by the victim's own weakness, they saw that the problems were caused by the absence of alternatives and a dearth of leadership, which "had allowed local government to fall into disrepair until the low and vicious set the tone of community life. Guilt at the desertion of duty by those who had been trained to lead impelled Toynbee to take up his residence among the poor" (Farrell, 1967, p. 45).

The would-be reformers found that it was not enough to work with the personal failings of individuals. They had to repair the social conditions that lead to personal failings. So the reformers' desire to save their own souls, assist others, and spread Christian virtues was transformed into a desire to make the government responsible for the conditions of its citizens. Toynbee and his associates had been influenced by Jeremy Bentham's (1879) economic utilitarianism. Bentham taught that formal principles should be subject to social consequences; politics should be governed by reason; opinions should be based on evidence; and the duty of those who govern was to advance the happiness of the governed.

In sum, what began as a mid-nineteenth-century effort by Christians acting individually and trying to save their own and others' souls was transformed into the Progressive Movement which pressed for—and still presses for—institutionally based and government-backed social action. In America, the movement, as Louis Menand (2001) points out, was assisted by the Civil War, which sent its veterans home with lessened respect for personal enthusiasm and greater respect for professional competence. It was later assisted by Marx's view of modern countries as economies whose politics and culture are shaped by the way production is organized. And for the purpose of trying to illustrate Jane Addams's education, it is fair to say that she traveled the whole way. From a mid-nineteenth-century Christian child trying to save her soul by doing for others to a woman who came to embody the nineteenth-and-twentieth-century movement to make government responsible for its citizens' welfare.

Eager to emulate what she had seen in London, in March 1888 Addams wrote that "it would be a good thing to rent a house in a part of a city where many primitive and actual needs are found, in which young women, who had been given over too exclusively to study, might restore a balance of activity along traditional lines and learn of life from life itself" (Addams, 1910/1998, p. 59).

Jane and Ellen Starr, whom she had known since college, traveled to Chicago, found and furnished—with their own funds—a large older home where they would emulate what they saw at Toynbee Hall. So began America's second and Chicago's first neighborhood settlement. Called Hull House after its original owner, it was located in Ward 19 of the Fourteenth Precinct, an area that contained 50,000 people—most foreign born—seven missions, two churches, and almost 2,000 saloons. The immigrants had been drawn to Chicago's rail and water transportation and industrial and manufacturing opportunities, and to that neighborhood because rents were low and there was no limit to the number of people landlords could cram into the houses. The immigrants were strange to the country, socially despised, uneducated, exploited, and often living in hovels or unheated tenements. Schools were primitive, there was no family assistance, welfare, or juvenile courts. Industrial work was life-and-limb threatening, and politicians behaved like privateers.

> [W]orkdays lasted sometimes sixteen hours. There were no limits to how old or young a worker might be, and even children as young as four years were taxed beyond limit. . . . There were no sanitation standards, and sweatshops were often hotbeds of smallpox and tuberculosis. (Elshtain, 2002, p. 128)

The neighborhood and its inhabitants needed assistance. Addams and Starr needed something to do. Ellen maintained that "Jane's idea, which she puts very much in the front and on no account will give up is that [Hull House] is more for the people who do it than for the other class" (Himmelfarb, 1991, p. 241). Jane agreed. Like Arnold Toynbee (1884/1920), she believed that one's "best self" was beyond personal interest and should be directed toward doing for others. John Dewey, who admired Addams and who later served as a consultant to Hull House, maintained that moral action is rooted in the desire for an improved self: "Moral action results from the ideal which a man forms of himself and occurs in order that he may realize himself" (Dewey, 1891, p. 411). Whatever the combination of motives, Addams and Starr set about doing what they could in those days when charity was more a personal than an institutional enterprise: "From the first, it seemed understood that we were ready to perform the humblest neighborhood services. We were asked to wash the newborn babies, and to prepare the dead for burial, to nurse the sick and to mind the children" (Addams, 1910/1998, p. 75).

Jane and Ellen sheltered abused women and unwed mothers, organized reading sessions, established a nursery and kindergarten, and encouraged evening clubs and classes. Attending to the aesthetic as well as the physical and educational, they established the (now) oldest little-theater group in America. Hull House provided refuge, entertainment, a free public meeting hall, an alternative to saloons; and from the beginning, the facility was in constant use. In the first year, Hull House recorded 50,000 visitors, and in the second year, 100,000: "The little children who came to the kindergarten in the morning were followed by the afternoon clubs of older children, and those in turn made way for the educational and social organizations of adults, occupying every room in the house every evening" (Addams, 1910/1998, p. 100).

And more to the point of this story, Addams and Starr learned from their clients. Among the first lessons was that the people they had come to help had richer and more complex lives and were more charitable to one another than the two had imagined: "We were constantly impressed with the uniform kindness and courtesy we received" (Addams, 1910/1998, p. 76). Addams recounts the visitors' generosity and the way that she and her colleagues came to respect their visitors as social and cultural equals. Like Tolstoy, she relinquished any notion that she and Starr were in any way superior to the poor. "The young woman . . . is chagrined to discover that in the actual task of reducing her social scruples to action, her humble beneficiaries are far in advance of her, not in charity or singleness of purpose, but in self-sacrificing action" (Addams, 1902, p. 69).

They also found also that those they came to help, although "overburdened with toil" (Addams, 1910/1998, p. 177), were themselves people of culture and learning. Addams speaks of a 90-year-old woman, poor, ignored, mumbling to herself, and regarded as crazy until it was discovered that she was speaking Gaelic, and then "one or two grave professors came to see her," whereupon the woman's mental state and social status rose (Addams, 1910/1998, p. 74). Promoting the culture and learning that existed in the community became a more appropriate type of instruction than Addams and Starr had initially assumed. Wrestling with the problem faced by Tolstoy—how to break down social barriers—their answer was to integrate Hull House into the community cultures, not to change those cultures or to encourage their own culture, which might have set Jane and Ellen aside in a class by themselves. The two had already created at Hull House "an attractive, refined, and welcoming facility" (Addams, 1910/1998, p. 66). In that setting, they encouraged the visitors' "own handicrafts, and occupations . . . folk songs and folk lore, the beautiful stories which every immigrant colony is ready to tell . . . the [things that] softened and interpreted life and have endowed it with value" (Farrell, 1967, p. 92). They encouraged their visitors to practice traditional skills such as stick spinning, basket weaving, sewing, and cooking. Showcasing these abilities put elders in the position of teachers, thus gaining them some respect from their families and encouraging in their children "instincts of workmanship and creativity" (Farrell, 1967, p. 102). Equating labor learning with cultural learning, Hull House "was a place of civic education . . . a vehicle for the creation of community and the sustaining of identities" (Elshtain, 2002, p. 153). Encouraged by John Dewey, who believed that knowledge is an instrument of action—"We don't act because we have ideas; we have ideas because we must act" (Menand, 2001, p. 364)—she started a labor museum where young people who worked in factories could gain some deeper understanding of their occupation.

Addams speaks of other things she learned from her neighbors, such as the importance they attached to funerals. Briefly, a child was abandoned at her nursery and despite staff efforts, the child died and Jane arranged for a county burial. The Catholic neighbors were shocked, not at the child's abandonment and demise, but at the prospect of sending him off without a mass and buried in unconsecrated ground from whence his soul might be denied entrance to heaven, and they took up a collection for a respectable service. Reflecting on the matter, Addams said:

> It is doubtful whether Hull House had ever done anything which injured it so deeply in the minds of its neighbors. We were only forgiven . . . on the ground that we were spinsters and could not know a mother's heart. No one reared in the community could possibly have made a mistake like that. (Elshtain, 2002, p. 187)

More broadly, like Arnold Toynbee and his friends, Addams and Starr were learning about social and governmental conditions. They learned about laid-off workers with no resources, about the sweating conditions under which women and children worked, and about the factories that demanded unlimited work for low pay. They learned about untended children left at home, and children who refused Christmas candy because they worked in a candy factory 6 days a week, 12 hours a day. They learned of young girls beginning work at 6:30 A.M., of factories where one could hardly breathe for the dust in the air.

They learned of men without overcoats waiting 2 hours in the sleet, hoping for a chance at a few hours of street sweeping, and about the nursing mother who scrubbed floors "with her mother's milk mingled with the very water with which she scrubbed and who returned home at midnight . . . to feed her screaming child with what remained in her breast" (Addams, 1910/1998, p. 117). They learned about mothers raising children with their husbands out of work, drunk, or in prison; about children left alone and locked in the house for fear of thieves. They learned of men with ruined health, no longer able to do the only work they knew, and of one old woman reduced to living in a trunk; of old people deprived of everything and sent to the county poorhouse; of pregnant girls wronged by lovers and rejected by families. And Addams, a lifelong supporter of the Women's Christian Temperance Union, learned to understand the drinking, which gave some relief from "unceasing and brutalizing toil" (Addams, 1902, p. 16) and which left the young women vulnerable to "lurid and exciting pleasures . . . pale listless girls, who worked regularly in a factory returning from work debilitated and exhausted only too easily convinced that a drink and a little dancing . . . was what they needed to brace them" (Addams, 1910/ 1998, p. 136).

And they learned about the limits of giving advice. To a husband and father who came to Hull House for assistance, she suggested he take a job digging canals, and against his wishes he "worked for two days digging on the canal where he contracted pneumonia and died a week later. . . . wisdom to deal with a man's difficulties comes only through knowledge of his life and habits as a whole and . . . to treat an isolated episode is almost sure to invite blundering" (Addams, 1910/1998, pp. 109–110).

As well as learning about herself and the people she came to help, Addams was moving from personal to institutional intervention. Like Arnold Toynbee, she learned those in "need" were not responsible for their condition; responsibility lay with man-made accommodations, and what was needed was institutional change. Among the first steps was to enlarge the mission of Hull House. A group of young women had been fired for trying to improve conditions at their shoe factory. At a Hull House meeting, one of them said: " 'Wouldn't it be fine if we had a boarding club of our own and then we could stand by each other in a time like this?' We discussed all the difficulties of such an undertaking . . . and on the first of May, 1891, two comfortable apartments near Hull House were rented and furnished" (Addams, 1910/1998, p. 93). That effort was so successful that a whole building was soon constructed to house women in time of need. Among Hull House's other expanding facilities were a kitchen to teach cooking, a gymnasium, a nursery, library, reading room, and art studio.

Then there was the matter of Chicago politics, which Jane saw as responsible for the deplorable health of the neighborhood residents. In the Nineteenth Ward, uncollected garbage generated child-killing typhoid fever, schools were overcrowded, streets were unmaintained, and bus fares were higher than average. The ward's political system was kept in place by vote buying, payoffs to elected officials, jobs for 2,600 party loyalists—68 of the 72 aldermen were on the payroll—and free drinks on election day. Appalled at the politicians' unprincipled behavior, Addams got herself appointed sanitation inspector and followed the refuse collectors to make sure they did their jobs. Later, she and Hull House supporters took on the system in an election. They lost, but she learned about the power of bossism and the tenacity of patronage-ridden politics.

As much as by the political corruption, Addams was dismayed by the factory owners who took no responsibility for conditions therein. Speaking of a boy who was injured on a faulty machine, the factory owners "did nothing whatever, and I made my first acquaintance then with those pathetic documents signed by the parents of working children, that they will make no claim for damages resulting from carelessness" (Addams, 1910/1998, p. 132).

We note that from her own accounts and those of her biographers, Jane Addams's transformation from a young woman trying to live a personally moral life to involvement in institutional politics was unaccompanied by the existential soul searching she went through between her 21st and 27th years. Once in Hull House with something to do, even in the face of adversity, she was at ease with herself, and her reflections are no longer about her personal angst or her health, which was never good. Rather, her reflections are about what needs to be done and how to go about doing it.

Nor did she allow antagonism to deter her. She told John Dewey of "the stones thrown at Hull House, windows smashed, break-ins . . . and said 'She would give the whole thing up before she would ask for a policeman or increase the conflict'" (Martin, 2002, p. 166). She even told him of "a time when 'a man spat straight into her face in the street

and she simply wiped it off and went on talking without noticing it'"
(p. 166). Although personally attacked because "she suggested that women
should have a role outside the home and a public voice" (Faderman, 1999,
p. 117), she folded knowledge into action and found a completeness, reflecting perhaps the pragmatic philosophy of William James: "The knower
is not simply a mirror floating with no foothold anywhere . . . the knower
is an actor and co-efficient of the truth" (Menand, 2001, p. 357).

A recurring theme in this book is how the subjects continue their
learning in progressively larger cooperative enterprises. Jane Addams was
a master of cooperation. She needed the neighbors to expand her perspective, and she needed civic-minded and wealthy women, often wives
of influential husbands, who would support her projects. She had created
a welcoming and convenient place for the like-minded to meet, and she
became part of several emerging organizations. Female bookbinders accepted her dinner invitations, later joined Hull House, and helped organized the American Federation of Labor. The Women's Shirt and Cloak
Makers were organized at Hull House, as was the Dorcas Federal Labor
Union. To do something about the long hours and low wages of department store girls, she joined with the Consumers League, an association
of women—Eleanor Roosevelt later among them—who boycotted es-
tablishments with a reputation for treating women workers unfairly. She
was among the founders of the NAACP and American Civil Liberties
Union. She and other residents joined with others to limit child labor,
and their efforts led to Illinois's first factory legislation limiting the workday and ending child labor. Recalling that effort, she said, "I very much
disliked lobbying . . . [but for three months, I] addressed the open meetings of trades-unions and benefit societies, church organizations and social clubs" (Addams, 1910/1998, p. 135). "The discussion opened up
situations new to me and carried me far afield in perhaps the most serious
economic reading I had ever done" (Addams, 1910/1998, p. 109).

Jane Addams was an admirable person, but alone, she could never
have accomplished what she did. She had an unusual ability to pull together sets of like-minded people, fold her efforts into larger contexts,
and operate at the nexus of overlapping groups working to expand wom-
en's rights, end child labor, limit the workweek, reform government, and
later oppose militarism. Part of her appeal was her willingness to mediate,
to accept the other's point of view, to avoid worsening conflict. An example was her effort to mediate the Pullman Palace Car Company strike
in 1894, which was joined nationwide by 125,000 workers and tied up
20 railroads, and wherein President Cleveland called out the army to
suppress the strikers. Addams was committed to the strike but she saw
the social cleavage it fomented leading to a bitterness that could end in

worse, not better, working conditions: "There had been nothing in my experience to reveal the distinct cleavage of society, which a general strike at least momentarily affords" (Addams, 1910/1998, p. 142). Not a revolutionary, she advocated a continual "chipping away at the capitalists' position, wear them down, erode their resistance, and build their support bit by bit, law by law, contract by contract so that their children and their children's children . . . would feel no urge to avenge [their] death" (Brown, 1999, p. 141).

She carried that reasoning into all of her endeavors. She reasoned simply and directly that "government was a wider and more efficient instrument" (Farrell, 1967, p. 133) to accomplish her ends "because the very sentiments of compassion and desire for social justice were futile unless they could at last find expression as an integral part of corporate government" (Addams, 1910/1998, p. 187).

This is not a biography of Jane Addams. There is no need to describe all of her learning, only her education, the pillars of which were in place by her middle years. So we need not detail her later years when she traveled widely and became a symbol of international progressivism and engaged in larger efforts: the Women's Peace Party, which attempted to prevent America's entry into World War I; her trips to Europe to stop the war; her efforts in passing the Twentieth Amendment, which in 1919 gave women the right to vote; nor her later work on behalf of the League of Nations.

Nor need we recount the personal attacks on her during the "Red Scare," begun in 1919 by Attorney General Mitchell Palmer, in which anyone remotely connected with the peace movement might be deemed a socialist or a Marxist. Jane Addams resisted "isms" and had little patience with political reformers who "have in mind political achievements which they detach in a curious way from the rest of life and they speak and write of the purification of politics as of a thing set apart from daily life" (Addams, 1910/1998, p. 223). She shared with Lincoln and Franklin the ideal of joining the old with the new: "I thought that life had taught me at least one hard earned lesson, that existing arrangements and hoped for improvements must be mediated and reconciled to each other, that the new must be dovetailed into the old" (Tims, 1961, p. 66).

There is certainly no need to recount the nadir of her career, when her opposition to America's entry into World War I earned her the sobriquet of "Poor Bleeding Jane" by Theodore Roosevelt and when she was expelled by the Daughters of the American Revolution for attempting "to destroy civilization and Christianity" (Faderman, 1999, p. 134). As she says, those events "brought me very near to self pity, perhaps the lowest pit into which human nature can sink" (Elshtain, 2002, p. 232). Nor do we need to describe her later years, when even with failing health she worked with Herbert Hoover to feed Europe's starving masses, eventually becoming recognized in 1931 with a Nobel Peace Prize and seeing her efforts embedded into President Roosevelt's New Deal Legislation. It is enough to say that capitalizing on her combination of Quakerism and evangelical Christianity, awareness of social injustice, and a resulting desire to personally translate Christian principles into social action, she lived her life within and came to embody the major currents of her time. She died in 1935, then the most famous woman in the world.

CONCLUSION

Jane Addams was materially more advantaged than Franklin and Lincoln, but barriers of class and gender made hers the more difficult road. Had she not found her calling, those barriers might have killed her and in her mid-20s they almost did. But otherwise, her educational path was similar, and she built her education on similar pillars. There was a religious background that stressed obligation and responsibility, and connected learning to virtue. Jane Addams read widely and early, took a disciplined approach to study, and found colleagues with whom to share ideas. Having the benefits of school, she shows how much education can be found there if one personalizes the experience. Finally, learning about the events of the age gave meaning to youthful ideals. It was not Emerson's transcendentalism that inspired her social efforts; it was what she saw happening to boys and girls who worked 72 hours a week. Also in Jane Addams, one sees the educative power of like-minded companions and engagement in communities where she was energized and where academic learning took shape. Further, one can see the importance of opposition and conflict that force one to reflect, consider alternatives, or modify action.

CHAPTER 5

W. E. B. Du Bois
1868–1963

Especially do I believe in the Negro race: the beauty of its genius, the sweetness of its soul.

(Du Bois, 1920/1969, p. 3)

William Edward Burghardt Du Bois was a scholar, teacher, editor, novelist, poet, propagandist, Marxist, pan-African, and NAACP founder who would never accept lesser status for himself or his race. From valedictorian of his high school class, to Fisk University for his bachelor's degree, then to Harvard for a second bachelor's and a master's, to the University of Berlin, where his doctorate was denied only because he did not have the money to fulfill the residency requirement, and back to Harvard for a doctorate, Du Bois is the book's most schooled subject. One cannot give an account of all that he knew any more than one could account for all that Jane Addams or Abraham Lincoln knew, but it is possible to illustrate the pillars of his education and the way he used those pillars to lever learning into life.

William—only later did he become known as W. E. B.—was born in 1868 in Great Barrington, Massachusetts. He was raised in his mother's family—the "Black Burghardts," as he calls them (Du Bois, 1968a, p. 62)—which in his childhood consisted of his mother and her nine brothers and sisters. Long established in the area, the Burghardts were "farmers, barbers, waiters, cooks, housemaids, and laborers" (p. 63). Great-great-grandfather Burghardt gained his freedom by volunteering in the American Revolution; his son had fought in the War of 1812. On the paternal side, the Du Bois family was descended from French Huguenots driven out of France by Louis XIV. Generations later, a Dr. James Du Bois owned a plantation in the Bahamas where he had two boys by his mistress, "a beautiful little mulatto slave" (Du Bois, 1920/1969, p. 7). One of those boys was Du Bois's grandfather, so William was "born with a flood of Negro blood, a strain of French, a bit of Dutch, but, thank God! no Anglo Saxon" (p. 9).

William's father, Alfred, was a wanderer and a sometimes preacher, "a dreamer, romantic, indolent, kind and unreliable [who] had in him the making of a poet, an adventurer or a beloved vagabond" (Du Bois, 1920/1969, p. 7). But Alfred left in his son's infancy and William "never saw him and know not where or when he died" (Du Bois, 1968a, p. 73). William says little more of his mother, but by all accounts, he was devoted to her as she was to him. Never in good health, she took what jobs and housing she could to support her promising child. "She did not try to make me perfect; to her I was already perfect" (Du Bois, 1920/ 1969, p. 11). Mother insisted that he finish high school, the town's only black and the first of her family to do so; and she lived long enough to see him graduate, but "that very year, she lay down with a sigh of content and has not yet awakened" (p. 12). He added that when she died, "of my own loss, I had then little realization" (pp. 12–13).

William reports a secure childhood although "already in my boyhood, this matter of color loomed. My skin was darker than that of my schoolmates . . . my family confined itself not entirely but largely to people of this darker hue" (Du Bois, 1940/1968b, p. 5). "The shadow [of race] swept across" him during a school Christmas card exchange that was "quite merry till one girl, a tall newcomer, refused my card—refused it peremptorily, with a glance. Then it dawned on me with a certain suddenness that I was different from the others . . . shut out from their world by a vast veil" (Du Bois, 1903/1961, p. 16).

That concept of a "veil" separating blacks and whites would appear often in his later writings where he elevates his personal experience into an account of how a fictional black man comes to learn about the world: "He first noticed now the oppression that had not seemed oppression before, differences that erstwhile seemed natural, restraints and slights that in his boyhood days had gone unnoticed or been greeted with a laugh" (Du Bois, 1903/1961, p. 170).

The topic is Du Bois's education, not his inner life. But there may be a connection between his early awareness that he was different and later independence of thought for which he was noted. Sigmund Freud (1935) noted that because of his own Jewishness, he was made aware "at an early age . . . of the fate of being in the opposition and put under the ban of the compact majority. The foundations were laid for a certain degree of independence of judgment" (p. 11).

William, however, accepted and was accepted by his white classmates, shared their prejudice against the Irish and Germans who worked in Great Barrington's mills and that he, like the other respectable townspeople, "cordially despised. . . . None of the colored folk I knew were so poor, drunken, and sloven" (Lewis, 1993, p. 31). He sensed the distinctions of race only on occasion, as in the Christmas card exchange or when another black boy came to the school, and William was ashamed because the new boy "did not excel the whites as I was quite used to doing" (Du Bois, 1940/1968b, p. 20). If there is anything notable about William's childhood, it was that early on he, like Jane Addams and Benjamin Franklin, had a sense of himself doing important things. He began to recognize that in some way, for some reason, "I wasn't clear at all about it—I sort of had to justify myself" (Lewis, 1993, p. 31).

The family practiced the Congregational faith, which had come down from Puritanism and which stressed literal interpretation of the Bible, personal examination, and individual striving. William may have been influenced by that creed's self-reliance, suspicion of authority, respect for community, and verbal restraint. "It was not good form in Great Barrington to express one's thought volubly, or to give way to excessive emotion. We were even sparing in our daily greetings" (Du Bois, 1940/1968b, p. 19). In that latter respect he resembled his paternal grandfather, "a man who held his head high, took no insults, made few friends . . . he was not a Negro. He was a man" (Du Bois, 1968a, p. 71).

When he was fifteen, William was sent to visit his "elegant and iron willed" (p. 40) paternal grandfather, "a proud free man of color," one who resented distinctions based on race, did not like being invited to "Negro" gatherings, and had been involved in an earlier attempt to resettle American Blacks to Haiti. Grandfather taught William how to behave in company:

> They . . . talked seriously; finally my grandfather arose, filled the wine glasses and raised his glass and touched the glass of his friend, murmuring a toast. I had never before seen such a ceremony . . . I suddenly sensed in my grandfather's parlor what manners meant and how people of breeding behaved. (Du Bois, 1968a, p. 98)

William's awareness of race was enlarged when, on his way home from Grandfather's, he saw "ten thousand Negroes, of every hue and bearing, saw in open-mouthed astonishment the whole gorgeous gamut of the American Negro World; the swaggering men, the beautiful girls, the laughter and gayety, the unhampered self-expression. I was astonished and inspired" (Du Bois, 1968a, p. 99).

William attended Barrington's public schools from age 5 until he graduated at 16, the valedictorian and youngest of his class. The early curriculum was reading, writing, spelling, arithmetic, grammar, geography, and history. Principal Hosmer, who had fought in the Civil War and was later to run a missionary college in Hawaii, and who had kept William from being sent to a reform school for stealing grapes, encouraged him to take the additional courses in algebra, geometry, Latin, and Greek; the mother of a friend purchased the books. William describes school as a businesslike enterprise where one went to learn the curriculum; and in the 1950s, he attributed white resistance to school integration as reflecting the fact that schools had become more social than academic. William gave the valedictory speech on the life of Wendell Phillips, an early black abolitionist and socialist.

In school, he coedited the school paper and acted in plays. Out of school, he worked what jobs he could find, read illustrated weeklies, reported for the local paper, and bought, on a weekly installment, Macaulay's five-volume *History of England.* Attention to detail and a reputation for responsibility obtained him a postgraduation summer position as timekeeper and paymaster for a construction project. Not having the money or encouragement to attend his preferred Harvard, he accepted the suggestion—and $25 a year for 4 years—from Principal Hosmer and three additional contributors to attend Nashville's Fisk Free Colored School, one of the southern institutions founded after the Civil War to train former slaves and, it was hoped, black leaders.

Being sent south was for William an early lesson in the importance of race, more important to his Great Barrington elders than his intelligence, industry, or promise. "I was Northern born and bred and instead of preparing me for work and giving me an opportunity right there in my own town and state, they were bundling me off to the South" (Du Bois, 1940/1968b, p. 23). Reflecting on the encouragement to go south, he "did not thoroughly realize, the curious irony by which I was not looked upon as a real citizen of my birth-town, with a future and a career, and instead was sent to a far land among strangers who were regarded as [and in truth were] mine own people" (Du Bois, 1920/1969, p. 13). Later and even more sanguinely, he wrote, "Black folk were bound in time to dominate the South. They needed trained leadership. I was sent to help furnish it" (Du Bois, 1940/1968b, p. 24).

Created right after the Civil War by the Tennessee Freedman's Bureau and the Congregationalist Church, Fisk attracted 200 former slaves the first day, 600 the first year, 1,000 the second. As Booker T. Washington later said, "Suddenly, as if at the sound of a trumpet, a whole race that had been slumbering for centuries awoke one morning and started off for school" (Lewis, 1993, p. 57). Headed by former northern abolitionists and Civil War veterans, Fisk had begun with an understandably elementary curriculum, including "Webster's *Blue Backed Speller*, McGuffey's *Reader*, Davis's *Primary Arithmetic*, and General Fisk's *Plain Counsels for Freedmen*" (Lewis, 1993, p. 57). By the time William arrived in 1884, the school had been transformed into a New England–like liberal arts college, designed to help students think clearly and logically and live their lives as free men and women.

William studied Greek, Latin, French, chemistry, physics, music, moral philosophy, history, and religion. The curriculum was designed to provide habits of disciplined study, exercise the intelligence, expose one to big ideas, inspire broad social goals, and leave one with knowledge of the world. Later, as a professor at Atlanta University, Du Bois would defend such a curriculum against Booker T. Washington's widely popular Tuskegee curriculum where black students were taught manual and domestic arts, an arguably appropriate set of studies for former slaves and their children taking their first steps on the road to equality.

As did Washington's, Du Bois's beliefs about schooling reflected his experience. His Great Barrington and Fisk teachers and curricula stressed American notions of individual rights and democracy, social progress, and freedom. He had learned that human nature worked for the good and, while the world needed improvement, "universal suffrage, common schools, and a free press would solve social problems" (Adams, 1918, p. 11). But such progressive notions collided with what he learned in Nashville about race. "The public disdain and even insult in race contact continually took my breath; I came into contact with the sort of violence I had never known in New England" (Du Bois, 1940/1968b, p. 30). He was spat upon by a white woman with whom he brushed shoulders. He spoke of the public murder of an editor whose racial views were unpopular, of the regular lynching of blacks and the public display of victims' body parts, and of his fellow students—themselves from the South—who were familiar with all this and went about armed. He learned more when, because Fisk was created to train teachers, he spent two summers teaching in a black, rural school where "all the appointments . . . were primitive: a windowless log cabin, hastily manufactured benches, no blackboard; almost no books, long, long distances to walk . . . I saw the hard ugly drudgery of country life and the writhing of landless, ignorant, peasants. I saw the race problem at nearly its lowest terms" (Du Bois, 1940/1968b, p. 31).

And so William, like the book's earlier subjects, who as children attached themselves to large ideas, decided to direct his efforts toward creating a nexus between what the white world—with its progress, goals, and ideals—was doing and the fact that he and people like him were refused entry into that world. Brought up in "the primary democracy of a New England village" (Du Bois, 1940/1968b, p. 28), he watched the "increasing triumph of democratic government" in the United States, France, England, Japan, and Ireland (p. 29). Accordingly, he asked, "How, into the inevitable and logical democracy which was spreading over the world, could black folk in America and particularly in the South be openly and effectively admitted. . . . The difficulty here, however, was in securing any real and exhaustive knowledge of facts" (p. 29).

Following Plato, who argued that the best sort of happiness is found in the rule of reason, William decided he would study the racial situation, illuminate its irrationalities, and prove empirically that it was as bad for whites as blacks. Reason, or at least reasonably exercised self-interest, would in time compel whites to stop supporting racist practices. Reason is the core of the Western tradition that identifies ignorance as the source of evil, attributes social power to social science, and elevates the position of the scholar in society. William was by nature a scholar, and he reasoned that blacks needed their own scholars who would do the illuminating work that would lead to social justice. Thus he joined who he was with how he regarded himself and what he wanted to do. He also saw the promise of political power attached to being a black leader. "The South will not always be solid . . . and in every division, the Negro will hold the balance of power" (Lewis, 1993, p. 73).

His thinking coincided with another choice he made at that time, to remain black. Light of color and having grown up mostly with whites, William could have, like other Burghardts, "passed" over into the white world. But at Fisk, he learned about black people, large numbers of whom he had not known. "I willed and lo, my people came dancing about me—riotous in color, gay in laughter, full of sympathy, need and pleading; darkly delicious girls—'colored girls'—sat beside me and actually talked to me while I gazed in tongue-tied silence" (Du Bois, 1920/ 1969, pp. 14–15). Along with being smitten by the opposite sex, he decided that he was "quite willing to be a Negro and to work with the Negro group" (Lewis, 1993, p. 73). He was "thrilled to be for the first time among so many people of my own color or rather of such various and extraordinary colors" (Moore, 1981, p. 22). "Into this world, I leapt with enthusiasm. A new loyalty and allegiance replaced my Americanism. Henceforward, I was a Negro" (Du Bois, 1968a, p. 108).

So at the age of 18 or 19, William committed his life and his work to reducing racial discrimination. He did not deny racial distinctions and spoke in his most poetic voice of the black race: "the beauty of its genius, the sweetness of its soul" (Du Bois, 1920/1969, p. 3). He was black, proud of being black, proud of his black culture, and "would not bleach his Negro soul in a flood of white Americanism for he knows that Negro blood has a message for the world" (Du Bois, 1903/1961, p. 17). He wanted blacks to take pride in their cultural uniqueness and contributions, and not "deprecate and minimize race distinctions" (Du Bois, 1971, p. 176). His goal was not integration, which he saw as continuing white supremacy; rather, it was to end the institutionalized segregation that restricted blacks and closed the doors of opportunity to talented blacks like himself.

Indeed, for him, why should they have been closed? Save for inherited wealth—the long-term benefits of which are dubious—he had all the advantages. He was intelligent, good-looking, energetic, male when that mattered more than it does now, and the son of a long-established, respected, and hardworking family from progressive New England. His forebears fought America's wars. He was valedictorian of his high school class, and a college (Harvard) graduate. He had all the advantages save one, skin color. And in late nineteenth- and twentieth-century America, that one element overwhelmed everything else. In the collision between himself and society's idea of him was born his mission: "Had it not been for the race problem, early thrust upon me and enveloping me, I should have been an unquestioning worshipper at the shrine of the social order and economic development into which I was born" (Du Bois, 1940/1968b, p. 27). Instead, William vowed "to make my name in science, to make a name in literature, and thus raise my race" (Moore, 1981, p. 25), and thus he became, in Hannah Arendt's (2000) terms, a "possibility . . . one needs a definite ideal . . . [an] imaginary revision of the world to transform himself into a . . . possibility" (p. 60).

Because all of the book's subjects were influential in the currents of their time—indeed, that is why they were selected—and because their education took shape in those currents, we need here to pay some brief attention to America's racial situation during Du Bois's lifetime. In 1865, the South had acquiesced to the North's military victory, but not to a change in the status of slaves, preferring, in the words of James Goodman (2002) to keep them "landless, illiterate, disenfranchised, and dependent" (p. 21). To force the South to change slaves' status and conditions, Republicans in Congress passed both the Constitution's Thirteenth Amendment, which forbids "slavery [and] involuntary servitude . . . within the United States" (Scaturro, 2000, p. 7) and the first Civil Rights Act, which guaranteed "citizens of every race and color [the same rights] as enjoyed by white citizens" (p. 7). To enforce the Thirteenth Amendment and the Civil Rights Act, the government had created the Freedmen's Bureau, which sent federal agents—900 of them by 1868—to assist former slaves with land ownership, education, finance, and legal matters, and to counteract the "Black Codes" that were being passed by southern states to maintain slavery under a different name. To press the matter further, Congress added in 1867 the Constitution's all-important Fourteenth Amendment:

> All persons born or naturalized into the United States . . . are citizens of the United States and of the states wherein they reside. No state shall make or enforce any law which shall bridge the privileges or immunities of citizens of the United States, nor shall any state deprive any person of life, liberty, or property, without due process of law. (Scaturro, 2000, p. 9)

To carry out the provisions of the Thirteenth and Fourteenth Amendments, and to counter the efforts of the Ku Klux Klan and other associations created to intimidate blacks back into servitude, Congress in 1867 divided the South into military districts and sent in an occupying army. But after a few years, it became apparent that the efforts of the Freedmen's Bureau, the army, President Grant—who had tried to treat former slaves as citizens and voters—the Thirteenth and Fourteenth Amendments, and military enforcement were not sufficient. The problem was that the Freedmen's Bureau was seen, even by its own people, as a temporary solution to a temporary problem. The long-term solution was extending suffrage to blacks and then allowing political enfranchisement and democracy to solve the persistent issues. "Negro suffrage [was seen] as a final answer to all present perplexities . . . [and so] the Freedmen's Bureau died . . . it leaves a legacy of striving for other men . . . and its child was the 15th Amendment" (Du Bois, 1903/1961, p. 40).

> Fifteenth Amendment: The Right of Citizens to Vote
>   Section 1: The right of citizens of the United States to vote shall not be denied or abridged by the United States or by any State on account of race, color, or previous condition of servitude. (World Almanac, 2003, p. 549)

But a few years after the war, popular support for black equality had weakened, and there was a national desire to put the war in the past, and the "best men"—former slaveholders and Confederate veterans—in control of the South. The close and contested presidential election of 1875 brought in Rutherford B. Hayes, who had come with southern support and an electoral, not popular, majority. Hayes, a Civil War general and committed abolitionist, agreed to the Compromise of 1877 by which federal troops were withdrawn and the South received home rule. By the late 1870s, the national effort to provide equality for former slaves was, for practical purposes, abandoned, and in 1884, with the election of Grover Cleveland, the South was allowed to literally nullify the Fourteenth and Fifteenth Amendments as they applied to blacks who, as Du Bois says, were "left bewildered, half-free . . . weary, wondering" (Du Bois, 1903/1961, p. 19).

Not immediately, but between 1885 and 1909, southern states passed a series of "Jim Crow Laws"—the origin of the term is obscure—which excluded blacks from white churches, schools, transportation and recreation facilities, restaurants, hospitals, orphanages, prisons, asylums, funeral homes, morgues, courts, and cemeteries. Blacks had no reliable recourse to a legal system and whites could do literally anything they wanted to blacks and get away with it. Whites and blacks drank at separate fountains, entered public buildings by separate doors, and worshipped in separate churches. Urban blacks were driven to marginal occupations, rural blacks into legalized peonage. The system was kept in place at the top by a court system that would convict 10 innocent blacks rather than let one guilty man go free, and a political system of poll taxes, exclusion from voting for petty crimes, and literacy tests that demanded would-be black voters recite obscure passages from state constitutions. All designed, as Virginia senator Carter Glass said, "with a view to the elimination of every Negro voter who can be gotten rid of legally, without materially impairing the numerical strength of the white electorate" (Redding, 1918, p. viii).

This system extended into the federal government, including the military, and into northern as well as southern institutions, from the top where Woodrow Wilson in 1914 dismissed the government's black employees to the bottom where it was enforced with KKK-style murder, lynching, and night riding. In 1892, the number of blacks who were publicly murdered reached 235 (Du Bois, 1968a, p. 208), and in 1906 white rioters in Atlanta killed 25 black people. Jim Crow was accompanied by an organized system of continuous insults. Du Bois describes a black waiting room at the railroad station:

> you stand and stand and wait and wait until every white person at the "Other Window" is waited on. Then the tired agent yells [because all the tickets and change are over there] "What d'y' want? What? Where?" He browbeats and contradicts you, hurries and confuses the ignorant . . . and sends all out on the platform burning with indignation and hatred. (Du Bois, 1968a, p. 234)

The system was declared legal by the Supreme Court in—among other cases—*Plessy v. Ferguson* (1896), which upheld a Louisiana law separating blacks and whites in transportation facilities. As Woodward (1957/1974) argues, Jim Crow was not a return to the old South. It was a new South that combined race hatred, economics, and religion: "'God Almighty drew the color line and it cannot be obliterated,' proclaimed the Richmond Times" (p. 96). The system did not show serious cracks until President Truman's (1945–1952) second term, when lynching was made a federal crime, segregation in interstate transportation was outlawed, and the military was integrated. In 1954, the Supreme Court under Earl Warren overturned *Plessy v. Ferguson*, countering the southern argument that while states could ban segregation, there was nothing in the Constitution to compel them to do so, by affirming that race relations were a constitutional matter and subject to federal intervention. Accordingly, in 1957 President Eisenhower sent troops to Little Rock, Arkansas, to enforce school integration. It was not until the 1960s, however, when the system's incongruities with democracy were embarrassing a country competing with Russia for influence in the third world, and when President Kennedy was elected with black support and President Johnson was in a position to demonstrate his commitment to equality, that this system began to break up.

Having attended to the broader picture and the racial situation Du Bois would spend his life opposing, let us return to his education. Early on and instinctively, he understood that study and learning pay off; whether the lectures were exciting or boring, pointed or irrelevant, and whether the teacher was more or less attentive or personable made little difference. He describes the Fisk curriculum as "limited but excellent" (Du Bois, 1968a, p. 113), and he found Fisk teachers "in subtle sympathy feeling themselves some shadow of the Veil and lifting it gently that we darker souls might peer through into other worlds" (Du Bois, 1920/1969, pp. 14–15). Later comparing Fisk's to Harvard's faculty—the latter he acknowledges as "fine men and fine teachers" (Du Bois, 1968a, p. 132)—he noted that at Harvard he "did not find better teachers, but only teachers who were better known, who had wider facilities for gaining knowledge" (p. 133).

Following graduation from Fisk, William went to Harvard, then under the direction of Charles Eliot and beginning to admit non-upperclass New Englanders, "provided that with their poverty . . . they bring capacity, ambition and purity" (Lewis, 1993, p. 81). Seeking a second undergraduate degree, Du Bois found Harvard rich, reactionary, and sufficiently racist to exclude him from the glee club despite his singing ability. But he had learned in the South to avoid whites, to "forget as far as possible that outer white world" (Du Bois, 1968a, p. 135), and he found friends and companions among Boston's black community. He was, as he says, "at, but not of, Harvard, [living] on his island within and it was a fair country" (p. 139): "I was encased in a completely colored world, self-sufficient and provincial, and ignoring just as far as possible the white world which conditioned it. This was self-protective coloration, with perhaps an inferiority complex, but with belief in the ability and future of Blackfolk" (Du Bois, 1971, p. 15).

At Harvard, he studied chemistry, history, economics, geology, and social science, and he concentrated on philosophy to get hold of the basis of knowledge and "pursue my dream of a Negro self-sufficient culture" (Du Bois, 1968a, p. 136). He also studied writing because "I believe foolishly perhaps but sincerely, that I have something to say to the world" (p. 145) and because he realized that "solid content with literary style carries a message further than poor grammar with muddled syntax" (p. 144). Like Addams, he studied events outside the classroom and began his lifelong and leftward intellectual path: "I began . . . to realize something of the meaning of the new Populist Movement in its economic aspects. I believed in the 'muckrakers' whom Roosevelt eventually attacked; [who] were revealing the graft and dishonesty in American political life" (Du Bois, 1971, p. 588).

The sum of William's formal education at Great Barrington, Fisk, and Harvard was distinctly "Western," which, because it is the intellectual tradition followed by all of this book's subjects, needs some brief explaining. According to Popper (1965), the Western tradition comes down from the pre-Socratic Greeks—among them Thales—who tried to understand the world through observation and reason, without reference to supernatural forces. As an approach to education, the Western tradition passes on society's accumulated lore, teaches a coherent view of human progress, and asks students to behave in time-honored and respectable ways. As well, it teaches that knowledge is subject to reason and its approach to learning is characterized by observation, accumulation of facts, and drawing conclusions from data. So while teaching respect for convention, the Western tradition subjects everything to reason, and nothing—save empiricism, inference, and the assumption that the two, properly exercised, lead to personal and social improvement—is sacred. The Western system appears to honor tradition, but the tradition it honors most is critique.

As a contrast, consider medieval scholasticism in which the task of the scholar was to treat certain texts as sacred and interpret them correctly. For more modern examples consider national states—some Islamic—where knowledge is again the correct interpretation of sacred text. Or for a view of knowledge and action even more foreign, consider the Taoist approach, which advises its adherents not to study, apply, and achieve, but to accept: "In the pursuit of Tao, every day something is dropped—Less and less is done—until non-action is achieved—When nothing is done, nothing is left undone" (Lao Tsu, 1972, no. 48).

After taking his bachelor's and master's degrees at Harvard, William applied for and received a Slater fellowship at the University of Berlin where he "began to see the race problem in America [with] the problems of peoples in Africa and Asia" (Du Bois, 1940/1968b, p. 47). He reports also being influenced by the ethical idealism of Fichte (1762–1814), a German philosopher and teacher, who preached a combination of principle and practice and who, like an older Du Bois, was forever in trouble with authorities and colleagues for his uncompromising stands. Fichte (1970) believed that "the kind of philosophy which one adopts depends on the sort of man one is, for a philosophical system is not a lifeless piece of furniture that one might take or discard . . . but is animated by the soul of the man who has it" (p. 434).

William was influenced also by the philosophy of Hegel whose idea of life was that it is a dialectical journey combining the idea with the thing, the method with the results, and the way of knowing with the object known:

> To consider a thing rationally means not to bring reason to bear on the object from the outside . . . but to find that the object is rational on its own account . . . the sole task of philosophic science is to bring into consciousness the proper work of the reason of the thing itself. (Weiss, 1974, p. 12)

Hegel preached an additional lesson on the importance of experience: "The individual mind must navigate the turbulent waters of experience to reach the stage of genuine knowledge" (Weiss, 1974, p. 38). William understood that lesson. A proud and scholarly man with degrees from Fisk and Harvard, as well as the author of several books, he was, in America, just "a N_____" (Du Bois, 1903/1961, p. 155) who daily endured the institutionalized insults of whites. To William, there was nothing abstract or academic about America's racial issue. His whole life was a Hegelian journey of experience, observation, argument, and opposition, all combined to bring into consciousness the irrationality of racial injustice.

In Europe, William gained an idea of a world where race was not a barrier, where he was judged on his behavior and personal qualities. He was accepted as an American, not a black American, and he was respected for his intelligence and social grace. He smoothed out some of his impatience and admittedly rough edges: "I came to know Beethoven's symphonies and Wagner's Ring. I looked long at the colors of Rembrandt and Titian. I saw in arch and stone and steeple the history and striving of men and also their taste and expression" (Du Bois, 1940/1968b, p. 45).

His sojourn ended when "after two long years I dropped suddenly back into Nigger hating America" (Du Bois, 1968a, p. 183), back to Harvard where he received his Ph.D. and laid out his life plan: "I was going to study . . . any and all facts, concerning the American Negro and his plight, and by measurement and comparison and research, work up to any valid generalization which I could. I entered this primarily with the utilitarian object of reform and uplift" (Du Bois, 1940/1968b, p. 51).

Twenty-eight years old, his formal schooling finished, W. E. B. Du Bois embarked on his career, first as chair of the Classics Department at Wilberforce University in Ohio, a small black, denominational college where his "rather inflated idea of a university and his terrible plainness of speech" got him immediately into trouble (Du Bois, 1940/1968b, p. 186). At an early meeting, the moderator announced, "Dr. Du Bois will lead us in prayer." "No, he won't," was his reply, after which the agnostic and in his own words "tactless" scholar had to do some explaining to keep his job (p. 56). Du Bois had resented Christianity's support of slavery but respected black churches for offering to blacks solace and protection, refuge, and recreation. He was particularly impressed with Alexander Crummell, "the first of his race ordained in the Episcopal faith" (Lewis, 1993, p. 44), from whom he took one of his central ideas, that "the masses must be guided by a natural aristocracy of talent" (Lewis, 1993, p. 165). A race was civilized, according to Crummell, when it produced "letters, literature, science, philosophy, poetry, sculpture, architecture" (p. 170), and talented blacks would not only prove the worth of the black race, but their "knowledge of modern culture could guide the American Negro into a higher civilization. . . . Without this, the Negro would always have to accept white leadership and such leadership could not always be trusted" (Du Bois, 1968a, p. 236).

But Wilberforce, with its religiosity, lack of funds, and inbred politics hampered a man so dedicated to work—"I shirk not. I long for work. I pant for a life full of striving" (Du Bois, 1968a, p. 154)—and one who envisioned himself doing the work that would lead "to the emancipation of the American Negro" (p. 192). Having as he said, "the wild intolerance of youth and no experience in human tangles" (Du Bois, 1920/1969, p. 10), Du Bois left Wilberforce for Philadelphia where, with funds from some well-intended benefactors, he undertook a study of that city's blacks.

> My vision was becoming clearer. The Negro problem was in my mind a matter of systematic investigation and intelligent understanding. The world was thinking wrong about race, because it did not know. . . . The cure for it was knowledge based on scientific investigation. (Du Bois, 1968a, p. 197)

For Du Bois, an opportunity to study "the condition of the forty thousand or more people of Negro blood" was a chance to practice the kind of scientific sociology that he had been planning since Harvard (Du Bois, 1899/1967, p. 1). The condition of blacks in Philadelphia was one of poverty, despair, and corruption. Race riots were common; newly arrived German and Irish immigrants were pushing blacks out of the laboring jobs; racial relations had bottomed out. Into this world, into Philadelphia's Seventh Ward, Du Bois moved himself and his new family—he had married at Wilberforce—where for a year "we lived . . . in an atmosphere of dirt, drunkenness, poverty, and crime. Murder sat on our doorsteps, police were our government and philanthropy dropped in with periodic advice" (Du Bois, 1968a, p. 195).

Modeling his work after studies of London's East End, he trekked house to house, described the way people lived, recorded population trends, occupations, recreation habits, income, alcoholism, marital patterns, poverty, family size, church attendance, crime, amusements, literacy, property, prostitution, corruption, ignorance, and aimlessness. Du Bois's book *The Philadelphia Negro* (1899/1967), a model of sociological observation, was the first important scientific study of an American racial group. Even while Du Bois admitted that many of those he studied were given to indolence and drink, the most industrious and skilled among them were denied opportunity.

> E_____ is a painter, but has found it impossible to get work because he is colored. F_____ is a telegraph line man . . . When he applied here he was told that Negroes were not employed. H_____ was a cooper, but could get no work after repeated trials, and is now a common laborer. L_____ was a first class baker; he applied for work some time again near Green Street and was told shortly, "We don't work no N_____s here." (Du Bois, 1899/1967, p. 330)

Du Bois described how immigrants had taken black jobs; and the unions would not allow blacks to join, except in the event of a strike when union membership would keep them from replacing whites. He wrote too about how industrialists played upon the immigrants' fear of blacks to keep wages down. He saw that the problem was not racist attitudes, but a capitalistic system that pitted blacks against whites in the competition for jobs. Black problems were a symptom, not a cause, of discrimination, and he advised whites to challenge racist practices that are "morally wrong, politically dangerous, industrially wasteful, and socially silly" (Du Bois, 1899/1967, p. 394). He laid out the history of the issue, the situation as it existed, the evil that it generated, and the costs of doing nothing about it. As well, he was further continuing his education: "I had become painfully aware that merely being born in a group does not necessarily possess one of complete knowledge concerning it. I had learned far more from Philadelphia Negroes than I had taught them concerning the Negro Problem" (Du Bois, 1968a, p. 198).

Finished with the study, he left Philadelphia for Atlanta University, which had been founded by northern Congregationalists to educate black leaders. Du Bois and Atlanta were philosophically on the same track, with the college committed to providing a New England–style, liberal arts education. As he envisioned it, students would "listen to the tales of Troy divine . . . wander among the stars . . . wander among men and nations . . . nothing new, no time-saving devices, simply old time . . . delving for Truth, and searching out the hidden beauties of life, and learning the good of living" (Du Bois, 1903/1961, p. 69). More practically, students would have their minds and worlds expanded, prepare themselves for membership in the talented tenth, and later provide their race with leadership.

Atlanta University's and Du Bois's educational ideas contrasted with those of Booker T. Washington, the founder and president of Tuskegee Institute. Because conflict between the two stimulated Du Bois and some like-minded friends to create the Niagara Movement and later the NAACP, and because it was in opposition that Du Bois honed his learning, some attention must be given to Washington's position and his education. Booker was born in 1858 of a Virginia slave whose task it was to prepare her owner's meals. By his own account, he was given no last name, no education, and no encouragement; he was cared for indifferently by his constantly cooking mother and fed on the floor as were the dogs. After the Civil War, and having given himself a surname, Booker T. Washington worked in West Virginia's salt mines and later in the home of a white woman from the North where he learned, among other things, how to clean a house. Anxious for uplift, he walked from West Virginia to Virginia's Hampton Institute, begun in 1868 by a Civil War general to give former slaves practical training. Booker proved his qualification for entrance by cleaning the admission officer's rooms, just as he had learned.

Shortly after graduation, he started—with nothing save an idea—Tuskegee Institute, where students grew their food, made the bricks from which they constructed the buildings, and learned manual and agricultural arts. Having pulled himself up by labor, Washington decided that labor should be the path for all blacks who would improve themselves and prove their worth by becoming craftsmen, farmers, and tradespeople. He disparaged the liberal learning practiced at Atlanta University and the ex-slaves' "craze for Greek and Latin and the desire to hold office" (Washington, 1901, p. 80). He "had no patience with any school for my race in the South which did not teach its students the dignity of labor" (p. 73). Subsequently, at Tuskegee, students learned "how to bathe; how to care for their teeth and clothing . . . what to eat, and how to eat it properly, and how to care for their rooms . . . a practical knowledge of some one industry, together with the spirit of industry, thrift, and economy" (p. 126).

According to Washington, and also to Frederick Law Olmstead (1861) who had studied the matter, slavery had ruined any respect for labor, among whites as well as blacks. When describing his mother's three-walled cabin, Washington (1901) describes also the slave owner's house "with falling plaster, doors off the hinges, unpainted and broken fences and windows" (p. 18). Olmstead too described a pre–Civil War South where whites thought labor was beneath them, blacks had little interest in working for whites, and it took 30 slaves to do the work of 6 free men.

All of which led Washington to conclude that former slaves needed to learn honest labor, even of a menial kind, to take care of themselves and through solid, respectable, and personal improvement begin their ascent to equality. In 1895 Washington made a famous speech explaining his educational approach and arguing that "there is as much dignity in tilling a field as in writing a poem. It is at the bottom of life that we must begin and not at the top" (Ravitch, 2000, p. 39). And more popularly, he augmented a gradualist approach, by promising that blacks would recognize their deficiencies, abstain from agitating, accept—temporarily—their lesser social roles, and work their way into social, political, and economic equality.

Whites were ecstatic. They had found an articulate, successful, and educated black man who shared their views of ex-slaves' backwardness, who "knew his place" and the place of his race, and who would accept a someday-but-not-now approach to equality. And in the latter nineteenth to early twentieth century, he was America's most famous black, the official voice of black America, and the filter through which charitable money was channeled to black institutions.

Both Washington and Du Bois regarded education as the key to advancement, but each regarded the other's approach as self-defeating. Washington thought liberal arts would encourage wrongheaded notions about equality and justice, create dissatisfaction among blacks and whites, and alienate philanthropists upon whom black institutions depended. Du Bois had agreed that right-out-of-slavery blacks needed to learn labor and had advised blacks to do less complaining: "work, though done in travail of soul and sweat of brow, must be so impressed on Negro children as the road to salvation" (Du Bois, 1971, p. 390).

But while he understood the absurdity of "a lone black boy poring over a French grammar amid the weeds and dirt of a neglected home" (Du Bois, 1903/1961, p. 43), Du Bois thought that Washington had supported white opinion of black inferiority and had compromised with northern industrialists—only after making their money did they become philanthropists—who used the threat of black labor to keep white wages depressed. Du Bois considered Washington's patient and practical solution a defacto giving-in to disenfranchisement and thought his educational program offered blacks only a sharecropper education. Moreover, he saw Washington as supporting white opinion that blacks—not institutional racism—were responsible for their situation. And what Washington had asked in return—that blacks be allowed to progress and that rednecks be reined in—had not been delivered. Lynchings were increasing, Jim Crow laws were becoming more restrictive, and white immigrants were taking the jobs that Washington was telling blacks to wait for. Du Bois argued that Washington had denied the existence of the Ku Klux Klan, and was telling only that part of the story which his northern industrialist backers approved. And what, Du Bois asked, would blacks learn "spending one hour at the spelling book and ten hours at the plow?" (Du Bois, 1903/1961, p. 50). What too would they gain from remaining "a patient, hardworking group of laborers, whose ultimate destiny would be determined by their white employers?" (Du Bois, 1968a, p. 230).

Particularly galling was Washington's acceptance of "the disenfranchisement of the Negro, the creation of distinct status of civil inferiority, [and] the withdrawal of aid from institutions for higher training of the Negro" (Du Bois, 1903/1961, pp. 48–49), and dismissing the idea of progress through the black's own talented tenth, among the most prominent of whom was W. E. B. Du Bois.

But Washington's "compromise" had captured the industrial and commercial spirit of an age which revered work and thrift as the path to improvement, and Washington was—until his death in 1915—the most popular and powerful black man in America. He lunched with President Teddy Roosevelt, had tea with Queen Victoria, received an honorary degree from Dartmouth, and as Du Bois admitted, "was the most distinguished southerner since Jefferson Davis" (Du Bois, 1903/1961, p. 43).

Among blacks, he was variously referred to as "the great accommodator" or "the great conciliator" or sometimes, "the wizard." He was consulted on political appointments. Philanthropists and capitalists—Andrew Carnegie among them—were fascinated by his story and consulted him before dispensing money to black schools, which made it difficult for liberal arts institutions like Atlanta University.

Washington and Du Bois treated each other warily. Washington respected the latter's efforts, intelligence, and literary gifts. Du Bois respected Washington for his slave origins—"he bears the mark of the lash" (Lewis, 2000, p. 569)—as well as his personal accomplishments and influence. But Washington was willing to wait and Du Bois was not, and Du Bois considered Washington's compromise to be nothing more than a "collusion with oppression" (Lewis, 1993, p. 313). Moreover, Du Bois had become noted for his studies of black rural southern life, studies that were praised by William James and Max Weber, among others, and which illuminated how racism operates at the bottom of the system:

> "Own land", said the wife . . . "We did buy seven hundred acres up yonder and paid for it; but they cheated us out of it. Sells was the owner." "Sells!" echoed the ragged misfortune who was leaning against the balustrade . . . "He's a regular cheat. I worked for him thirty-seven days this spring, and he paid me in cardboard checks which were to be cashed at the end of the month. But he never cashed them, kept putting me off. Then the sheriff came and took my mule and corn and furniture." "Furniture? But furniture is exempt from seizure by law." "Well he took it just the same." (Du Bois, 1903/1961, p. 103)

In *The Souls of Black Folks* (1903/1961), Du Bois argued for, among other things, a public school curriculum that would help the South get over being "an armed camp for intimidating Black folk" (p. 80). The book was described by southern reviewers as "dangerous for the Negro to read and [one which] will only excite discontent" (Du Bois, 1903/1961, p. x). But that book identified Du Bois as a serious intellectual, one who did not need a someday approach to equality. Washington offered Du Bois a professorship at Tuskegee, and later gave limited support to his effort to become chief administrator of black schools in Washington, D. C. Du Bois declined the professorship, did not get the school job, and was further discouraged by a lack of money to continue his studies.

Around the turn of the twentieth century, America's racial situation was worsening, and neither Du Bois's scholarly approach nor Washington's vocational approach seemed to improve conditions. Race riots and lynchings were increasing. President Theodore Roosevelt summarily discharged one of the army's only black regiments. The State of Georgia ordered separate lounges for white and black faculty at Atlanta University; one of Du Bois's friends, Monroe Trotter, was arrested for verbally attacking Washington in a public meeting. Du Bois was perhaps ready for an illuminating moment, one that Elias Canetti (1999) describes as when "a door suddenly [flies] open where one had expected not anything to be and one [finds] oneself in a landscape with its own light" (p. 204).

That moment came in April 1899. Sam Hose, a mentally retarded black Georgian, had killed his white employer in a dispute about wages. As the story spread, it was alleged that Sam had also raped the employer's wife. In response, Du Bois had written out a characteristically thoughtful statement and was on his way to the *Atlanta Constitution* office when he learned that

> Sam Hose had been lynched and . . . his knuckles were on exhibition at a grocery store. . . . I turned back to the University. . . . One could not be a cool, calm, detached scientist while Negroes were lynched, murdered and starved. . . . I regarded it as axiomatic that the world wanted to learn the truth if the truth were sought. . . . That was of course but a young man's idealism. (Du Bois, 1971, p. 38)

And for the purposes of this chapter, his recognition of the limits of reason and subsequent choice of politics and advocacy as more useful tools were among the experiences through which he became W. E. B. Du Bois.

Sharing the frustration of other blacks at the sight of Booker T. Washington acquiescing to white opinions, and finding dissenters like himself marginalized, Du Bois had learned, as Lewis (1993) explains, that "the force of an idea is only as good as the politics of the people advancing it" (p. 311). And in July 1905, he organized a meeting of 29 black men—"educators, lawyers, publishers, physicians, ministers and businessmen" (Lewis, 1993, p. 316)—at Fort Erie, Ontario, across the Niagara river from Buffalo, where no hotel would accommodate them. The anti-Washington gathering concluded with a resolution "to oppose firmly present methods of strangling honest criticism; to organize intelligent and honest Negroes; and to support organs of news and public opinion" (Du Bois, 1968a, p. 248). This direct challenge to Washington's position had as its goal to provide

> every single right that belongs to a freeborn American, political, civil and social . . . [and] opposed any proposal to educate black boys and girls simply

as servants or underlings . . . to make Negroes politically free from disenfranchisement, legally free from caste, and socially free from insult. (Du Bois, 1968a, p. 256)

A few years later, in 1910, the Niagara Movement was absorbed in the newer National Association for the Advancement of Colored People (NAACP) initiated by a mixed group of progressives that included Jane Addams. Joining the NAACP's staff, Du Bois left Atlanta University, then suffering from a lack of funding, partly due to the school's refusal to limit its curriculum and partly due to its support of his studies of black life. "I insisted on my right to think and speak; but if that freedom is made an excuse for abuse of and denial of aid to Atlanta University, then with regret I shall withdraw from Atlanta University" (Du Bois, 1968a, p. 229). And so he stepped out of his "ivory tower of statistics and investigation" (p. 229) and became director of publications and research and editor of the NAACP's major publication, *Crisis*, spending the next 22 years articulating and opposing the irrationalities and incongruities of institutional racism.

His goal was to educate blacks and to throw "down the gauntlet to those false collaborators who call themselves philanthropists, and Christians and gentlemen" (Lewis, 1993, p. 470) and to see that educated blacks themselves would guide their race. He attacked Harvard's president for excluding blacks from dormitories (Du Bois, 1971, p. 199), President Taft for reducing appointments of blacks, and President Wilson for dismissing the government's black employees. He congratulated the young such as future NAACP president, Roy Wilkins, for "being elected president of the Mechanical Arts High School Literary Society" (Lewis, 2000, p. 277), and at his poetic best, he wrote about the black "song—that vivid burst of sorrow, burst of joy, our love of life—the wild beautiful desire of our women and men for each other" (Du Bois, 1971, p. 103). And he kept up attacks on lynching, against which he exercised his most biting sarcasm. After one lynching, he praised "the inalienable right of every free American to be lynched without tiresome investigation and penalties . . . one which families of the lately deceased doubtless deeply appreciate" (Lewis, 1993, p. 412). Finally, he encouraged black writers of the 1920s Harlem Renaissance by publishing their work.

The influence of *Crisis* and of Du Bois's editorials was enormous. By 1919 *Crisis* had a circulation of 100,000; and at least 250,000 people read Du Bois editorials every month. Lewis (2000) says, "several hundred thousand young people were coming of age in households where

Du Bois was admired. . . . The habit of gauging one's thoughts by what Du Bois thought and the psychic safety-valve effect of doing so, was . . . deeply engrained" (p. 463).

This book is about its subjects' educations, not their whole life, and it is enough to conclude that Du Bois's mind was never at rest. Fiercely independent, he was often in controversy, sometimes with his own views. While opposing Booker T. Washington, he admitted blacks' educational deficiencies. He opposed America's entry into World War I, but later reversed himself and advised his readers to "close ranks" and support the effort. He supported the talented tenth, but excoriated their college-attending children for spending their energies on "liquor, extravagance, and fur coats" (Rudwick, 1969, p. 246). In the 1940s, he attacked President Truman's Marshall Plan for rearming western Europe: "We want to rule Russia and we can't rule Alabama" (Rudwick, 1969, p. 290). Later, he attacked presidential hopeful Adlai Stephenson and the Democratic Party for acquiescing to the southern caste system.

And he moved continually leftward. Unlike the book's next subject, Eleanor Roosevelt, he did not believe that economic capitalism could be made compatible with social justice, and in his Harvard years had become a Progressive. By the turn of the century, he proclaimed himself a "socialist of the path" (Lewis, 1993, p. 338), and advocated a "doing away with private property" (Du Bois, 1920/1969, p. 80). In 1926, after a visit to Russia, he admitted to being a Bolshevik. In the 1930s, he was at odds with the Communist Party, accusing it of using blacks as shock troops in the labor wars, but in the 1950s, he joined the party. His leftward leanings put him at odds with the NAACP, which pressed for backing Constitution-based remedies, and he was totally surprised by the Supreme Court's 1954 *Brown v. Board of Education* decision. His views also put him at odds with his government, which in the 1950s denied him a U.S. passport and arrested him for being an agent of a foreign power. The judge threw the government's case out of court, and with passport restored, he was honored in Russia, China, and Africa.

Underneath the controversies, there was his consistent and lifetime advocacy for racial justice, penetrating scholarship, absence of fear, and poetic way with words. In Heidegger's terms, he spent his life "liberating his inherited possibilities" (Heidegger, 1949/1976, p. 115); and as much as any one person can, he deserves credit for launching the civil rights movement that was beginning to change American life at the time of his death on August 26, 1963. On the next day, A. Philip Randolph told the 250,000 people gathered in Washington for a civil rights march that "W. E. B. Du Bois calls us here today" (Lewis, 2000, p. 570).

CONCLUSION

W. E. B. Du Bois's 95 years were coterminous with America's most volatile period of race relations. The government was legislating a limited form of equality; the South was trying to force blacks back into slavery; educators were trying to undo more than 200 years of enforced ignorance; emerging capitalists were using black labor to keep costs down; socialists were using race relations to make their points; and blacks were trying to figure out how to deal with it all. And in the middle was W. E. B. Du Bois arguing—and at odds at one time or another with almost everybody—that his people be treated with basic human decency.

Underlying his effort was his education which, like those of our previous subjects, was built around early literacy, early attachment to serious ideas, early awareness of the power of expression, and personal involvement with major currents of the time. Later there were mentors, communities of the like-minded with whom to pursue goals, and a lifetime participation in the confluence of human events. Also illustrated in the case of Du Bois is the contribution of opposition, which forces one to reflect, reeducate, and re-create himself.

CHAPTER 6

Eleanor Roosevelt
1884–1962

Knowledge of how little you can do alone teaches you humility.
(Hareven, 1968, p. 260)

America has no long-established aristocracy, but a few immigrant families got in early on our nation's "good thing," and generations later emerged with a great deal of money made from real estate, trade, manufacturing, shipping, timber, and mining. They purchased estates, protected their wealth through inheritance and intermarriage, and created for themselves an entitled and insular world described in the novels of Edith Wharton (1920, 1905/1964). The New York City Roosevelts, into which Eleanor was born in 1884, were such a family. In addition to Roosevelts, Eleanor came from a line of Dutch and English families that also made fortunes in America's emerging economy: Her maternal grandfather owned much of Sixth Avenue between Fourteenth and Eighteenth Streets when that area was the center of New York City. Eleanor's maternal grandmother had come from a wealthy, southern family, some of whom served the Confederate cause. She was the niece of President Theodore Roosevelt and married her fifth cousin, Franklin Delano Roosevelt, who was also descended from wealth. Eleanor was brought up in a self-assured society that in her words, "thought itself all important" (E. Roosevelt, 1961/1992, p. 3).

Members of her social class sometimes justified their money and position with reference to the theories of Herbert Spencer, who argued that among humans there is a self-regulating mechanism that operates so that the pursuit of personal interest by each will result in the greatest benefit for all. Included among Spencer's beliefs was the idea that "in the early stages of evolution natural selection was the main factor but in the course of time, it was gradually superceded by inheritance of acquired characters" (Elliot, 1917, p. 262). Loosely translated, that meant that

91

social traits could be passed on genetically, giving the already wealthy the assurance that they were not only personally rich and socially useful, they were congenitally superior. Notions of superiority combined with another belief that had come down through Eleanor's Dutch Reformed, Huguenot, and Puritan ancestors, that since the rich had been appointed by God as the world's stewards, they had an obligation to assist those less fortunate. Compassion, however, did not extend to changing the conditions of the less fortunate. The rich might practice charity, but still believed that the poor were victims of their own failings and that no one who was sober, industrious, and God-fearing went hungry.

In the late nineteenth century, however, many of Eleanor's class were influenced by the liberal and progressive thinking discussed in the chapter on Jane Addams. In effect, they moved from the right side of liberalism with its belief in individual freedom to the left side with its belief that individual freedom combined with aggressive capitalism resulted in an unbalanced, unstable, even un-Christian society. While not desiring any diminution of acquired capital, they worked to improve other peoples' chances by altering the role of government relative to society. Eleanor Roosevelt was early on influenced by such ideas, and to notions of Spencerian individualism she added liberal progressivism and spent her life encouraging people to be more responsible for themselves and government to be more responsible for people.

Money and social standing did not protect the family from tragedy. Eleanor's father, Elliott, the charming and good-looking brother of President Theodore Roosevelt, was an impossible alcoholic, unable to hang on even to the bottom rung of a career. Undisciplined, moody, reckless, attracted to horses, hunting, and his male friends, Elliott was drunk, disorderly, and unfaithful. At the insistence of Theodore, he was periodically institutionalized, thereafter going through periods of remorse and resolution to improve. But such periods did little for his wife, Anna, who was unhappy, in ill health, and angry about her married-but-without-a-husband role and about being left with the family responsibilities. Anna died of diphtheria in 1892, after which Elliott was denied custody of his children. Eleanor was deeply in love with her father and described the fantasy world into which she then retreated and where "some day we would have a life of our own. . . . He told me to write him often, to be a good girl, not to give any trouble, to study hard, to grow up into a woman he could be proud of. . . . When he left, I was all alone to keep our secret" (E. Roosevelt, 1937, pp. 20–21).

When Eleanor was 12, Elliott died after an extended binge, and Grandmother did not allow Eleanor to attend his funeral. But as she later said, "I knew in my mind that my father was dead, and yet I lived with him more closely, probably than I had when he was alive" (E. Roosevelt, 1961/1992, p. 34).

As a result of her father's drinking, his attempts to dry out, and her mother's efforts to accommodate both, Eleanor had been shuttled about. When she was 5, she attended a convent school in France, a few years later she went to live at Grandmother's house, later to an aunt's, and when her mother died in 1892, she returned to Grandmother's. Although orphaned, passed around, and reluctant to ask for anything because they were taking her in, Eleanor was treated not unlike children of a class that leaves its offspring to nurses and nannies. Other than a recollection of one tyrannical governess whom Grandmother dismissed, and occasional references to her lack of youthful beauty (which troubled her mother), Eleanor does not make a great deal out of childhood trauma and neither will we. An appealing trait that she shares with the rest of the book's characters is a pre-Freudian absence of self-pity. The people in this book regard themselves as subjects, not objects, and their reflections are not about injustices suffered but about how to better do what they want to do. Existentialists all, they made their choices, created themselves, and took responsibility for their lives and actions. Eleanor was more concerned about what needed to be done than what was done to her.

Among Eleanor's class, education was taken seriously, and like the book's other subjects, she benefited from an encouraging environment. Her father was well schooled and had admonished her to achieve "that curious thing they call 'education'" (Cook, 1992, p. 82). Her nurse had taught her to speak French before English, and when she was 6, an aunt taught her to read. After that, her mother "monitored her daughter's lessons for hours each day, corrected her spelling, supervised her reading, and read aloud to her three children every afternoon" (p. 70). Anna insisted that Eleanor recite daily verses from the Bible and she created a private school for Eleanor and some of her friend's children. Family members and governesses supervised reading. Tutors were engaged for music, languages, deportment, and dancing.

Much is made of Victorian restrictions on women, but Eleanor grew up surrounded by literate and intelligent people who respected learning and did their best to educate her according to their customs. The roles that young women were educated for were restricted but serious: marriage; raising children; managing servants and large, often multiple, households; launching sons into business and daughters into society. All of this depended upon a suitable marriage. A woman who did not possess the accepted stock of information, who did not know how to behave with the correct mix of rectitude and reticence might not marry or might marry someone unsuitable or someone who would leave her and her children unprotected, or worse, poor. Suitable education leads to suitable marriage to a suitable male, which lead to survival of the family, preservation of capital, and continued dominance of the class.

Among the important lessons to be learned were the unwritten rules and unspoken understandings, the codes, conventions, manners, modes of behavior, and assumptions by which members of that class identified and distinguished themselves. All classes share such understandings, but those with more—and more to lose—observe them more rigidly. The sum was a high degree of formality. "I think it would be very difficult for anyone in these days to have any idea of the formality with which girls of my generation were trained" (E. Roosevelt, 1961/1992, p. 109):

> you were kind to the poor . . . assisted in the hospital, and did something for the needy. You accepted invitations to dine and dance with the right people only; you lived where you would be in their midst. You thought seriously about your children's education, you read the books that everybody read. (1961/1992, p. 4)

Eleanor learned the rules, and all of her life she was socially at ease, considerate, and well-mannered; later she used those traits to her own and her husband's advantage. Even in hard-fought political fights, she was a model of graciousness and decorum, embodying in the best sense the manners she had learned as a child. But she did not let the rules of that society define her life. A more powerful motivator was her sense of having to do the right thing, which became "the motivating force in my life, often excluding what might have been joy or pleasure. I looked at everything from the point of view of what I ought to do, rarely from the standpoint of what I wanted to do. . . . I almost forgot that there was such a thing as wanting anything" (E. Roosevelt, 1937, p. 173).

Along with the appropriate instruction and indoctrination into a tight social world was the moral and religious environment. Grandfather had a Puritanical sense of sin and personal unworthiness, and although he died before Eleanor came to live in his house, Grandmother continued the atmosphere of piety and restraint, duty and discipline. Eleanor had to "bathe in cold water . . . walk with a book on her head for exercises . . . wear black stockings and woolen underwear no matter what the weather . . . read [only] devotional books on Sunday . . . hide her feelings and cry in private" (Hareven, 1968, p. 5). Moral lessons were enforced by modest dress, daily prayers, disciplined study, and long walks. On Sundays, along with church, there were spiritual readings as well as hymn singing in the evenings, all designed to instill in her what she later called this "sense of obligation that was bred in me. I couldn't help it. It was nothing to be proud of" (Lash, 1971, p. 84). At the same time, there were her youthful aunts and uncles, trips on the Hudson River, excursions to a summer home in Bar Harbor, parties, plays, and dancing lessons.

Still she was often alone and spent much of her time reading popular novels of Dickens, Scott, Thackery, as well as the romantic poets, Tennyson and Longfellow. She took pleasure in reading and later commented that nothing "could bring me out of the world between the pages" (Cook, 1992, p. 99). If on occasion the novel she was reading generated some embarrassing questions and then disappeared, there were others. She had her own pony, even her own little house in the woods with a stove on which she could learn to cook. The older members of her family took an interest in her and encouraged her. She reciprocated in kind and early on learned the importance of personal relations "which has served me in good stead many times . . . that the most important in any relationship is not what you get but what you give . . . out of [the relationship] may grow an inner development in your self and sometimes a relationship of real value" (Cook, 1992, p. 96).

By her early teens, Eleanor was conventionally well read, conversant in French, literate, reflective, and judging from her early letters, articulate. She was surrounded by and comfortable with adults, anxious to please, and more serious than other girls of her age. She was also tall, a bit socially awkward, perhaps from spending so much time alone, and dressed, by her frugal grandmother, in outdated clothes. But adolescent awkwardness is rarely terminal, and Eleanor was on the verge of becoming her own person. When she was 15, an aunt convinced Grandmother to send Eleanor to England to study with Marie Souvestre, the headmistress of Allenswood School.

Descended from and respected among European intellectuals, Mlle. Souvestre had no use for then-current ideas about the harmful effects of intellectual effort on women's reproductive organs or now-current ideas that discourage teachers from making intellectual demands on adolescents. She assumed that the young could learn large amounts of information more quickly than at any other time of life, and that women would benefit just as would men from intellectual stimulation, a radical idea when education for women was considered "dangerous to a woman's health, the pathway to madness and sterility" (Cook, 1992, p. 104). And unlike modern high schools where the curriculum is filled with options among which students choose, Allenswood limited the options and made the choices. Each day was strictly organized: Breakfast, a walk on the commons, classes taught in French, time for preparation and practice, lunch, more classes, 2 hours for exercise, 15 minutes to dress for dinner, after which study, mail, roll call, and bed. One rose on time, made one's bed, followed the dress code, ate in communal dining rooms, ate everything on one's plate, kept one's bureaus and closets neat, and took brisk walks. Eleanor later said that Mlle. Souvestre "exerted the greatest influence, after my father, on this period of my life" (E. Roosevelt, 1961/1992, p. 35).

Allenswood's curriculum—Greek and Roman traditions; English, French, and American literature; European languages; a modest amount of science and mathematics—was designed to stretch students' minds, train their memories, and teach them to respect accuracy. Like the curriculum that Jane Addams studied at Rockford and W. E. B. Du Bois taught at Atlanta University, it is based on the Western notions of human progress, and in the words of former Harvard president Nathan Pusey, designed to "educate free, independent, informed, and vigorous minds" (Yarrow, 2001, p. D11). It was hoped then, as it is today, that such a liberal and liberating set of studies will provide students with the capacity to create themselves and a worthy society, to think freely and critically, and to behave in time-honored and respectable ways.

The Western tradition has its critics and advocates. Among the former is Foucault (1994) who says the curriculum overemphasizes the individual and reason, and puts knowledge at the disposal of power. Some Islamic critics disparage its ignorance of "permanent, immutable, transcendental [and] divinely revealed, moral and spiritual values" (Jameelah, quoted in Hoodbhoy, 1991, p. 53). And a long line of vocational and career educators criticize its unrelatedness to practical matters. Among its advocates is Diane Ravitch (2000) who traces the problems of today's schools to a sliding away from such a curriculum, and Ted Sizer (1984) who argues that if studied by all, such a curriculum would better promote equality. But even admitting the limits of backward mapping from our subjects' achievements to what they studied in school, the curriculum seems to have done—at least for Eleanor—what it was intended to do.

Eleanor loved Allenswood. No longer an orphan living with aunts and uncles who, however kind and well disposed, were still aunts and uncles, she reveled in the companionship of people her age. Quick-witted, well-read, and practiced in expression, she thrived in languages and literature, and proved reasonably competent in art, music, and algebra. She was also learning about her own learning. Relating how Mlle. Souvestre would often talk about things Eleanor had no knowledge of, she says that she used the "quickness of my mind to pick the minds of other people and use their knowledge as my own. A dinner companion, a casual acquaintance, provided me with information which I could use in conversation" (E. Roosevelt, 1961/1992, p. 27).

Mlle. Souvestre was impressed with Eleanor's maturity and knowledge of French and valued her assistance with younger girls. Eleanor became her favorite pupil; she taught Eleanor to dress well, to think of herself as an attractive person, and to use, rather than be ashamed of, her height and intelligence. Later she wrote of Eleanor, "As a pupil she is very satisfactory, but even that is of small account when you compare it with the perfect quality of her soul" (Cook, 1992, p. 110). In her second year, Souvestre took Eleanor on a European tour, taught her how to behave while traveling, and how to handle her own affairs. Later she told Eleanor's family, "I have not found [Eleanor] easily influenced in anything that was not straightforward and honest" (Lash, 1984, p. 9).

Eighteen years old and back in New York, Eleanor was expected to "come out," that is, to engage in the premarital round of dinners, dances, concerts, and other social activities that would culminate in a suitable union with a suitable and suitably situated male. Not attractive at first glance, older than her years, somewhat high-minded, and embarrassed by play, Eleanor was also well mannered, well schooled, and well-off with an independent income of $7,500 a year, in a time when a working man earned $500. She was finding a set of artistic friends, beginning to do some entertaining on her own, and demonstrating her maturity by taking care of an emotionally wrought aunt and an alcoholic uncle.

She also was enlarging her sense of social responsibility. She quickly tired of the coming-out parties and vowed "she would not do another year of . . . the social rounds" (E. Roosevelt, 1961/1992, p. 39). With other young women of her class, she began to visit and teach classes at New York's Henry Street Settlement. She was among the early members of the Junior League, and worked with the Consumer League, an association of women committed to improving working conditions in garment factories and clothing stores by refusing to purchase clothes made in sweat shops. Her volunteer work took her into the lower East Side where she was particularly interested in the young. Helping poor children was a family tradition. Grandfather, Father, and Uncle Theodore had supported homeless newsboys and had helped found the Children's Aid Society. Grandmother, Mother, and aunts had volunteered at hospitals and put on Christmas parties for orphans.

However, Eleanor was still steeped in the codes of her class, and she had to interrupt her personal trajectory and attend to the all-important matter of reproduction. During the social rounds, she met or remet her fifth cousin, Franklin Delano Roosevelt. Eleanor wrote different versions of her life, but all of them are as much about Franklin and their tandem careers as they are about her. And because she married a man who later became New York's governor and four-time elected president, and because of the roles they played in one another's life and education, and because for the remainder of American history they are Franklin and Eleanor, it is necessary to look specifically at the education of Franklin D. Roosevelt.

Franklin was born at the apex of the American establishment, "that small group of men who come from established and moneyed families and move from New England prep schools to Ivy League colleges to New York law firms, and later take time out for government service" (Berger, 2002, p. A20). He was born in 1882 into another wealthy branch of the Roosevelt family; Franklin's father, James, had invested his inherited money in coal, steamships, railroads, and canals. James was older than his wife, Sarah, and his primary interest in his later years was his family and managing Springwood, his 1,100-acre estate on the Hudson River where Franklin was born and raised and where he and Eleanor are now interred. Franklin's mother came from a wealthy Huguenot family who made money in shipping, transportation, real estate, and manufacturing. Franklin, the couple's only child—there was an older half-brother on Father's side—was educated at home according to a strict schedule: "Up at seven, breakfast at eight, lessons from nine until twelve . . . games . . . lunch . . . studies until four" (S. D. Roosevelt, 1933, p. 6). Tutors supplied lessons in the mornings and afternoons in reading, arithmetic, French, German, and music. There were periods of recreation, and although there were, on occasion, other children, his regular companions were his parents, servants, and tutors.

He was a precocious child, and once when his mother became irritated with him because he was playing with his stamps on the floor while she read to him, he recited back what she had been reading. He told her, "Why, I'd be ashamed if I couldn't do at least two things at once" (S. D. Roosevelt, 1933, p. 33). Although loved and doted upon, Franklin was not restricted. He was riding horses with his father when he was 4, piloting the family's sailboat when he was 9, iceboating on the Hudson at 10, shooting birds, and learning taxidermy at 12. All the while, he was accompanying his parents to museums and concerts and taking part in other mind-improving activities. He was interested in science, he read adventure stories and science magazines, and early on he could absorb large amounts of information.

When he was 14, Franklin attended Groton, one of a group of church-related schools that were being founded in New England. Several factors stimulated such schools' growth. America's post–Civil War rich wanted their children to be educated, of course. They also wanted to emulate English aristocrats who sent their sons to private boarding schools to meet others of their class, prepare for the colleges that were now asking for formal schooling, and escape the Irish who were filling New York's and Boston's public schools. Groton and other schools answered the need by taking boys from the better families at age 12, sequestering them in a rural and Spartan setting, and offering a liberal and rigorous curriculum. The schools would "teach by example, discipline by persuasion, and bring nature's ministrations into the making of the good scholar and the good citizen" (Heckscher, 1980, p. 8). Studies consisted of Latin, Greek, French, German, English, and science, a set of studies that combined notions of Western empiricism with human progress. Paralleling the academic was the moral curriculum with its emphasis on "Christian ethics, vigorous sports—there were three football fields—clean and Spartan living, and a class-conscious comradeship" (Cook, 1992, pp. 147–148). Added was the communal living, dress codes—formal for dinner—set periods of study and rest, and mandatory participation in sports. The idea was that the school would train the mind, discipline the body, and strengthen the character, and the students would learn to handle the matters of life as they presented themselves.

Boarding schools are not for everyone. English novelist George Orwell (1956) savaged his own in his essay "Such, Such Were the Joys," and poet and Latinist, Robert Graves (1957) equated the character training of his boarding school as pure anti-intellectualism. Describing himself as "a scholar who really liked to work," Graves recounted that his habit of writing poetry was taken by his school as "strong proof of insanity" (p. 42). But Sarah Lawrence-Lightfoot (1983) praised the boarding school she studied for the way it combined manners and morals with mental preparation, which is the way Roosevelt biographers describe Groton under Rector Endicott Peabody.

Coming from a long-established, Puritan and wealthy family, Peabody had studied in England and come under the influence of reformers who combined notions of class and wealth with notions of Christian service. He "looked upon social problems as basically moral in nature" (Greer, 1958, p. 766) and to his lectures about hierarchy and discipline, he added Christian living and social responsibility. Years later when Franklin was president and pressing for social legislation to aid the Depression poor, he told the rector: "More than 40 years ago, you said, in a sermon in the Old Chapel something about not losing boyhood ideas in later life . . . those were Groton ideals and your words are still with me" (Freidel, 1952, p. 37).

Along with academics and morals was the matter of learning how to behave relative to one's peers, a serious business that Franklin took seriously. He had entered Groton at 14, two years after others in his class, and was regarded as somewhat sissified. But he had been raised in the company of adults and had to learn about the give and take of those his own age. He was not much good at football, baseball, or crew, but he cheered at events, managed the baseball team, debated, and played tennis and golf. He worked at being accepted by his peers, even going out of his way to receive some black marks for violating the rules. He was also pursuing the all-important art of getting along. Learning how to behave discretely, guard one's tongue, take advice gracefully, and earn colleagues' esteem are serious life lessons, all of which he studied. One can imagine Franklin listening to the advice given by an older Yale classman to the fictional Dink Stover:

> Get to know everyone right off. . . . Get to know them by name; but hold yourself apart. Make fellows come to you. Don't talk too much. Hold yourself in. . . . keep yourself well in hand . . . now you've got to do a certain amount of studying here. Better do it the first year and get in with the faculty. (O. Johnson, 1968, pp. 28–29)

After Groton, Franklin went to Harvard where, unlike the socially isolated Du Bois, he majored in the politics of the institution. He joined the clubs appropriate to those of his set, and got himself elected to a host of offices including chairman of the class. He edited the newspaper, and in one of his editorials advised new students to "be always active. The opportunities are almost unlimited. There are athletics . . . a dozen kinds . . . and athletic management, literary work on the university publications and the outside press, philanthropic and religious work, and the many other interests that are bound to exist" (Freidel, 1952, p. 62). Noticeably absent from that list is studying, but Franklin was mentally disciplined and well read when he entered college. He could afford to spend his time practicing politics and putting the finishing touches on that aristocratic sense of completeness and entitlement for which— among other things—he was later famous.

In his senior year, at one or another social event, he met Eleanor. He admired her seriousness; she liked his intelligence; they were of the same social set, even the same family, and in 1903 they married. Along with Franklin, Eleanor acquired his widowed, disapproving-of-the-marriage, and hanging-onto-the money mother, Sarah, who helped to drive Eleanor back into that dependent state and restricted world in which she grew up. Barely out of her teens, Eleanor was totally enveloped. She had to please her husband, taking whatever he said as "the gospel truth" (E. Roosevelt, 1961/1992, p. 51), and please Sarah, who rather than giving up a son, had adopted a daughter. She had also to attend to her younger brother, Hall; learn the role of the young society matron; give birth to and raise six children, one of whom died; and frequently move the family from one of their homes to another. She did not do it by herself. Mother-in-law, who built a house for herself adjacent to the New York house she built for Eleanor and Franklin, handled the big things and 11 servants handled the small ones. And although "fitting into the pattern of a conventional, quiet, young society matron" (p. 55), Eleanor "was beginning to lose some of my self-confidence and ability to look after myself" (p. 31):

> I sat in front of my dressing table and wept, and when my bewildered young husband asked what on earth was the matter with me, I said I did not like to live in a house which was not in any way mine, one that I had done nothing about, and which did not represent the way I wanted to live. (p. 162)

But life began to change in 1910, when Franklin was elected to the New York state legislature. That election was the beginning of his and Eleanor's political career and therefore needs some attention. It is not that Franklin created and developed Eleanor or that she just followed his views and actions. Indeed, it can be argued that she did more for him than he did for her. Her talents were there and had she not met and married Franklin, her career might have been as or more productive. But they met and married, and her later stature, if not predicated on, at least reflected the roles she assumed and the opportunities she exploited as FDR's wife. If in this brief account of politics, I drift ahead of the story, I am trying to account for a person's education, which has multiple sources; and in Eleanor's case, a major source was her husband's political career.

Following his graduation from Harvard, Franklin attended Columbia Law School and went to work for a New York law firm. His residence in those years was the family estate in Dutchess County; and in 1910 that county's attorney noticed Franklin's name, good looks, mother's money, and relation to cousin Theodore, and invited him to run as a democratic candidate for the New York state senate. Candidates were then selected by the political party, not primary elections; and although the Democratic boss did not like Franklin, he liked the name and the money. Franklin had few political beliefs and not even his mother took his candidacy seriously. But with Theodore's approval and mother's $2,500, Franklin visited every corner of the county and, to everyone's surprise, won. Whereupon he and Eleanor moved to the New York state capital, Albany, and embarked on their political lives.

Eleanor and Franklin were both social and both had the ability to attract and to learn from those they attracted. And both learned from an Albany newspaperman named Louis Howe, who early on "made up his mind that [Franklin] was a young man with a future" (E. Roosevelt, 1949, p. 23). For the next 25 years, Howe was a Roosevelt family retainer, friend, confidant, and advisor. He moved with the family to Washington when Franklin became assistant secretary of the Navy in 1914, and he lived with the Roosevelts until he died in 1936. When Franklin contracted polio, Louis worked with Eleanor to keep Franklin's political career alive; and in 1920 Louis engineered his nomination to the vice presidency, and in 1928 his nomination and later his election to the office of governor of New York. He was the main strategist in Franklin's first two elections to the presidency.

Along with Franklin's promise, Louis recognized Eleanor's intelligence as well as her frustrations with having to attend political meetings where she had no voice. When Franklin was running for vice president in 1920, Louis sought her out. He "began to break down my antagonism by knocking on my stateroom door and asking if he might discuss a speech with me. I was flattered and before long found myself discussing a wide range of subjects" (E. Roosevelt, 1961/1992, p. 110). Louis also saw the emerging power of women in politics, and encouraged Eleanor to stay active in the League of Women Voters and the women's branch of New York's Democratic Party. He taught her how to behave at meetings, worked with her on public presentations, and taught her to control herself: "He . . . sat in the back row when I was speaking and . . . once he asked me why I had laughed at a certain point in my speech. 'I didn't know I laughed . . . there wasn't any reason to laugh.' 'I know there wasn't, so why did you give that silly little giggle?'" (E. Roosevelt, 1949, p. 32).

Louis also encouraged her liberal and humanitarian sensibilities and encouraged her husband, when he was president, to use Eleanor as an emissary to those most hurt by the Depression. Before he died, Louis talked seriously to Eleanor about running for president. In turn, she, who judging from her letters was all her life eager for emotional relationships, developed a reciprocating affection for Louis. He was her friend, "confidant, mentor, and jolly chum" (Cook, 1992, p. 349), and when he died, she said, "I loved him and no one will ever be more loyal and devoted than he was" (p. 349).

Reform politics in general are characterized by attempts to open the political process, and the issue that got Franklin noticed involved the way parties selected candidates for state legislatures and legislatures selected candidates for the U.S. Senate. At the time, the system made candidates beholden to party bosses, and early in Franklin's first term, the Democratic Party proposed a candidate for U.S. Senate whom even Democratic legislators considered unqualified. The ostensible issue was the candidate; the real issue was the right of the party boss to select candidates and tell state legislators how to vote. Franklin became the leader of the reformers, assisted by the fact that, unlike his colleagues who lived in Albany's rented rooms, he and Eleanor lived in a large house where they held receptions and where he became the center of the party's reform wing. The ensuing dispute and eventual compromise identified Franklin with reform politics, and after supporting Woodrow Wilson for president in 1914, Franklin was invited to become assistant secretary of the Navy, a position that cousin Theodore had held. Louis accompanied the family to Washington and helped the new assistant secretary become a friend of the working man. Among other things, he told Franklin to "find out something about labor conditions in Navy yards . . . this was one of Franklin's first close contacts with labor; and there is no doubt . . . that it was one of the turning points in his development" (E. Roosevelt, 1949, p. 23).

From his Navy position, Franklin ran for the vice presidency in 1920. He and presidential candidate, Frank Cox, lost and he went back to practicing law, but his major effort in the early 1920s was learning to live with the polio that struck him in 1921. Along with Louis Howe, Eleanor "became his stand-in with the Democrats and kept his name before the public. She brought people to see him—key party officials and public personalities and the less well known whose points of view she felt should interest him" (Lash, 1971, p. 277). Franklin learned to live a restricted but politically active life, and in 1928 he supported New York governor Al Smith for president, and he ran for New York governor. Smith, who was fond of saying that he received his own education working in New York City's Fulton Fish Market, lost to Republican Herbert Hoover, but Franklin won his own election and served as New York governor from 1928 to 1932. He was elected to the presidency in 1932, 1936, 1940 and 1944, dying in April of 1945. His story is one of continued and increasing political power, abetted by what can only be regarded as phenomenal luck, beginning with the rain that kept Republican farmers at home and away from the polls in his 1910 election to the New York legislature.

Returning to Eleanor, when Franklin was elected to the legislature in 1910, she was 26 years old, dutiful, and carrying out her wifely roles. She attended to the children—or rather, she attended to the people who attended to the children—did the marketing, and ran an open house for Franklin's supporters. Franklin's views became her own. Regarding the campaign for women's suffrage, "I realized that if my husband were a suffragist, I probably must be too" (E. Roosevelt, 1961/1992, p. 68). Along with following Franklin's opinion, she followed the prevailing customs. When the family moved to Washington in 1914, Eleanor believed that "my duty as the wife of a public official was to do exactly as the majority of women were doing" (p. 75). So she spent her afternoons continuing the tradition of officials' wives, paying a series of 10 to 30 calls every afternoon at the homes of other wives of government officials. What went on during those calls, one wonders, but the visits stopped in 1917 when America entered the European war, and Eleanor found better things to do: "Instead of making calls, I found myself spending three days a week at the [Red Cross] canteen down at the railroad yards, one afternoon a week distributing free work for the Navy League, two days a week visiting the naval hospital, and contributing whatever time I had left to the Navy Red Cross and the Navy Relief Society" (Lash, 1984, p. 33).

She was also learning to use her access. Among her charitable visits was one to a veterans hospital where she found shell-shocked veterans wandering around unattended: "I could hardly wait to reach Secretary [of the Interior] Lane to tell him that I thought an investigation was in order" (E. Roosevelt, 1961/1992, p. 92). Lane appointed a committee, the committee wrote a report, and appropriations for veterans hospitals increased.

Eleanor was learning to be a public person. She was intelligent, energetic, socially and politically connected, and wealthy enough to leave—except for an hour before dinner—child raising to help. She was thinking things out for herself, becoming an individual, and "not allowing myself to be stampeded by the likes and dislikes of a nurse or governess" (E. Roosevelt, 1961/1992, p. 97). "I was learning to have a certain confidence in myself . . . and in my ability to meet emergencies and to deal with them" (Hareven, 1968, p. 17).

The growing independence was caused, or accompanied, by her growing apartness from Franklin, who preferred the company of others to wife and children, and was accustomed to being served, not serving. As he admitted to an aide, "I always do what I want to do" (Cook, 1992, p. 366). Characteristically deferential, Eleanor excused his lifestyle and absences, saying, "My husband's duties made it impossible for him to travel with us" (E. Roosevelt, 1961/1992, p. 80). But it was not only his work. Franklin—rich, successful, and attractive—was involved with another woman, a subject this book would omit were it not for the effect on Eleanor, who said that when she learned of the matter, "the bottom dropped out of my particular world and I faced myself, my surroundings, my world, honestly, for the first time" (Lash, 1984, p. 34).

Eleanor offered Franklin a divorce; his mother told him if he took it she would cut him off. Franklin needed his family, his mother's money, and his job as assistant secretary of the Navy, which Secretary Lane would have terminated had he divorced. He promised to end the affair (although the woman was with him when he died), and for public purposes he and Eleanor treated the matter with a reserve characteristic of their class. They stayed together in a state of what biographer Cook (1992) calls "sustained compatibility" (p. 409), strengthened by Franklin's polio through which Eleanor nursed him and in the early stages of which he came to rely upon her. But the distance between them increased. After he learned to live with his restrictions, he bought a house in Warm Springs, Georgia, which he turned into a polio treatment center. She had her apartment in New York and her cottage at the Hyde Park estate. But all of that came later. The point here is that when Eleanor was in her mid-30s, she found that the traditional role as wife to the most suitable of all males had created as many problems as it solved.

Characteristically, she turned the experience inward, reflected on the lesson learned, and concluded that the problem was hers to solve.

> I cannot meet the need of someone whom I dearly love . . . [I] must learn to allow someone else to meet the need, without bitterness or envy . . . [and] you have to learn to accept what other people are unable to give. You must learn not to demand the impossible or to be upset when you do not get it. (Lash, 1971, p. 297)

In those difficult days, Eleanor spent a great deal of time alone in Washington's Rock Creek Cemetery Park where she rode her horses and took long walks. If she was not having a breakdown, it was at least a transition: "I had spent most of my life in an atmosphere where everyone was sure of what was right and what was wrong, and as life progressed I . . . became a more tolerant person, far less sure of my own beliefs and methods of action . . . I knew more about the human heart" (Cook, 1992, p. 230).

Later friend Joseph Lash credits Eleanor with having been influenced by not only her Puritan grandmother but also the stoic philosopher and emperor, Marcus Aurelius (161–180 A.D.), who preached a "life of austere self denial; simple, virtuous, and detached," and who advised that "one should neither expect, nor even want, outward satisfaction" (Everitt,

2003, p. 256). Eleanor seems to have taken the lesson of emotional self-reliance seriously.

> Somewhere along the line of development, we discover who we really are, and then we make our own decision for which we are responsible. Make that decision primarily for yourself because you can never really live anyone else's life. . . . The influence you exert is through your own life and what you become yourself. (Lash, 1971, p. 238)

Sadder, but certainly wiser and stronger, she stayed in the marriage and capitalized on the things it offered, familial stability and political access. In turn, she arranged the married side of Franklin's private life, attended to his children, his mother, his household, proved a gracious hostess to his gatherings, and played the role of political wife with grace and aplomb. She taught him to be a better speaker, more careful with facts, and more concerned about his poorer constituents.

He taught her to pay attention to details. He could not walk so she was frequently his emissary, and when wanting to know about New York state hospitals, he asked her to look into the cooking pots (to find out if the inmates were getting the food advertised) and to see if beds were kept in closets (which would indicate that the institution was over-crowded). When she went to Canada, he "wanted to know about everything I had seen on the farms . . . the kinds of homes and the types of people, how the Indians seemed to be getting on and where they came from" (E. Roosevelt, 1961/1992, p. 177). "I learned to watch . . . [and] by the end of our years in Albany, I had become a fairly expert reporter" (Hareven, 1968, p. 38). He also encouraged her progressive associations and liberal undertakings, and if some of her later activities were publicly criticized (as they often were), or if they got in the way of his own programs, he simply disavowed them. "Well, that is my wife. I can't do anything about her" (Hareven, 1968, p. 123).

As governor, he supported her work as a teacher and sometimes administrator in a New York private school, and during the Depression, he gave moral support—Eleanor was financially independent—to the furniture factory that she and her friends started at Hyde Park. He helped her plan her own house at the family estate, and he accepted the male and female companions with whom she spent her time. He even accepted the continued presence of one bodyguard who became her intimate friend and traveling companion. Later when president, he sent her on serious missions, as in 1940 to the presidential convention to make sure Henry Wallace would be nominated as vice president. Many of his colleagues came to value her work and her intelligence and, along with Louis Howe, took seriously the idea that she should run for president when Franklin's polio and lifestyle had begun to wear him down. He taught her the machinery of politics, the importance of patience and timing, how to set and control an agenda, how to make her points in meetings, how to speak publicly, how to "checkmate a masculine opponent . . . [or better] to make an ally of that opponent" (Lash, 1971, p. 288). He also taught her the most important lesson, one at which he was a master: how to create alliances. If he was distant from his wife, so he was with everyone: "Roosevelt was like an interstellar black hole, sucking information in . . . but giving nothing out. What he really thought was a mystery even to his family" (Powers, 2002, p. 11).

The sum of it all is that together and for outward purposes, Eleanor and Franklin maintained a principled relationship; and if their lives went in different directions and they lived more apart than together, they were among that class of people to whom marriage is as much about family and fortune than it is about companionship and love. Paradoxically, freedom from an emotional relationship with her husband allowed—perhaps forced—Eleanor to find a personal life. Describing the network of female and male friends and associates, and the life she lived, biographer Cook (1992) says that she lived "an outrageous life with her own set of friends and lovers, but she made compromises . . . with form and tradition. She avoided scandal, broke no fundamental ties with her husband or mother-in-law, and where her children were concerned allowed convention to rule" (p. 299).

Having attended to Franklin and to Eleanor with Franklin, I return to Eleanor's education. By her mid-30s, her children were growing and going—each left for boarding school at age 12—her husband was busy and absent, and she "did not look forward to teas, luncheons, dinners; the [First World] war had made that seem an impossible way of living" (E. Roosevelt, 1961/1992, p. 323). By necessity, Eleanor had to create her own life, and she did so by capitalizing on a central feature of democracy, noted by de Tocqueville (1946): the existence and importance of free-standing interest groups and associations, created around public issues, and designed to influence government. Just as Franklin was a master of governmental machinery and legislative politics, Eleanor became a master of such associations. Louis Howe had taught her that to be taken seriously, she had to be useful; and that meant surrendering some of the reticence that she had been taught was part of being a woman. As she later told a gathering of Democratic women, participation in elections was not sufficient. Women had to get in the game and stay in it. . . . To many women, and I am one of them, it is extraordinarily difficult to care about anything enough to cause disagreement or unpleasant feelings, but I have come to the conclusion that this must be done . . . until we can prove our strength and demand respect for our wishes. (Lash, 1971, p. 289)

She prepared for involvement in the most practical ways. "After the Cox-Roosevelt defeat of 1920, I mapped out a schedule. . . . I attended business school and took a course in typewriting and shorthand every day" (E. Roosevelt, 1961/1992, p. 323). After that, she joined with people and groups involved in progressive causes and associated with the Democratic Party. Easy and graceful, well-connected by birth and marriage, she was an immediate asset to any gathering; and in associations with others—mostly women—she began to turn her principles into practice. Along with working in the Henry Street Settlement, she was invited to join the board of the League of Women Voters, where she was assigned to study legislation of interest and write monthly reports. In that association she met two women, Elizabeth Read and Esther Lape, with whom she worked on league business and with whom she "spent many evenings at their little apartment" (E. Roosevelt, 1961/1992, p. 112). Because of her interests in Democratic politics, women, and labor, she met Marion Dickerman and joined the Women's Trade Union League. She met also Harriet Mills, who was prominent in New York's Democratic Party, and Nancy Cook, who invited her to join the Women's Division of the Democratic State Committee. Chairing the first women's platform committee of the Democratic Party, she and others presented a "Progressive Woman's Agenda" which recommended an 8-hour workday, the right of employees to bargain collectively, abolition of child labor, equal pay for women, universal health insurance, sex education, and an end to lynching. Other items on that agenda were "public housing and transportation, improved sanitation, parks and playgrounds, school lunches, workers' compensation, occupational and mandatory education, pure food and milk legislation, and the right of women to serve on political committees" (Cook, 1992, pp. 339–340). She worked with Jane Addams in the Women's International League for Peace and Freedom, and in 1926 she participated in a mass picket demonstration of 300 women in striking paper-box makers: "I was beginning to find the political contacts. . . . I drove a car on election day and brought people to the polls. I began to learn a good deal about party politics in small places. . . . I saw . . . how much of the party machinery was geared to crooked business" (E. Roosevelt, 1961/1992, p. 344).

In the process of supporting and working for an overlapping set of associations, Eleanor was learning leadership, a topic that will get more attention in the chapter on Robert Oppenheimer who, during the Second World War, went from running an academic department to running the Los Alamos Atomic Bomb Project. Steeped in broad and transcendental ideas early on, both Eleanor and Robert directed their intelligence and energies into areas associated with those ideas. They then worked with overlapping groups where they made substantial contributions, earned their colleagues' trust, and were assigned to articulate central ideas, and thus became publicly associated with the undertakings.

When Franklin was elected president in 1932, Eleanor had already left off some of the confines of family, mother-in-law, and wife: "In my early married years, the pattern of my life had been my mother-in-law's pattern. Later it was the children and Franklin . . . [now] I began to do things on my own, to use my own mind and abilities for my own aims" (E. Roosevelt, 1949, p. 349).

Eleanor was determined not to allow the ceremonial nature of the White House job to confine her. She had known Ida McKinley, who had been driven insane by the role of First Lady; President Wilson's first wife, who died in the job; and President Taft's wife, who had appeared insane while her husband was president but regained her senses as soon as he left office. Eleanor had hoped for a direct appointment, which would give her something to do and bring her and Franklin closer, and suggested she take care of Franklin's mail. But when he gave the assignment to his longtime secretary, Eleanor "knew he was right and that it would not work," and she had to find her own way, and her own set of activities (Lash, 1984, p. 57).

It did not take long. "Somebody had asked me to 'come and let us show you what is happening here' and being interested I went. Then another invitation came and I accepted that. And each thing I saw proved so fascinating I found myself going more and more, farther and farther" (Hareven, 1968, p. 42). Already accustomed to operating on her own—she did not like having bodyguards and as a compromise carried a pistol in her car—she created a role as an unofficial link between the administration and the people. She not only went out to meet people, she invited them back to her place, and turned a theretofore isolated White House into a conference center for "student organizations, delegations of school children, youth from mining communities and rural areas, Negro girls from reform schools, lobster fisherman from Maine, organizations of professional women" (Hareven, 1968, p. 41). And because most of her activities were inspired by the Great Depression of the

1930s, and because of the consistent argument that the book's subjects create their education in the currents of their times, some brief attention must be given to that Depression.

Capitalism depends on a free flow of capital—the accumulated financial wealth generated by private enterprise—and capital had begun to wither with the 1929 stock market crash. With capital went investment; and with investment went credit, production, and consumption; and with credit, production, and consumption went employment. In 1933, there were 13,000,000 unemployed—25 percent of America's workforce—and more were marginally employed or had dropped out of the system. There had always been periods of recession as business expanded and contracted, but the severity of the 1930s Depression brought into question our democratic and capitalistic system. Politicians and policy makers were trying to correct the problems with government actions; Communists, who saw the decline of capitalism predicted by Marx, were trying to undo the system. Add in international tariff wars, agitation from the left and right, declining birthrates, an increase in lynchings, urban race riots, European wars with the fear that America would be swept into one, and local governments that were fearful and reactionary. The country was closer to revolution than it had been since the Civil War, and it was for good reasons that the 1930s were called the "Devil's Decade."

As New York governor, Franklin had established programs for unemployment relief, industrial welfare, conservation, and public control of utilities. In Washington, his administration set about to end child labor, limit working hours, expand credit, electrify rural areas, steady banks, reduce foreclosures, establish production limits, set price supports for farmers, and assist sharecroppers, tenant farmers, and farm laborers. The Depression and her unofficial position in FDR's reform administration offered Eleanor an endless array of opportunities to pursue her ideals.

She worked on behalf of the Civil Works Administration, the Civilian Conservation Corp, the Fair Employment Practices Commission, and the Farm Security Administration. She helped set up a National Youth Administration to provide jobs and vocational training for young people; and when the officials of that organization were brought up before a House Un-American Activities Committee, she sat in the front row of the hearing and later invited the witnesses to a White House dinner.

Although she sometimes restrained her inclinations in order to serve her husband's political alliances, as in the early 1930s when she restrained her criticisms of Hitler's anti-Semitism in order to avoid alienating German American voters, her overall trajectory was of democratic inclusiveness. She was involved with the League of Women Voters, joined or supported and worked closely with the American Civil Liberties

Union, the American Association of University Women, the American Friends (Quaker) Service Committee, the NAACP, and the American Foundation, which supported the World Court. Beyond attending meetings, she visited factories, slums, coal mines, impoverished rural communities, industrial towns, and military hospitals. She lectured, traveled, gave radio talks, and wrote a newspaper column 6 days a week, wherein she described her life, dispensed advice on how to be a better person, and preached the president's policies.

The topic of this book is the subjects' educations, not their whole life. Accordingly, at a certain point in life the pillars of education are in place, and one is ideationally, ethically, and vocationally established. For Eleanor, those pillars were an ethically based commitment to social justice, familiarity with broad ideals, awareness of limits as well as possibilities, an abiding faith in the power of reason for good, and the political astuteness to pursue her goals. Her efforts ranged from her 1930s sponsorship of a government-backed effort to create a model and self-sustaining community, to the Second World War when she visited American soldiers all over the world, to her postwar efforts in relocating refugees, and to the United Nations where she chaired the committee that put out the now widely admired and used Universal Declaration of Human Rights. She worked for the election of Adlai Stephenson in 1952 and 1956, and in the 1960s, when Russians and Americans were evil-eyeing one another in Berlin and Cuba, she served as an informal liaison between President Kennedy and Premier Kruschev.

Her progressive involvements sometimes seemed to trip over one another, and earned her the vituperation of conservatives such as James Burnham who accused her of "directionless feeling," and William F. Buckley who accused her of "perilous intellectual habits" (Hareven, 1968, p. 266). But to Eleanor, idealism was realism writ large, and psychologist Abraham Maslow said after interviewing her that "although she had no outstanding talents, no brilliant mind, no special training, no artistic genius . . . [she] fitted most the criteria for the self-actualizing personality" (Hareven, 1968, p. 277). She died in 1962, like Jane Addams before her, the then most famous woman in the world.

CONCLUSION

Eleanor Roosevelt's educational journey reminds us again of the importance of early encouragement to read, write, express one's ideas, and connect oneself to larger ethical and moral ideals. Through her peripatetic and emotionally charged childhood, she learned that life is a serious matter and needs be taken seriously. Although she had only 2 years of formal schooling, Eleanor capitalized on the institutional experience, identified with her teachers, and received in return their best efforts. Like FDR and her fellow students, she practiced in school the social behaviors so important to the remainder of her life.

Like Jane Addams, Eleanor learned that the world she was brought into and the roles she was expected to play no longer held and that to stand still would be to relegate herself to the sidelines. That was not where Eleanor wanted to be, and so she made herself into a different person. She learned to type, to contribute to meetings, to make points, to engage with paupers, press, politicians, and all sorts of people from different worlds whom she needed to pursue her ends. This second education cojoined the first, and her earlier learned notions of morality and responsibility, propriety, courtesy, and loyalty came to characterize her public life. Thus in a harsh political world, she became an unusual and unusually attractive person. Eleanor reminds us that the power of education to transform cannot be underestimated.

CHAPTER 7

J. Robert Oppenheimer
1904–1967

When it has once been given you to do something rather reasonable, forever afterward your work and life are a little strange.
(Einstein to Oppenheimer, in Oppenheimer, 1956, pp. v–vi)

"I'm Oppenheimer" (Royal, 1969, p. 50), he said as he walked into Berkeley's physics laboratory for the first time, as if there were no one there who had not heard of him. Nor was there. Everyone knew about the smartest physics student at Harvard who had studied in England with the great Rutherford and taken a Ph.D. at Gottingen, where his intelligence had intimidated his professors; he was the quixotic young theoretician who combined science with philosophy. He was already a first-rate physicist, a writer of 16 respected articles, and later would be the administrator of the project to develop the first atomic bombs. Everyone at Berkeley knew of him then, just as everyone in the United States and beyond would know of him later.

Robert's early years were characterized by acquiring knowledge and emerging as a scientist. His middle years were characterized by work in physics and his assignment to oversee the construction of the first two atomic bombs. His later years were notable for important government posts in which he worked on ways to handle newly acquired knowledge about atomic power. Those later efforts—combined with his reputed reluctance to build or see others build hydrogen bombs and his earlier flirtations with leftist organizations—led the U.S. government in 1954 to revoke his security clearance. That the man who had "fathered" the atomic bomb was no longer to be trusted with the country's secrets was a huge and, for him, life-altering event. He died in 1967, worn out by controversy, but universally respected for his science, war efforts, and concerns about nuclear weapons.

Robert Oppenheimer was a gifted child. And in this book about education, one might ask, What does the quality of gifted look like in a child? For Albert Einstein, it may have been when at the age of 5, he received a compass and wondered if because it pinpointed North, there were not something physically important between the compass and the North Pole (Clark, 1971). For philosopher Ludwig Wittgenstein, it may have been at the age of 10 when, "with the most careful observation and deep and concentrated reflection," he created from wood and wire a sewing machine (McGuinness, 1988, pp. 44–45). For Galileo, it may have been an early fixation on the ideas of Euclid and Archimedes, and for Isaac Newton, a "sober, silent, thinking lad" (Bailey, 1988, p. 20), an early wondering about the progress of the sun across the sky. Those mentioned, even young, seemed to stretch beyond themselves, exhibiting what Heidegger (1949/1976) terms a "running forward in thought to [their] potentiality" (p. 61). Robert Oppenheimer was that kind of gifted. His later science contributions were about dying suns, black holes, and neutron stars that, at the time of his writing, had not been discovered. His originality, as Rhodes (1986) says, was "not so much ahead of his time as outside its frame" (p. 150).

Robert was born in 1904 in New York City. His father, Julius, had come from Germany as a teenager and had gone to work for his uncles who imported lining for men's suits. By dint of hard work, attention to detail, and the adoption of ready-made suits by American men, Julius and the company did well. By the mid-1890s, he was made partner, later president, and prior to Robert's birth had already become a wealthy man. He was liberal, cultured, artistically inclined, and married to Ella Friedman, an equally sophisticated artist and teacher. The Oppenheimers lived in a nine-room apartment on Manhattan's Upper West Side, surrounded by servants, impressionist art, and intellectual conversation at dinner. Later in life Robert would say, "my childhood did not prepare me for the fact that the world is full of cruel and bitter things" (Royal, 1969, p. 16).

Robert was early literate, treated by his parents as an intellectual equal, and conversant with topics beyond his years. He liked to be read to, and if he showed interest in an author, his parents bought all of the author's works. When he was 5, he wanted to know about buildings, and his parents bought him prints and books on architecture. When he was 7, he wanted to be a poet and they bought him volumes of poetry. Watching his mother paint, he decided to be an artist and was given lessons, books, and supplies. On an early European trip, he became interested in minerals—"with crystals, their structure . . . what you saw in polarized light" (Rhodes, 1986, p. 119) and his parents helped him explore the geology of Central Park and supported his rock collection.

Early fascinations took root. All his life, he retained an interest in
architecture. His love of poetry continued and his second reaction to the
initial atomic explosion was a line from the *Bhagavad Gita*, "I am become Death, the shatterer of worlds" (Royal, 1969, p. 123). He enjoyed
impressionist art and extended his interest in minerals by joining the
New York Mineralogy Society. When he was 11 years old, that society,
unaware of his age, invited him to give a lecture. He had a facility with
languages and, like John Stuart Mill who could read Greek at 4 and
Latin at 8, Robert is reported at the age of 9 to have challenged a cousin,
"Ask me a question in Latin and I will answer you in Greek" (Bailey,
1988, p. 153). When, as an adult, he was invited to lecture in Holland,
he learned Dutch in 6 weeks and when he wanted to read Hindu poetry,
he learned Sanskrit, and later, Egyptian hieroglyphics. As early as 5, he
could identify obscure pieces of classical music.

Robert attended New York's School for Ethical Culture. His parents
were members of the school's parent organization, the New York Society
for Ethical Culture, founded by Felix Adler (1892, 1927), son of an
immigrant rabbi, and an early campaigner for social justice. Because Adler and the Oppenheimers were Jewish, and because Adler and his society
were rooted in Jewish thought, some brief attention should be given to
that topic. Such attention will extend the argument, made in earlier
chapters, that the subjects' educations are characterized by spiritual and
ethical, as much as by intellectual, matters.

Orthodox Jews do not accept the distinction between the spiritual
and physical world. Rather, they believe that "the law and the commandments are the instruments by which man becomes partners in the process
of creating and supporting the world" (Menes, 1960, p. 381). Further,
like Puritans described in the chapter on Benjamin Franklin, they believe
that study may bridge the distance between man and God, and so they
study God's word and through those words struggle to make sense of
his will and his world. Among Jews, "scholarship was not an intellectual
release, not a matter of curiosity or upward mobility; it was a pathway
to God. A man's . . . position depended . . . on his learning" (Howe,
1976, p. 8).

Traditional Jewish scholars, such as the Russian Jewish grandfather
of conductor Leonard Bernstein, spent their lives studying the Jewish
laws, traditions, and history (Bernstein, 1982). As the village's resident
scholar, and with his wife maintaining the family, Bernstein's grandfather
served as the community sage, studying, giving advice, rendering judg-
ments, and helping others live according to God's word. Among Jews,
however, scholarship was not an esoteric undertaking open only to those
willing to spend their lives in its pursuit. It was "not an inheritance of

priests or Levites or Israelites only; it is the possession of the whole house of Jacob" (Menes, 1960, p. 381). It was a means of social as well as personal fulfillment: "Every evening artisans and others in the crowd gather around separate tables to catch a 'good word' from the reciters . . . [of the Pentateuch and the Talmud] . . . and other philosophical and edifying books" (p. 381).

In the first half of the nineteenth century, the Enlightenment, the French and American revolutions, and English liberalism had relaxed social and political restrictions on Jews in western Europe. At the same time, Russia and other eastern European countries had increased those restrictions, compelling many Jews to immigrate westward, some to America. Easing of restrictions in the West and migration from the East combined, in Paul Johnson's (1987) words, to turn Jews' "inward and sacerdotal intellectualism and their endless sharpening of critical faculties to secular matters." The result was that "this ancient and highly efficient social machine for the production of intellectuals . . . instead of pouring all its efforts into the closed circuit of rabbinical studies . . . unleashed a significant and ever-growing proportion of them into the secular world" (p. 341).

Felix Adler was part of that unleashing. The Adlers were a German rabbinical family, and in the mid-nineteenth century, Felix's father, Samuel, had immigrated to America and moved from Orthodox to reformed Judaism. His goal was to present American Judaism as an enlightened and monotheistic religion emphasizing "inner devotion and ethical sanctification" (Kraut, 1979, p. 6). Felix's early goal was to extend his father's mission, but to his rabbinical studies in Germany, he added science at Columbia University, and after some intellectually tortured years, departed from a belief in God into a belief in personal ethics. To Felix, whether there was or was not a God was a subject that could not even be approached, and he distained religions that "spin the gossamer threads of an abstruse and subtle philosophy which few . . . minds are fine enough to grasp" (pp. 120–121). For him, the "God of theology was gone but the moral law was a power actually working in the world" (p. 69). One's obligation was "to act upon another as to evoke in him, and conjointly in oneself, in the same movement and counter movement, the consciousness of the interlacedness of life with life" (p. 148).

Accordingly, Felix founded the Ethical Culture Society, then the Ethical Culture School, which was "dedicated to the ever increasing knowledge and practice and love of the right" (Bailey, 1988, p. 153). (That school is, at this writing, still strong and successful.) Inside an academic curriculum of science, history, mathematics, literature, languages, classics, and art, the school promoted "right habits, right ideas as well as regularity, punctuality, silence, and industry: good conduct, high moral vision and respect for the authority combined with an emphasis on study and the uses to which such study would be put" (Kraut, 1979, p. viii).

Robert was the school's top student. He took all the courses the school offered, and spoke highly of his teachers, such as Ms. Newton with whom he read Homer and Mr. Klock who "loved the sciences . . . and the view of nature—part order, part puzzle. . . . But above all he loved young people to whom he hoped to give some touch, some taste, some love of life, and in whose awakening he saw his destiny" (Royal, 1969, p. 23).

In addition to school, where he studied five languages and did college-level work in several subjects, Robert had the benefits of growing up in a wealthy and cultured home in New York City. He attended concerts, plays, and museums and spent his summers at the family's Long Island home. But all those advantages did not make him happy. "I'm the loneliest man in the world" (Royal, 1969, p. 23), he had remarked to an English teacher, and his social isolation was such that he did not even know his advantages were advantages. He was described by those who knew him as

> hunched over . . . driven everywhere he went, attended by servants . . . smarter than any contemporary and not accustomed to friends. . . . He desperately wanted to be liked, even popular. (Michelmore, 1969, p. 7)

Independent of Robert's studiousness and social isolation is a question of whether he was more educated than the book's other subjects. A stock of referential information is necessary for education, and Robert, like Du Bois and Franklin, may have known more than the book's other subjects. But mastering information is a necessary, but not a sufficient, condition for education. Rather, education occurs, as our stories illustrate, when the individual takes a personal position relative to issues, participates in the associated endeavors, and searches out new ways of thinking about and acting toward related matters. In that searching out and solving of problems, knowing is transformed into action, knowing and action are transformed into education, and education into the person one is.

The question ever since the advent of universal and compulsory schooling is to what degree schools can turn information acquisition into education. Efforts in that direction are the subject of long-running, broad-based, emotional, and often-acrimonious debates of the type described by Suzanne Wilson (2003) in her study of mathematics teaching and the politics of mathematics teaching in California. However, the stories presented in this book suggest that the gap between information acquisition and education may not be an issue schools can address; more likely, it is a wall against which they will forever bash themselves. It is only in maturity when individuals make a personal decision to position themselves relative to the issues and to explore the vagaries and uncertainties therein that education as defined here occurs. And that happens not in school and not in youth, and not until the information one acquires, perhaps in school but more often outside, becomes acted upon in pursuit of adult goals.

Although Robert did not participate in sports or activities, he was not unadventurous. Julius bought him a 28-foot sailing sloop, and like Albert Einstein to whom sailing was a series of problems to be solved as well as a passion, Robert became an accomplished sailor. And in response to Robert's late adolescent funk, his father asked one of his teachers to take his intelligent but then-alienated son to New Mexico for an outdoor experience. In the hiking, horseback riding, and Spartan living, Robert demonstrated stamina, a way with horses, and an indifference to physical discomfort. His love of the desert impelled him to later purchase a New Mexico ranch, an event of some significance when, in the Second World War, the country was looking for a place to build atomic bombs.

After his time away, Robert entered Harvard and completed the curriculum in 3 years, graduating summa cum laude. Like all of our subjects who understood that they are the net gainers in the educational exchange, Robert took advantage of formal schooling. Of the years at Harvard, he later said it "was the most exciting time of my life. I really had a chance to learn. I loved it. I almost came alive. I took more classes than I was supposed to, lived in the stacks, and just raided the place" (Michelmore, 1969, p. 11).

He also began to think of what he would do with his life. He had begun majoring in chemistry and proved an intuitive theoretician: he "immediately grasped the concept, formulated equations, and . . . arrived at a conclusion before the professor finished" (Royal, 1969, p. 30). When he began to think about physics and accepted the offer of a professor to attend those classes, it came over him that "what I liked in chemistry was very close to physics; it's obvious that if you were reading physical chemistry and you began to run into thermodynamical and statistical mechanical ideas, you'd want to find out about them" (Rhodes, 1986, p. 123).

More attention will be given to Robert's scientific studies further on when the events leading up to the atomic bombs are reviewed. An important point here is that he augmented science with philosophy and mysticism. At Harvard, he had found Alfred North Whitehead—coauthor with Bertrand Russell of *Principia Mathematica*—with whom he conversed about philosophy and poetry. He was drawn to the mystical writings of St. John of the Cross and the philosophy of Spinoza, Hobbes, and Aquinas; the poetry of Dante, Donne, Rilke, Baudelaire, the *Bhagavad Gita*; and the novels of Dostoyevsky and Proust. And from the Bible, he read the book of Ecclesiastes, with its existential lament: "For what hath man of all his labor and of the vexation of his heart" (2:22). In a later essay, Robert addressed his efforts to join science with a broader understanding of the world, and of the "the ceaseless change and wonderful novelty and the perishing of all earthly things, and the eternity which inheres in every happening . . . between growth and order, between the spontaneous and changing and irregular and the symmetrical and balanced . . . between the individual and the community" (Oppenheimer, 1989, p. 67).

Robert saw no contradiction between the spiritual and the scientific. Rather, he saw them as complementing each other. "These two ways of thinking, the way of time and history and the way of eternity and of timelessness, are both part of man's effort to comprehend the world in which he lives" (Oppenheimer, 1989, p. 53). Moreover, he saw science as offering only a partial solution to the problem of being, as he indicated in a later letter to his brother, Frank: "I believe that through . . . discipline, though not discipline alone, we can achieve serenity and a certain small but precious measure of freedom from the accidents of incarnation and charity and that detachment which preserves the world which it renounces" (Royal, 1969, p. 28).

And Robert saw the limits of scientific knowledge. He shared the view of philosopher Leo Strauss (1964/1978), that "science cannot teach wisdom . . . [it] can only bring about a further increase in man's power . . . to manipulate man still better than ever before" (p. 31).

Characteristic of all of the book's subjects is evidence of an interior life that they develop through sensing, observing, reading, and reflecting and that they use to carry on a self-correcting and often critical dialogue with their acting selves. Roth (2004) explains the interior life as an "autobiographic memory which forms the foundation of the self and self awareness" (p. 37), and Pauen (2004) explains it as "a kind of core containing the most fundamental personality traits and convictions that define a human being" (p. 47). Lincoln said little about his interior life, but Franklin, Addams, Du Bois, and Eleanor Roosevelt left autobiographical accounts that show their interior lives as exhibiting the rational and purposeful thinking they exhibited in their actions.

Robert was as or more self-revealing about his interior life, but his public ruminations left the impression that he was detached, perhaps too taken with metaphysical speculation, which after he had worked on the atomic bomb was interpreted by his more security-conscious colleagues as even-leftist and not-to-be-tolerated ambiguity. When, in 1953, the Personnel Security Board of the Atomic Energy Commission recommended the removal of his security clearance, it was neither for disloyalty nor treason. It was for intellectual detachment, which came across as moral ambivalence and was deemed incompatible with the hypernationalism of the time and with Robert's position as an insider in security matters. The board noted that Dr. Oppenheimer had exhibited "substantial defects of character" (Strout, 1963, p. 44), as well as "consistently plac[ing] himself outside of the rules that govern others" (p. 55). But Robert was always an outsider, and his intelligence was always tinged with ambivalence, even melancholy. He once said that "My ideal man would be one who was good at a lot of things but would still look at the world with a tear-stained countenance" (Michelmore, 1969, p. 18). And one of his favorite passages from the *Bhagavad Gita* (1979) was

> That man I love! Who dwelling quiet eyed
> Stainless, serene, well balanced, unperplexed
> Working with me yet from all works, detached. (p. 113)

Vannevar Bush, a scientist and administrator who worked with Robert during the war, referred to him during the security hearings as a profoundly complex character who "had strong opinions and had the temerity to express them" (Bailey, 1988, p. 191). And I. I. Rabi, one of the physicists who worked with him at Los Alamos, said that he

> was overeducated in those fields which lie outside the scientific tradition, such as his interest in religion, in the Hindu religion in particular which resulted in a feeling for the mystery of the universe . . . he saw physics clearly . . . [but] he tended to feel that there was much more of the mysterious and novel. (Rhodes, 1986, p. 149)

Intellectual detachment and moral ambivalence notwithstanding, the world demands that young people get on with life and Oppenheimer decided, in his 20th year, to be a physicist. And with his father's support, he went off to study with the world's best. First to the Cavendish Laboratory at Cambridge University in England, then run by Ernest Rutherford of whom more further on. Then on to the University of Göttingen, where he received a Ph.D., and where he worked with the great men of physics, including Max Born and Paul Dirac. He also studied at the University of Leyden and later in Switzerland. Returning to America in 1928, as Michelmore (1969) says, "to bring the new physics to America and to make it flourish" (p. 31), Oppenheimer was invited to—among 11 other schools—the University of California at Berkeley where, within a few years, he was a professor of theoretical physics. As well, he served part-time on the faculty at the California Institute of Technology.

Much of Robert's education took place inside the world of science and, in order to understand his education, we need to pay some attention to science learning. Oppenheimer lived in what philosopher Michael Polanyi calls "the open republic of science" (Oppenheimer, 1989, p. 66). To Polanyi, science knowledge is craft knowledge "characterized by freedom of speech and openness of communication" (p. 34). Learning the craft and learning to become part of the scientific community requires "a full initiation . . . [which comes from] close personal association with the intimate views and practices of a distinguished master" (Rhodes, 1986, p. 32). Similarly, Robert described science as an edifice that

> does not appear to have been built upon any plan but to have grown as a great city grows. There is no central chamber, no one corridor from which all others debouch. . . . All about the periphery men are at work studying the . . . mechanisms by which life proliferates, alters, and endures. (Oppenheimer, 1989, p. 64)

Science is undertaken by individuals, but the knowledge is cumulative, with the important entity being the community that has its own history, language, and accumulated lore. Alan Turing, who during the Second World War developed a machine to break the code used by German submarines and so contributed to the invention of computers, explained that for an individual to develop any scientific contributions, he must "be immersed in an environment of other men, whose techniques he absorbs during the first twenty years of his life. He may then perhaps do a little research of his own and make a very few discoveries which are passed on" (Hodges, 1983, p. 384).

However brilliant, Oppenheimer had to learn the accumulated lore and direct his efforts around common concerns. He had to join in the community where "the search for truth is based on communication with other people, on agreement as to results of observation and experiment and on talking in a common tongue about the instruments and apparatus and object and procedures" (Oppenheimer, 1989, p. 6). The cumulative nature of the enterprise means that in science, unlike the humanities in which one need not know one artist to appreciate another, one has to spend years mastering the cumulative findings.

This is why the student spends many long years learning the facts and arts
. . . of science, [and that is why science] is so discouraging for the layman
to enter. (Oppenheimer, 1989, p. 19)

The nature of science knowledge raises a question as to whether this
book's science subjects are more educated than others. In other words,
did Benjamin Franklin and Robert Oppenheimer "know" more than
Jane Addams or Abraham Lincoln? The argument here is that they did
not. Scientific knowledge accumulates, but so does every other form.
Lincoln did not simply "know" in an abstract sense about the politics of
slavery in the mid-nineteenth century, nor did Jane Addams, W. E. B.
Du Bois, and Eleanor Roosevelt simply "know" about progressive politics. Just as did Robert with subatomic physics, they had eliminated the
distance between themselves and what they knew and their knowledge
was at the core of who they were. Robert Oppenheimer could no more
easily access what Lincoln knew about the politics of slavery in the nineteenth century than Lincoln could access what Oppenheimer knew about
subatomic physics in the twentieth. In a later speech, Oppenheimer said
as much, illustrating Lincoln's "genius" by citing his decision, which was
met with widespread disapproval at the time, to put the preservation of
the Union ahead of freeing the slaves.

As the stories of the individuals show, education is not merely
"knowing" in an abstract sense. Nor does it exist apart from the person
one is. It is the accumulated learning, habits of thought and expression,
experience in and participation in common endeavors. It is a way of
thinking, looking at, and going about one's affairs in a consistent and
intelligible manner. It is at the core of one's intentional as well as one's
acting life. And because Robert Oppenheimer's education was in subatomic physics, and because in this chapter, the effort is to explain Robert's education, some brief attention must be given to the events in
atomic physics up to and during his lifetime.

Twentieth-century physics is the story of developing techniques to
examine the interior of atoms, developing theories about atoms, and fig-
uring out how to apply the theories. The story has a long line of contributors, and illustrates Jenny Uglow's (2002) argument that "innovation
is found in groups; that it tends to arise out of social interaction—
conversation, interaction, validation, the intimacy of proximity" (quoted
in Gladwell, 2002, p. 104). The background begins with Democritus,
who in about 400 B.C. suggested that matter is composed of indivisible
particles, which he called *atoms* and which Newton later termed "solid,
massy, hard, impenetrable, moveable particles . . . [which] should they
wear away or break in pieces, the nature of things depending on them

would be changed" (Oppenheimer, 1989, p. 143). Progress accelerated in the early 1800s when Dalton showed the atomic constituents of compounds, and described the properties of materials according to the weight and number of their constituent atoms. Parallel to and equally important is the story of electricity and its contributors, among them Benjamin Franklin, who described the characteristics of magnetism and electricity, and James Clerk Maxwell who showed how changing a magnetic field produces electricity and changing an electric field produces a magnetic field. Maxwell noted further that a back-and-forth action between electricity and magnetism would produce electromagnetic waves that provided a tool—electromagnetic radiation—which might be used to explore the properties of atoms.

Toward the end of the nineteenth century, England's J. J. Thompson passed electricity through gas and showed that atoms are composed of much smaller particles, some of which he called *electrons*—negatively charged, pointlike entities. In 1895 Wilhelm Roentgen demonstrated that electrons could be stripped away from their atoms, travel through empty space, and give off energy, which he termed *radiation*. Then Thompson determined that the stripped away electrons remained intact, and Ernest Rutherford, with whom Robert studied in England, applied Newton's laws on the physics of moving bodies to the behavior of electrons. Rutherford used chargeless (alpha) subatomic particles to map the interior of atoms and found that when radioactive particles penetrated the nucleus—one 10,000th of the dimensions of the atom as a whole—other particles—neutrons and protons—emerged. In sum, over an extended period, a series of experimentalists had demonstrated the existence of atoms, the presence in atoms of electrons, the presence in the atom's nucleus of protons and neutrons, and showed that atoms could be penetrated, their elements could be freed, and the freed elements could produce energy. Rutherford also described the nucleus of an atom as having the density of

> many millions of tons per cubic inch. . . . [and that] when fast [radioactive] particles penetrated [the nucleus] things other than [radioactive] particles emerged. . . . [Rutherford] knocked out of the nucleus of nitrogen a nucleus of hydrogen . . . and started a chain of events which led . . . to man's release of atomic energy. (Oppenheimer, 1989, p. 24)

How much energy could be released and how the released energy could be controlled became matters for further investigation. In 1934 Frédéric Joliot and Irène Curie, the daughter of Marie Curie, figured out that penetration would release additional neutrons, and that it was possible not only to "chip pieces off the nucleus . . . but also to force [the nucleus] to artificially release some of its energy in radioactive decay" (Rhodes, 1986, p. 202). Thinking about such matters in 1934, I.I. Rabi wrote that since the neutron "carries no charge, there is no strong electrical repulsion to prevent its entry into nuclei. . . . When a neutron enters an [atom's] nucleus the effects are about as catastrophic as if the moon struck the earth" (Rhodes, 1986, p. 209).

Experiment, method, theory, and serendipity had produced a working model of the atom and hinted at the power it contained. There remained the questions of whether the power could be released in a controlled manner and what elements might expedite that end. Uranium is among the heaviest of elements, and Henri Becquerel—quite by accident—had found that photographic plates sprinkled with uranium salt emitted radiation, giving impetus to the Curies' work on purifying radium from uranium ores. Enrico Fermi in 1934 extended that knowledge with his own experiments on uranium, and in 1938 Lise Meitner, a German Jewish refugee living in Sweden, and Otto Hahn penetrated uranium atoms with neutrons and found that neutrons split into lighter and unstable atoms of roughly equal size but with an overall loss in mass and an enormous release of energy. The result was termed *fission*:

> the uranium atom, when hit by a neutron, splits into lighter atoms with a loss in mass and an enormous release in energy. . . . If there were enough of them, the released neutrons might split other uranium atoms into a multiplying chain reaction. (Davis, 1968, pp. 96–97)

Albert Einstein's energy-mass equivalence formula ($e = mc^2$) allowed Meitner to calculate the amount of energy locked in an atom's mass and, similarly, an amount that might be released from the mass and through fission turned into energy.

Meitner and her colleague Hahn published their results in 1939, and physicists everywhere began to think about a multiplying chain reaction. Leo Szilard, a Hungarian/German Jewish refugee living in America, figured out that "If we could find an element which is split by neutrons and which would emit two neutrons when it absorbs one neutron, such an element, if assembled in sufficiently large mass, could sustain a nuclear chain reaction" (Rhodes, 1986, p. 28). Thinking further, two British physicists, Frisch and Peierls, calculated that 5 kilograms of uranium 235—an isotope that contains extra neutrons and adds a necessary instability to the element—would have the explosive power of several thousand tons of dynamite. As indeed, in 1945, it proved to have.

The theory of atomic energy was in place. Enrico Fermi, working with others at Columbia University in 1942, found that the release of energy from uranium atoms did produce vast amounts of energy. In December of that year, Fermi and Szilard, working at the University of Chicago, created the first controlled nuclear reaction. When the uranium pile began its self-perpetuating series of exploding atoms and the controlled release of atomic energy was a reality, Szilard commented, "this day would go down as a black day in the history of mankind" (Rhodes, 1986, p. 442).

Robert was in the loop but had not made his own contributions. Nevertheless, he was respected, known as one of the country's smartest physicists, and had created at Berkeley a physics department that equaled those in Europe. He had worked with Ernest Lawrence on the cyclotron, which was used to create isotopes, and it was likely that he would be excited by the work on fission. And so he was, as one of his Berkeley colleagues, Luis Alvarez, recounted: When Luis told Robert that fission had been observed, Robert first said, " 'That's impossible,' [but] I invited him over to look . . . in less than fifteen minutes, Robert had decided that it was indeed a real effect and . . . that some neutrons would probably boil off in the reaction and that you could make bombs and generate power. . . . Within a week, Robert had drawn a picture of a bomb" (Rhodes, 1986, p. 274).

The story is getting ahead of itself. Before describing Oppenheimer's work with the bomb, one needs to ask why, as soon as the knowledge about atomic energy was emerging, it was directed toward making bombs. Why not toward power plants or, as Lawrence had demonstrated on his own mother, the arresting of cancer? The answer is that discoveries about atomic energy intersected with the emerging European war and subsequently with national and international politics. This book's subjects write their lives in the currents of the time, and when currents intersect, they continue their education in the confluence. Just as his community efforts and the French and Indian War opened the way for Benjamin Franklin, and the Depression and her husband's career opened the way for Eleanor Roosevelt, so the discoveries in physics and the emerging Second World War opened the way for Robert Oppenheimer. It is necessary, therefore, to recount, in the briefest way, the military and political situation that brought this atomic physicist out of the laboratory and into the larger political world.

In September 1939 Germany, flush from successes in Austria and Czechoslovakia, invaded Poland. England and France, then allied with Poland in an effort to halt the Germans, were drawn into the fray, and the United States, although not in the war until December of 1941 was sympathetic to England. Hitler had earlier asserted the emerging knowledge about atomic energy was "Jewish physics," and had emptied German universities of Jewish scientists, including Einstein, Rabb, Szilard, Fermi, and Meitner. Since there never was any secret about atomic energy, the expelled scientists, several of them then living in America, were fearful that German physicists would create an atomic bomb. To counter the possibility, Szilard at Columbia University enlisted the help of some others, including Albert Einstein, and wrote a letter to President Franklin Roosevelt expressing concern that German scientists might be working on an atomic bomb and asking the president to initiate a comparable effort. There was no question about Roosevelt's anti-German sympathies and he provided a modest amount of support to, as he put it, "see that the Nazis don't blow us up" (Rhodes, 1986, p. 314).

There was, however, a minor issue, which later became a major one. In the later 1930s Robert Oppenheimer had supported with modest contributions and attendance at meetings some leftist social causes. That he was involved in political matters is surprising. In his Berkeley years, he owned no radio, read no newspapers, and even while having his earlier Berkeley income augmented by inherited investments, was unaware until 1930 that the stock market had crashed the year before. Although interested in philosophy, poetry, and history, he said of himself in those years that he "had no understanding of the relations of man to his society" (Royal, 1969, p. 54). But no one could long ignore the larger world that, in the late 1930s, had become a disconcerting place.

As explained briefly in the chapter on Eleanor Roosevelt, the Depression began in 1929 and continued for over a decade. Capital withered, the banking system collapsed, unemployment and underemployment were as high as 30 percent, wages were abysmal, spending and production were down, poverty was rampant. FDR's New Deal legislation had begun to ameliorate some of the hardships, but the situation worsened in 1936–1937 and convinced many—W. E. B. Du Bois among them—that Marx was right, capitalism had failed, and the revolution was at hand. In the 1936 presidential election, America's Communist Party garnered 80,000 votes.

The American Communist Party operated, in part, as an arm of Russia's International Comintern, which was designed to promote the world revolution. The Comintern supported the Republican side of the Spanish Civil War, which lasted from 1936 to 1939, and pitted Spanish Republicans, supported by Russia, against Spanish Fascists, supported by Germany and Italy. As part of its agenda, the Comintern intended to take over America's Left, and to further that end, operated through "front" organizations, that is, small, often local, quasi-autonomous efforts to promote regional issues. So if one joined a local organization to improve

working conditions for stevedores or teachers, or came to a neighborhood meeting to protest German and Italian bombings of Spanish cities,
one might find oneself unwittingly assisting a communist-affiliated association.

Robert saw his students unable to support themselves and find jobs
when they graduated, saw his colleagues thrown out of Germany, and
along with his brother, helped his expelled Jewish German relatives relo-
cate to America. He had been involved with a woman who had been a
Communist, and he later married a woman whose former husband, a
Communist organizer, was killed in the Spanish Civil War. His brother
Frank was a member of the Communist party, and Robert had attended
anti-Fascist meetings and contributed funds to Spanish Republicans. All
of which drew him into organizations that might have been sponsored
by Russia's Comintern. Although later disillusioned by Stalin's non-
aggression pact with Hitler, he said that what he had learned from his
involvement was "an essential part of becoming a whole man; if it hadn't
been for this late but indispensable education, I couldn't have done the
job at Los Alamos" (Halberstam, 1993, p. 331). Independent of that,
all such affiliations ended in December 1941 when the Japanese attacked
Pearl Harbor. Robert then decided that he "had had about enough of
the Spanish cause and that there were other and more pressing crises in
the world" (Rhodes, 1986, p. 446).

The war was on and there were things to do. Physicists knew about
the energy locked up in atoms, knew that atoms could be split, and
knew, because Fermi and Szilard did it at the University of Chicago, that
a nuclear reaction could be set off and controlled. But they did not know
whether plutonium (uranium 239) might produce a more effective reaction, whether to use graphite or heavy water to control the flow of neutrons, how to trigger an explosion, build a bomb, get the bomb into
an airplane, and deliver the bomb without blowing up the airplane. In
Oppenheimer's words, "would a bomb work and what sort of a thing
would it be, how much material would it need, what kind of energies
would it release; would it ignite the atmosphere in nuclear reactions and
end us all; could it be used to start fusion reactions" (Oppenheimer,
1989, p. 137).

Robert was among the most noted physicists in the country, had
done work in subatomic research, published papers on radiation, assisted
Lawrence with the cyclotron, and created a preeminent physics department. Marcus Oliphant, an Australian physicist working in England, was
in America trying to fire up the then-stalled effort to create the bomb.
In a conversation between Oliphant, Lawrence, and Oppenheimer, that
topic came up, and Oppenheimer suggested he, having no security clear-

ance, should leave. Oliphant replied, "But that's terrible, we need you" (Michelmore, 1969, p. 66). And so, as he says, because "I had begun to think more intensely and on my own about how to make atomic bombs and made some calculations of efficiency, design, amounts of material and so on . . . I was able to give a little information about this aspect of the problem" (M. Wharton, 1955, p. 10). He was invited into the planning group and later was asked to organize the then-scattered efforts. And so Robert was drafted—as were 10 million other Americans—into the Second World War.

Because of his knowledge about physics and his skill at pulling ideas together, as well as his reputation as the "most competent in seeing the essentials of an intricate problem and in interpreting what he saw" (Rhodes, 1986, p. 383), Oppenheimer was asked to coordinate the efforts. At the age of 38, he was put in charge of creating America's atomic bomb. The openness of science presented a conflict with military security, so the project was brought to Los Alamos, New Mexico, where the scientists could have their openness and the military could patrol their fences.

No modern organization would take an academic intellectual whose administrative experience was limited to running a graduate department and turn over to him or her a multibillion-dollar, 10,000-person enterprise. But wars create exigencies and that is exactly what happened. Therefore, the issue of how Robert exercised leadership must be considered. First, there was the matter of his intelligence. General Groves, the Army's project officer, considered Oppenheimer the "most intelligent man [I] had ever met" (Michelmore, 1969, p. 90) and "a genius, a real genius. . . . he can talk about anything. Well, not exactly . . . he doesn't know anything about sports" (Rhodes, 1986, pp. 448–449). Added to his intelligence was his energy. Arthur Compton, chair of a national committee to investigate military uses of atomic power, found that under Oppenheimer, "something got done and done at astonishing speed" (Royal, 1969, p. 85). Along with intelligence and energy was his modeling of the effort. Everyone at Los Alamos worked hard but no one harder than Robert, who worked 20 hours a day, 6 days a week, plus overtime. He was "everywhere, encouraging, flattering, lighting cigarettes, darting in and out of offices and laboratories with suggestions" (Michelmore, 1969, p. 101). He was also ambitious to make a name for himself in science.

Oppenheimer's own assessment of his organizing abilities is perhaps too modest, but it reflects his understanding of the collegial nature of the undertaking. As he recounted in the 1953 security hearing, he described his job as being sure that people understood and that the decisions were properly made, and there were not many easy decisions. We did this through a system of groups, divisions, and coordinating councils, and a coordinating committee which finally made the determination of laboratory policy. (M. Wharton, 1955, p. 12)

To his list of organizational skills, add the element of persuasiveness. Neither Oppenheimer nor anyone else knew how to create a bomb, but the task required the best physicists, and he embarked on an aggressive recruiting policy, convincing scientists and often their families to move to a remote place in the New Mexico desert for the duration of the war. General Groves took a less sanguine view of the physicists and told his staff, "At great expense, we have gathered together on this mesa, the largest collection of crackpots the world has ever seen" (Michelmore, 1969, p. 103).

Knowing how to "work with people" has become a cliché, but large-scale endeavors require integrated effort. Successful administrators, as General Motors creator Alfred Sloan (1964) noted, are not rampant individualists; they know they need others and they are artful in the ways they show respect to and capitalize on others' efforts. Oppenheimer was a natural at bringing people together, encouraging their cooperation, and creating a unifying force: "Group discussion was Oppie's game, and soon it was his voice and his measured sentences that held the attention" (Michelmore, 1969, p. 105). "It wasn't that he contributed so many ideas or suggestions . . . it was his continued and intense presence that produced a sense of direct participation in all of us" (Royal, 1969, p. 104).

Bailey (1988) speaks of Robert's "consummate skill at summarizing discussions . . . even after a three day session . . . [he] could summarize their deliberations lucidly and comprehensively, giving each contribution its proper weight" (p. 168). And Hans Bethe, one of the physicists at Los Alamos, explained Oppenheimer's way with people: "We needed a unifying force and this unification could only be done by a man who really understood everything and was recognized by everybody as superior in judgment and superior in knowledge to all of us. This was our director" (M. Wharton, 1955, p. 135).

Edward Teller, who later worked on the hydrogen bomb and even assisted in the effort to remove Oppenheimer's security clearance, still commented on the way Robert combined scientific knowledge with an ability to create an encouraging informal environment. As Jack Welch (2001), later CEO of General Electric, explained, "Bureaucracy strangles; informality liberates . . . creating an informal atmosphere is a competitive advantage . . . passion, chemistry, ideas flow from any level at any place" (p. 384). Accordingly, there was little rigidity at Los Alamos: "Oppie knew several hundred intimately . . . their relationships with one another . . . and what made them tick. He knew how to organize, cajole, humor, soothe feelings—how to lead . . . without seeming to do so" (Rhodes, 1986, p. 539).

Always something of a know-it-all, Robert learned to mask his intellectual superiority. "Oppie didn't make anybody feel inferior, not anybody" (Rhodes, 1986, p. 570). Hans Bethe said that his administrative skill stemmed from his skill at teaching: "He always knew what were the important problems . . . he truly lived with those problems" (Rhodes, 1986, p. 447). Believing that, Robert protected the work from intrusions by the security-obsessed military: "There was danger in the fact that such decisions had to be taken secretly, not because the people who took the decisions were not wise but because the very absence of criticism and discussion tended to corrode the decision making process" (Bailey, 1988, p. 242). He arbitrated personnel differences, directed the construction of housing, and made the final decision on what lines of inquiry to follow and what to reject.

The bomb was tested on July 16, 1945, and one of the witnessing guards noted, "the long hairs have let it get away from them" (Oppenheimer, 1989, p. 137). There was no question that the bomb would be used. The war had taught the Americans that Japanese soldiers and even civilians would die rather than surrender; the coming invasion of the Japanese homeland could cost up to 1 million American and 10 million Japanese lives. There had been talk of warning the Japanese by inviting them to a demonstration, but no one believed that a big bang in a New Mexico desert would convince them to surrender. As Andrey Sakharov, who later developed the hydrogen bomb for Russia, said, "the atomic question was always half science, half politics" (Bailey, 1988, p. 238).

So the bomb was used on Hiroshima on August 6, 1945, and at Nagasaki on August 9; and 5 days later Japan surrendered. America's reaction was one of elation, but there were as many misgivings. Einstein later said that had he known that "the Germans would not succeed in constructing the atom bomb, I never would have moved a finger" (Rouzé, 1964, p. 114). And Arthur Venner, one of the American soldiers brought to Hiroshima to see the effects, said that he was "astonished at the flattened city and ashamed when he saw the ulcerated and half-dead survivors, their skin burned off on the side exposed to the blast" (personal communication, November 1998). Oppenheimer too had second thoughts: "There are people who say [the bomb] is not such a very bad weapon. . . . Before the test, we sometimes said that too . . .

after the test, we did not say it anymore" (Michelmore, 1969, p. 112). But the scientists had been told to build the bomb; they were not asked to provide lectures on politics and morals. Besides, the building itself had presented them with what Robert called, "a technically sweet problem . . . [and] when you see something that is technically sweet, you go ahead and do it and you argue about what to do about it only after you have had your technical success" (Rouzé, 1964, p. 87). He added later that the planned invasion of Japan would have been "much more terrible than the use of the bombs" (Oppenheimer, 1989, p. 138).

There was next the matter of what to do with knowledge about atomic weapons, and Robert had joined a committee to make recommendations. Their report suggested that, in the interest of "taming a force too dangerous to fit into any of our usual concepts" (T. W. Wilson, 1970, p. 40), atomic energy and research about atomic energy be turned over to a United Nations–based authority that would control the resources needed to build bombs, operate facilities for the creation of fissionable materials, control the research on atomic weapons, and promote "nondangerous use and wide distribution of atomic energy for beneficial purposes" (p. 41).

It was not to be. Russia's intransigence in the United Nations, its takeover of Eastern Europe, Communist parties in western Europe proclaiming that they would welcome Russian soldiers as liberators, Stalin's attempt to cut off western access to Berlin, and the Communist victory in China, all convinced America that their fears of Communism were founded. Worse, in 1949, with some technical assistance from Klaus Fuchs, who had worked at Los Alamos, Russia exploded its own atomic bomb and in 1952, under the direction of physicist Andrey Sakharov, its own hydrogen bomb.

Paranoia and hypernationalism reigned. Morgan (2003) argues that Communism and fear of Communism, combined with Russia's obtaining nuclear weapons, "precipitated a kind of American national nervous breakdown" (Powers, 2004, p. 21). Senator Joseph McCarthy, FBI Director J. Edgar Hoover, and the House Un-American Activities Committee were looking for Communists, would-be Communists, had-been Communists, or any fellow travelers who in the 1930s might have entertained a socialist idea. Schoolchildren practiced getting under their desks in case of attack; atomic fallout—strontium 90—was reputed to be in cows' milk; bomb shelters appeared in backyards; and atop the hills around Elmira, New York, civil air patrols scanned the skies for Russian bombers.

And in the center of it all was Robert Oppenheimer, nuclear technocrat, leading intellectual, father of the bomb, and, save for Albert Ein-

stein, the most famous scientist in the world. He had left Los Alamos
and returned to Berkeley, but he maintained a public presence; politicians and generals sought his advice on everything from the bomb to
how soon the Russians would have the bomb, to nuclear and military
policy, to whether to build hydrogen bombs. Oppenheimer hoped
to preserve America's advantage, but that ended when Russia got the
bomb.

Thereafter, he advocated for scientific openness, declassification of
most military secrets, public debates of military policy, and sharing nuclear knowledge with allies. He also advocated the development of "tac-
tical" or smaller atomic bombs that could be used on battlefields but not
against cities. Of America's then-superiority over the Russians, he said,
"Such superiority can probably only be maintained through continued
further development of both the technical and the underlying scientific
aspects of the problem . . . no government can adequately meet its responsibilities for defense if it rests content with the wartime results of
this project" (Rouzé, 1964, p. 82).

In 1949, along with several other scientists, Oppenheimer had opposed the creation of the hydrogen bomb, which he considered an evil
thing. "If [the H bomb] is successful, radioactive poisoning of life on
earth has been brought within the range of technical possibilities. . . . In
the end there beckons more and more clearly, general annihilation" (Bailey, 1988, p. 180). In fact, when a hydrogen bomb was detonated on a
Pacific island, the island itself was vaporized; "when told that 'the island
was missing,' President-elect Dwight D. Eisenhower visibly paled"
("Fifty Years," 2002, p. 79).

But Russia had both atomic and hydrogen bombs and those Americans in power were convinced that if military force were not massively
applied, the United States would go the way of Athens, Rome, Spain,
and the British Empire. Conflict dichotomizes and Oppenheimer became an opponent of the then-prevalent doctrine of massive retaliation.
For that and for his continued opposition to secrecy, which he termed
"rigid and dangerous . . . when even the men who know facts can find
no one to talk to about them, when facts are too secret for discussion,
and thus for thought" (T. W. Wilson, 1970, p. 160), and for being on
the minority side of the issue, and saying what others feared to say, he
was subject to a public trial. And like Plutarch's (1891) Themistocles,
the Athenian admiral who after giving his city the victory at Salamis, was
banished "to pacify and mitigate the fury of envy, who delights in the
disgrace of superior characters and loses a part of her rancor by their
fall" (p. 247), Robert was deemed no longer "entitled to the continued

confidence of the government and of this commission because of the proof of fundamental defects in his character" (Strout, 1963, p. 44).

Removed from the cutting edge of physics, in retreat from former friendships, smoking constantly, followed by the FBI, and "something of a loner" (Halberstam, 1993, p. 353), he became director of the Institute for Advanced Study at Princeton. He was also an international celebrity, and because of his contributions and his efforts to keep open discussions of atomic weapons, he remained a hero to the world's scientific community. In 1963, President Kennedy, attempting to right an old wrong, awarded him the Enrico Fermi Award, the nation's highest scientific honor, which he received from President Johnson in December 1963. Oppenheimer died in 1967.

CONCLUSION

J. Robert Oppenheimer was smarter than the rest of us, but he too had to create an education to do the things that he did. The elements of that education are plain. He had early encouragement from literate and caring parents, a cultural inheritance that valued learning and combined learning with ethics, substantial exposure to and affiliation with transcendental ideas, early induction into the scientific currents of the time, and later participation in a community of similarly engaged colleagues. It is the pattern followed by this book's previous subjects, and overall, quite like what a career counselor might project by way of personal advice. But as they did for the other subjects, the currents within and around Oppenheimer's life overlapped, and the resulting confluence was more than the career counselor might have foreseen. Robert's quest for intellectual unity led him into alternative ways of knowing, his Berkeley affiliations and the times lead him to politics, his science converged with the war, his talents led him to Los Alamos, and America's nervous breakdown over Russian bombs, British spies, and atomic fallout led to his public humiliation. In retrospect, and with apologies for the implied teleology, the elements add up and create the person that J. Robert Oppenheimer was or, at least, the person he was in American history. And for purposes of this book, the sum of that experience, by choice or chance, fate or will, was his education.

CHAPTER 8

Dorothy Day
1897–1980

I haven't the slightest idea what I learned in classes. All my education has come from outside.

(Day, 1938/1978, p. 61)

Like strong emotions, strong ethics are necessary for strong ideas. And for this book's subjects, ethics and education were enjoined. Brought up with rationalist assumptions about the connections between learning, knowing, and acting, each believed that humans are not hardwired with notions of responsibility, justice, and charity. A good person is a learned person, and both learning and ethical learning were influenced by religion. Franklin, Lincoln, Roosevelt, Addams, and Du Bois learned their ethics in Christian homes where the emphasis was on the authority of scriptures. Their families read the Bible, believed in salvation through Jesus Christ, and, to varying degrees, regarded life on earth as preparation for life in heaven. Accompanying learning and religion was a fundamentalist faith in relentless striving. Learning and effort were moral obligations as well as paths to personal betterment, and conversely, ignorance and indolence were sinful, or at least an affirmation of unworthiness. Oppenheimer had neither Christian nor traditional Jewish teachings, but his family's Ethical Culture Society had as institutionalized a system of ethics as any religion.

As these subjects grew, they tended to pay less attention to religion's rituals and hierarchies and less to inward notions of salvation and piety, but they directed their ethics outward toward faith in intelligence and social action. Ethics was not only a part of the subjects' educations; it influenced their learning, infused their knowing, guided their actions, and gave their lives coherence. And so without entering into a discussion of whether the Ten Commandments or silent prayer should be allowed in the schoolhouse, I present in this final description the education of a woman for whom ethics was the center of her life.

Dorothy Day was a convert to the Roman Catholic faith and, but for an early abortion, might be considered for sainthood. Saintly Dorothy may have been, but as well as religion, she was driven by the progressive ideals that influenced Jane Addams and Eleanor Roosevelt. However, there is a difference. While all three directed their efforts to helping the poor and the disenfranchised, Addams and Roosevelt directed their energies toward constructing institutions based on liberal and democratic values. They hoped that such institutions, supported by education and legislation, would mitigate the ill effects of unbridled capitalism and would insure, in bureaucratic form, some humanization of the social landscape.

Not so Dorothy Day. She did not create programs to feed the hungry; she fed the hungry. She did not improve housing through government subsidies; she housed the homeless. She did not work on behalf of the poor through institutions; she remained poor, and the organization she created, or more accurately inspired, remains a direct-action network of small, self-organized, locally funded, volunteer-staffed communities with no bureaucracy to sustain them. An anarchist, Dorothy resisted institutions and their inevitable accumulation of power. She believed that "responsibility for the poor must return to the parish . . . the group, the family, the individual" (Day, 1963, p. 192). Her life was one of direct action, which meant not sending tax-deductible contributions to progressive agencies, but "bringing ideas to the man in the street via picketing and leaflets, storming employment offices, marching on Washington, . . . boarding Polaris submarines and sailing boats . . . into areas where nuclear testing is going on" (Day, 1963, p. vii).

To personalist ideals, Dorothy added the self-abnegation of the Catholic Church, which teaches that the world is a vale of tears, temporal happiness is illusory, and the only lasting good is communion with God. In that respect, she emulated St. Therese of Lisieux, the saint of the personal act who believed that "sanctity was . . . bringing the love of God into the routine affairs of life" (W. D. Miller, 1982, p. 431). In accounting for Dorothy Day's education, we keep in mind the combination of anarchy and Catholicism that characterized her life and work.

Dorothy was born in 1897 in Brooklyn, New York. Her Scottish-Irish parents were from long-established American families, some of whom had fought in the Revolutionary War, and later the Civil War. Her father, John, was a journalist who specialized in horse racing, worked at tracks in Florida, and later served as a racing inspector for New York State. He was described by those who knew him as "gruff, surly, smart, respected . . . [a friend of] New York Giants manager John McGraw and New York Governor Al Smith" (W. D. Miller, 1982, p. 5). John's life was bounded by the triad of work, sports, and saloons that some men favor over the company of wife and children. In 1905 he moved the family to San Francisco where he took a journalism job, but in that city's 1906 earthquake, the newspaper plant went up in flames. The family then moved to Chicago and lived over a saloon while John drank, wrote a novel, and looked for work. He found work, moved the family around Chicago a few times, and in 1916 landed a journalism job back in New York City.

John had been brought up in the Congregational Church, and his wife in the Episcopal, but neither pushed religion into the home. As Dorothy writes, "In our family, the name of God was never mentioned. Mother and Father never went to church; none of us children had been baptized and to speak of the soul was to speak immodestly, uncovering what better might remain hidden" (Day, 1938/1978, p. 20). Any show of emotions was suspect as well. "We could never be free with each other . . . we were always withdrawn and alone, unlike Italians, Poles and Jews" (MacDonald, 1957, p. 38).

Dorothy, a serious and introspective child, was inspired by religious thoughts. Her "heart leapt when [she] heard the name of God" (Day, 1952, p. 10), and when she picked up the Bible, she "sensed the holiness in holding the book in my hand" (p. 19). The Bible's words made her feel as if she were "being introduced to someone and I knew almost immediately that I was discovering God" (p. 19). Religious stories instilled in her a "lofty enthusiasm . . . [and] my heart almost burst with desire to take part in such high endeavor" (p. 19). Of the San Francisco earthquake, after which the people of Oakland shared what they had with those displaced, she says: "I remember the joy of doing good, of sharing whatever we had with others" (Day, 1938/1978, p. 21).

A Methodist minister convinced her mother to bring the children to church, and, with the exception of John, who thought that "churches and hymn singing were a lot of bunk," the family attended services (W. D. Miller, 1982, p. 12). Dorothy enjoyed the singing, later attended and was baptized in the Episcopal Church, and began to read religious works. She was drawn to the sermons of John Wesley and Jonathan Edwards, and recalls reading Thomas à Kempis, whose *Imitations of Christ* was, as she later recalled, "a book that followed me through my days" (Day, 1938/1978, p. 7). And when there was nothing to do, as she says, she used "the time to think about fundamental things" (Day, 1938/ 1978, p. 31).

Serious thoughts were encouraged by her parents. John Day carried a Bible, read Shakespeare, and filled his newspaper columns with literary allusions. Mother had graduated from a business college and was a serious reader; and both parents provided an encouraging and literate atmosphere for their four children. Toward the end of her life, Dorothy talked about what she had learned from reading: "I really did love those books . . . I'm always telling people to read Dickens or Tolstoy, Orwell . . . I wanted to live by [those novels] . . . to take those artists and novelists to heart and live up to their wisdom" (Elie, 2003, p. 452).

As well as reading, which Dorothy had been doing since she was 4, the Day children were encouraged to write. "When I was eleven, we had started to type out a little family newspaper. We all liked to write, and I had been taught to write early, personally, subjectively, about what I saw around me and what was being done" (Day, 1963, p. 7). And for the family, there were reading times during which "no one was allowed to talk or violate the quiet" (Day, 1938/1978, pp. 33–34): "there was no blaring radio bringing in the news every hour on the hour so that you heard about the latest murder, train wreck, plane disaster, and political coup twelve times a day. There were no picture books . . . or what father called 'trash' around the house. We had Scott, Hugo, Dickens, Stevenson, Cooper and Poe" (Day, 1952, p. 27).

Books gave Dorothy a way to think about larger issues. And in the late nineteenth and early twentieth centuries, among the largest was social justice, a matter discussed in the earlier chapters on Jane Addams and Eleanor Roosevelt. Jacksonian democracy, liberal capitalism, and post–Civil War industrialism had brought—along with economic and technological revolution—a concentration of wealth, and power on one hand, and an unsettling degree of economic inequality on the other. One result was the increasingly militant workers' movement reacting against low wages, difficult working conditions, and the arbitrary exercise of owners' powers. Opposing the movement was the government, run by men who may or may not have voted for equality, but who believed that the government should not interfere with the God-given rights of individuals to accumulate wealth. "The rights and interests of the laboring man will be protected and cared for—not by labor agitators but by the Christian men to whom God in his infinite wisdom has given control of the property interests of the country and upon the successful management of which so much depends" (E. Morris, 2002, p. 137).

On the other side were a host of people and groups who wanted a different distribution of wealth and power and a different political and economic system. Unionists wanted to organize labor on a large scale, syndicalists wanted to organize labor on a small scale. Anarchists—believing that the domination of one human by another was the root of evil—wanted to abolish authority. Anarcho-syndicalists wanted all of society organized on a small scale. Socialists wanted to reorganize society from the top, and suffragettes wanted women to vote. Even President

Theodore Roosevelt (1901–1908) thought that the economic policy of laissez faire had gotten out of control, and that government should play a moderating influence in the economy. The sum of it all was a great ferment—in 1903 there were 3,000 strikes (E. Morris, 2002, p. 259). The movement was heavily infused by religion. As Jane Addams said, "The great awakening of social consciousness in the labor movement [was] one of the most deeply religious things of modern times" (Martin, 2002, pp. 164–165). And that combination of religion and radicalism made up the intellectual stream in which Dorothy Day would live her life.

As a young woman, Dorothy was inspired by proletarian novels such as *The Jungle* (1906/1984), in which Upton Sinclair detailed Chicago's meatpacking industry and the way European immigrants were worked to death in rat-ridden slaughterhouses. Exploited and cheated by employers, landlords, and lawyers, immigrant fathers were driven to drink, mothers to prostitution, and children died of overwork, typhoid, and consumption. Describing the competitive wage system that underlay all this, Sinclair says: "The workers were dependent on a job to exist from day to day and so they bid against each other and no man could get more than the lowest man would consent to work for. And thus the mass of people were always in a life and death struggle with poverty" (p. 372). Inspired by Sinclair's story, and already in the habit of asking questions about life, Dorothy took walks around the Chicago area where the immigrants lived.

Dorothy was influenced also by Jack London's quasi-autobiographical novel, *Martin Eden* (1909/1931). One of the more interesting and educated characters of that time, London was a voracious autodidact. Born of an often-absent father and unstable mother, he quit school and went to work at age 12. After that, he spent some years as a seaman, factory worker, hobo, and, for a few months, a member of Kelly's army of unemployed who during the recession of 1894 marched on Washington to ask for federal aid. During the march, London spent some time in a Buffalo, New York, jail, and after the march ended, went through a period of riding the rails. But he had always been determined to improve himself, and as a child had begun to read his way through the Oakland, California, library. Accordingly, he returned to high school where he studied for his diploma and began to write about his adventures. Combining what he saw, what he lived, and what he read, London gradually moved toward socialism.

Dorothy reports being influenced also by Peter Kropotkin (1899/1971), a Russian nobleman turned socialist, turned anarchist, who explains that his conversion to anarchy took place when he was an officer in the Russian army and had to undertake large-scale projects with small means: "And if all these things ended more or less successfully, I account for it only by the fact that . . . once the impulse has been given, the enterprise must be conducted . . . in a sort of communal way by means of common understanding" (p. 217).

Dorothy recounted too being affected by Kropotkin's essay in which he asks the reader to chose between a life that says "humanity can go to the devil" or one in which "you will join the ranks of the revolutionists and work with them for the complete transformation of society" (Day, 1938/1978, p. 46). After which, he proffers the advice Dorothy followed all her life: "Be among the people and the question will solve itself" (p. 46).

In high school and college Dorothy read about the efforts of socialist and presidential candidate Eugene Debs, of the Knights of Labor, and of Big Bill Haywood's International Workers of the World (IWW). She read about the insurrectionist Molly Maguires in Pennsylvania coalfields, and about women striking the New England cotton mills. She read about Chicago's Hay Market riot of 1886 where policemen were killed, anarchists blamed, and the latter's ensuing execution was for years a cause célèbre among the left. She read about labor organizers such as Mother Jones, Elizabeth Gurley Flynn, Carlo Tresca—who was mysteriously killed—and IWW organizer and construction worker, Joe Hill, who told the Utah firing squad assigned to execute him, "Don't mourn for me; organize" (Diggins, 1973, p. 59). She read Maxim Gorki, and—because Jack London had read him—Herbert Spencer. She read Tolstoy, Turgenev, and "everything of Dostoevsky" (Day, 1952, p. 15), who condemns materialism and self-interest, emphasizes the collective nature of guilt, and writes of "men and suffering" (p. 124). While it remained for her to grow up and experience the world she had read about, Dorothy had already embarked on her intellectual path. As to the underlying question, What is your place in all of this? she developed an answer that she took into her later life: "I wanted every home to be open to the lame, the halt, and the blind the way it had been after the San Francisco earthquake" (Day, 1952, pp. 43–44).

Dorothy enjoyed school, but says little of the experience except that she loved English composition and languages, studied Greek, admired her Latin teacher, and learned enough of that language to read the Roman poet Virgil. She describes herself in those years as serious, introspective, busy with her readings, and busy as well, as the eldest daughter, with the care of her baby brother. Her efforts paid off when she graduated and received a $300 a year tuition scholarship to the University of Illinois at Urbana: "I was sixteen and filled with a great sense of independence. . . . The idea of earning my own money by my own work was more thrilling than the idea of an education" (W. D. Miller, 1982, p. 31).

At Urbana, Dorothy led "a very shiftless life doing for the first time exactly what I wanted to do, attending only those classes I wished to attend, coming and going at whatever hour of the night I pleased. My freedom intoxicated me" (Day, 1952, p. 49). Finding her high school work sufficient, she skipped classes, received indifferent grades, got excused from requirements, and took little interest in assignments. The scholarship paid for tuition and books; for sustenance, she did housework, cooked, and babysat. Sometimes she had no money to eat, but she used the occasions to experiment with the voluntary poverty that would later characterize her Catholic Workers. She had already rejected a middle-class version of happiness, with its "smug disregard of the misery of the world" (Day, 1938/1978, p. 39). "I could have made my way safe and secure, but that is not what I wanted. I was not merely perverse . . . I was choosing another way . . . I had no right to regard my poverty or my hardships as any other than of my own choosing" (Day, 1938/1978, p. 54).

Equally important for this woman who would later make her living in journalism, she wrote a description of her 3 days without food and so was invited to join the staff of the campus newspaper, *The Daily Illini*, where she found a friend, Rayna Prohme, a woman similarly inspired by notions of social justice and who 10 years later moved to Russia to help build a Communist society. Dorothy, Rayna, and the latter's socialist boyfriend, Ralph, carried an idyllic friendship: "We wrote, we attended lectures, we listened together to the [visiting poets and socialists]. We saw Shakespeare's *Twelfth Night* and listened to symphony orchestras. . . . Ralph would sometimes call beneath our window to share some poem . . . which had fired him with enthusiasm" (Day, 1952, p. 54).

In 1916, Dorothy's father received an offer from the *New York Sun*, and the family moved east. Dorothy, then finishing her second year of college, was unwilling to be far from her family, so she quit school, went along, and for the rest of her life made her home and, as Catholics say, "found her vocation" in New York City. John opposed women working and living at home, so Dorothy moved to the lower East Side to live among the Jewish and Italian immigrants. A journalist with socialist leanings, she supported herself by writing for a series of leftist newspapers, *The Call*, then *The Collective*, and later, *The Masses*.

A profession connects one to the world and provides one with ideas with which to think about and behave toward the world. And among radical journalists in the early twentieth century, the dominant idea was to "build up indictments against the system" (Day, 1952, p. 74). Accordingly, this 18-year-old female reporter was carried along on a world of events: "One day listening to [Leon] Trotsky, and the next day interviewing Mrs. Vincent Astor's butler; writing articles about the Navy Department's charges against . . . munitions makers, then stories about child labor. . . . One fourteen-year-old boy working ninety hours a week" (Day, 1952, pp. 74–75).

Drawn to revolutionary striving, opposing America's 1917 entry into World War I, living among the poor, and working with anarchists and socialists, Day was also thinking through her position: "I was only eighteen so I wavered between my allegiance to Socialism, Syndicalism and Anarchism. When I read Tolstoi, I was an Anarchist. My allegiance to the Call kept me a socialist . . . and my Americanism inclined me to the I.W.W. movement" (Day, 1938/1978, p. 68).

Dorothy castigates herself for not being a real student of revolution, for not undertaking a serious reading of Marx. But she had little tolerance for theories of revolution and less for ideational infighting. She was more taken with people, and she was critical of socialists' tendency to concentrate on ideas rather than on the way individuals survive. "I still question this over-emphasis of human misery and under-emphasis of bravery, the courage of human beings, enabling them to make the best of their surroundings" (Day, 1938/1978, p. 75). Day would later build this emphasis on individuals and on attending to one person at a time into the Catholic Worker.

Continuing the experiment with self-denial that she began in college, Day lived in "vermin-ridden tenements with stray cats yowling at night . . . a smell in the walls . . . the smell of the grave" (Day, 1952, p. 58). Indeed, all her life she preferred, as she says, "the slums of the poor to the slums of the rich. A tenement is a tenement whether it is on lower Park Avenue or upper" (Day, 1938/1978, p. 67). So she subsisted on little, asked for less, and continued to seek out—as she said in a later story of her conversion—"the downward path that leads to salvation" (Day, 1938/1978, p. 2).

As did all of this book's subjects, Dorothy demonstrated an early intellectual maturity and a more-than-passing-acquaintance with serious ideas. By their late teens and early 20s, the subjects had read and studied, and then they set out to experience the world and find a place for themselves. Their paths differed, and differed in difficulty. W. E. B. Du Bois and Robert Oppenheimer slid easily from students to scholars and from scholars to researchers, administrators, and activists. Robert Oppenheimer's wealthy family protected his fiscal security, but family money may have complicated the transitions of Jane Addams and Eleanor Roosevelt.

Money was absent from the early manhood of Abraham Lincoln who went through several years of laboring, flat-boating, storekeeping, soldiering, and surveying before, in his late 20s, he settled into law and politics. Benjamin Franklin was without resources when—after some casting about—he got off the boat in Philadelphia, walked up Market Street, and began his adult life. And from his autobiography, we may infer that only after some extended period of self-examination was he able to put together his career as businessman, citizen, scientist, and diplomat. But whatever the circumstances, all of our subjects added to the awareness of larger events they had gained through reading the personal experience in which they would try out their ideas. And from that combination of ideas and experience, their lives and their education flowed forward into the future.

Along with her socialist politics and personal penury, there was an exciting life to be led in New York's Greenwich Village for a young female journalist of radical inclinations. Day was loosely affiliated with what Diggins (1973) calls the "lyrical left . . . an intellectual saturnalia in which everything was possible and nothing prohibited, a joyous springtime in which . . . barriers went down and people reached each other who had never touched before" (p. 45). Diggins describes Greenwich Village at the time as filled with "socialists, trade-unionists, anarchists, suffragists, poets . . . lawyers . . . psychoanalysts, I.W.W.s, single taxers, birth-controlists, newspapermen, artists" (p. 74). As were her friends, Day was convinced that the revolution in Russia was only the beginning, and that the Marxian view of a better, freer, more opportunity-filled and proletarian world was at hand. Youth and enthusiasm carried her along. "Rayna visited me, and we walked the streets . . . sat on the ends of piers singing revolutionary songs . . . dallied on park benches, never wanting to go home to sleep, but only to continue to savor our youth" (Day, 1952, p. 79).

Her youthful idyll faded some with the help of the Washington police when Dorothy was imprisoned for demonstrating on behalf of women's right to vote. Briefly, one of her journalism assignments was to accompany a group of suffragettes traveling to Washington to picket the White House on behalf of other suffragettes who had been arrested for similar activity. The reactionary right, in the person of U. S. Attorney General Mitchell Palmer, was then beating back attempts to change the social order, and the women—including Dorothy—were arrested, given 30 days, and transferred to a Maryland State Prison. They protested with a hunger strike and Dorothy "lay for six days and nights in the coldness, darkness and hunger, pondering in her heart the world and our part in it" (Day, 1952, p. 89): "I would never be free again . . . when I knew all over the world there were women and men . . . suffering constraint, punishment, isolation and hardship for crimes of which all of us were guilty" (Day, 1952, pp. 89–90). Characteristically, Day used the time to read the only book she was allowed, the Bible, which gave her a feeling of regaining "something of my childhood that I had lost" (Day, 1952, p. 91).

Embarrassed by its behavior, more by the attendant publicity, the government relented, gave in to the women's demands, fed, and released them. Dorothy went back to New York and became for a time, an intimate of playwright Eugene O'Neill, then writing for the Provincetown Players and drinking his way through Greenwich Village. She was described at the time by an O'Neill biographer as

> from a solidly republican and Episcopalian family . . . she turned socialist at college, worked as a reporter for *The Call*, been Floyd Dell's assistant on *The Masses*, picketed the White House with other suffragettes, and been thrown into jail. [She was] a tall rangy girl with a fine strong face and inexhaustible energy. . . . She sat in saloons for hours, matching the men drink for drink. (Sheaffer, 1968, p. 403)

Day loved O'Neill's mind and writing, thought him a genius, refused to sleep with him, and read what he recommended, Strindberg and Baudelaire among others. Their set of writers, drunks, poets, journalists, and street people hung around a Sixth Avenue saloon they called "the hell hole" where one night Eugene recited Francis Thompson's "The Hound of Heaven," in which that poet recounts his resistance to and ensuing acceptance of God:

> I fled Him down the nights and down the days;
> I fled Him down the arches of the years;
> I fled Him down the labyrinthine ways;
> Of my own mind; and in the midst of tears
> I hid from Him. (quoted in Day, 1938/1978, p. 8)

Thirty years later, Day recalled that with the recitation, O'Neill had "brought me to a consciousness of God" (W. D. Miller, 1982, p. 118). And often after a night of partying, she would stop in St. Joseph's Church on Sixth Avenue for morning mass. "I felt again and again the need to go to church, to kneel, to bow my head in prayer. It was a blind instinct . . . an act of will" (Day, 1952, p. 96). And although she believed in the brotherhood of socialism, she began to see that there could be no "brotherhood without the fatherhood of God" (Day, 1938/1978, p. 12).

Dorothy decided to change her life. The precipitating event occurred during an all-nighter when one member of the party died in Day's arms of a drug overdose. After that, having sequestered the evidence from the police and seeing O'Neill refuse to help with the corpse or the cleanup, she decided she had enough of "characters, bad free verse, drunkenness, and casual sex" (W. D. Miller, 1982, p. 117). It was during the First World War and the country needed nurses, so Dorothy became one. In contrast to her former life, she embraced "the order, the life, the discipline" (Day, 1938/1978, p. 95), the "sacrament of duty," as she called it, and a place "where one's life fell into efficient orderly lines" (Elie, 2003, p. 35). She embraced as well the humble tasks she was required to perform. And she came to admire her patients who "were poor, and did not expect too much . . . uncomplaining . . . accepting their suffering with stoicism" (Day, 1938/1978, p. 95).

The task is to account for Dorothy Day's education, not her life. But the two are inseparable. She read everything and crammed into her early years as much experience as they could hold, even to the point of recklessness. In a self-revealing novel—copies of which she later did her best to destroy—she says she "was capable of doing anything—capable of following her desires wherever they lead" (W. D. Miller, 1982, p. 123). Totally of the moment, easily finding whatever work she needed, encouraged by the ideals of socialism, and unhampered by the restraints on women, she was living the later twentieth-century feminist ideal of independence, self-reliance, and free choice. The only boundaries she recognized were her own.

But there are reasons for boundaries; they protect the unwary, and cannot be ignored for long with impunity. At the hospital she fell wildly in love with Lionel Moise, a self-educated and itinerant journalist whose writing was admired by, among others, Ernest Hemingway. Moise was talented, a socialist, and literary—he liked to recite Shakespeare—but he had an unfortunate propensity to drink himself blind and get into brawls. And when he and Day met, he was working as an orderly to pay the hospital where he had wound up after one such bout. Dorothy was ready for love. Miller (1982) refers to her as "a tinder box, ignited by a vagrant spark" (pp. 124–125). She thought Moise looked like an Egyptian pharaoh, decided she had to have him, and for a time they lived in a tempestuous, off-on relationship that drove her to thoughts of suicide. And despite her mother's pleading, "Don't get caught," she became pregnant. Moise wanted neither a long-term relationship nor a child and, to keep him, Dorothy had an abortion, but Moise left her that very day.

Perhaps on downward spiral, she then married Barkeley Tobey, a man of mysterious origins, wealthy, twice her age, and the founder of the Literary Guild of New York. In her autobiography, Dorothy speaks of the people they met and places they lived, of their honeymoon spent drinking, of waking up in Paris and not knowing how she got there. And she speaks of the books she read: "Balzac and de Maupassant and Victor Hugo were my companions" (Day, 1952, p. 110). But there is no mention of Tobey, and of the omission she says, "I have always wanted to tell of things that brought me to God . . . and I do not want to write about other people with whom I was intimately associated" (Day, 1952, p. 110). Mr. Tobey disappeared shortly thereafter (with the silver), just as he had with some of his other seven marriages.

Back in America, divorced, adrift, and hearing a rumor of Moise in Chicago, she went to find him. Not finding or at least not reconciling with him, she found work at another socialist newspaper, where her affiliations brought her again to the jailhouse. She and another woman journalist spent a night at the rooming house run by the International Workers of the World. Chicago's union-busting police, always looking for a reason to harass the I.W.W. and finding two unattached women on the premises, arrested the leaders for running a disorderly house and the women for prostitution. In jail again, Day writes that she was "caught, found out, branded, publicly humiliated . . . [and] I deserved it" (Elie, 2003, p. 38). As always, she was taken with the charity and kindness of the poor, in this case, the also-jailed prostitutes, who took her as one of their own and consoled her. Again in a cell, she spent her 4 days thinking of the words of socialist Eugene Debs: "While there is a lower class, I am of it, and while there is a criminal element, I am of it, and while there is a soul in prison, I am not free" (Day, 1938/1978, p. 102). She was ashamed for having put herself in that situation, but as she said, "It was a valid experience. I felt, and I was sharing, as I never had before, the life of the poorest of the poor, the guilty, the dispossessed" (Day, 1952, p. 120).

Across the accounts of Dorothy's life, from herself and from others, is a picture of a self-reliant, adventurous, and resourceful woman. She never doubts her ability to survive, to find housing and meals, to make money one way or the other, to find books and friends. Even when things do not work out, when she is jilted, on the edge, imprisoned, humiliated, poor, or depressed, her resilience holds her up. In that respect, she is like the book's other subjects whose outlook is always rooted in a longer view. Neither Day nor they complain; nor do any of them take refuge in drink, drugs, or self-pity. Dorothy regarded drink and drugs as human failings, but like Jane Addams, she regarded self-pity as the worst of sins. Whatever the experiences—prison, heartbreak, poverty, unfaithful lovers—she turns them inward, folds them into her education, and takes whatever blame upon herself, referring back to her choices that brought her to that place. She had thought through principles of equality, socialism, and anarchy; she understood the randomness of injustice, and she was attracted by the dignity of the poor and oppressed, and as well by the possibility of redemption. The combination sustains her in adversity, and even when she is on the edge of what others would call ruin, she is never ruined. Her openness to experience, self-reliance, and lack of fear support her, and she continues onward with her education, with her life.

Released from jail, she went with her sister to New Orleans, supported herself by writing for another socialist newspaper, worked on her novel, and continued her readings, which at the time included James Joyce, Blaise Pascal, and more Dostoyevsky. She clerked in Montgomery Ward, worked in a library, posed for art classes, borrowed quarters from her neighbors for the gas meter, and with her sister, lived on rabbit stew, rice, and shrimp. One of her newspaper assignments was to write an article about girls who were taxi-dancers, that is, women for whom a man would pay a nickel or a dime for a dance, and so, for a time, she became such a dancer. Throughout, she found herself drawn to church where "the very physical attitude of devotion of those about me made me bow my head . . . I remembered the lines from the *Imitation of Christ.* 'Who humbly approaching to the fountain of sweetness, doth not carry thence some little sweetness? Who standing by a copious fire, doth not derive there from some little heat?'" (Day, 1938/1978, pp. 108–109).

Back in New York, she continued writing for newspapers, fell in with another socialist literary group that included several later writers, John Dos Passos, Hart Crane, Malcolm Crowley, and poet Allen Tate, among them. Despite the prohibition on alcohol consumption that had come with the 1922 Volstead Act, Day lived in a world where there was a great deal of partying and drinking and where "bootlegging was a common failure" (Day, 1952, p. 130). More important, she sold her novel for $3,000 and bought a cottage with a small piece of land—20 by 80 feet—on the shore of Staten Island where she lived for 4 years and where, as Elie (2003) says, she changed her life from "bohemian to anchorite, loose woman to expectant mother, social radical to rosary-praying Catholic" (p. 43). Never alone for long, she fell in love with another quiet, literary socialist named Forster, who "lived day by day and insisted on the freedom of body and soul" (Day, 1952, p. 136). A mechanic by vocation and biologist by avocation, Forster taught her about gardening, fishing, and the stars, and together they spent long hours on the water, and "lived together in the fullest sense of the phrase" (Day, 1952, p. 130). Day found peace there but she continued searching. "My happiness made me know that there was a greater happiness to be obtained from life than any I had ever known. I began to think, to . . . consciously pray more" (Day, 1952, p. 132).

She became pregnant, and after delivering her daughter, Tamar, she decided to have the baby baptized, "cost what it may. I knew that I was not going to have her floundering through many years as I had done, doubting and hesitating, undisciplined and amoral" (Day, 1952, p. 155). Forster loved Dorothy and his daughter but not the idea of marriage or religion.—"It was impossible to talk about religion or faith with him" (Elie, 2003, p. 49)—and he would have nothing to do with her if she embraced it. She understood his jealousy at having to share her with God, but acting against her desire to have Forster as a husband and father, she asked him to leave and decided to live, as she says, "in conformity with the will of God" (Day, 1952, p. 287).

Among her first steps was finding a sympathetic nun who instructed her in the Baltimore Catechism, the history of the Church, how to say the rosary, and what to do at mass. And she continued her spiritual readings, studying the lives of the saints, the New Testament, and—as always—Dostoyevsky. Besides costing her the man she loved and the father of her child, Catholicism had been a hard choice for other reasons. The Catholic Church was regarded by her socialist friends as an opiate of the people. They opposed its historical alliance with power and property, and in Catholic countries, with reaction. Even in America where its primary work was with immigrants on their way to the middle class, socialists saw the Church as putting aside the teachings of Jesus in favor of political, nationalist—often militaristic and capitalistic—goals. Charles R. Morris (1997) described the American—then Irish-dominated—Church with its millions of adherents and its "network of Catholic institutions that forced religious/ethnic identity and protected lay people from the virus of free thinking" as a virtual "state within a state" (p. viii). In the early to mid-twentieth century in America's large cities—Chicago, Boston, Los Angeles, and New York—Cardinals Stritch, Cushing, McIntyre, and Spellman respectively exercised enormous political power.

But Day's was not the church of bricks and mortar, cardinals and bishops. Hers was the church of the cross, the sacraments, of Jesus, Mary Magdalene, Therese of Lisieux, and Francis of Assisi; the church of the poor, the church of the masses. "My very experience as a radical, my whole makeup, made me want to associate myself with the masses, and [the Catholic Church] held the allegiance of masses of people" (Elie, 2003, pp. 50–51). Further, Dorothy never attacked church doctrines or authority. Her mission was social, not religious, reform, and when on a few occasions she was directed by the Church to alter her teaching, she

did so. As well, Day had the intellectual authority of two recent popes—
Leo XIII (2002) and Pius IX (2002)—each of whom had written encyc-
lical letters disparaging unrestrained capitalism, supporting labor, and asserting that the interests of the people were more important than the
interests of property. Dorothy felt certain her Catholic Church would
not deter—rather it would strengthen—her quest for social justice. So
she came to inspire and set an example for a whole generation of Catholics who were, like her, attracted to the Church's spirituality but not to
its temporal and institutional power.

Our subjects never stopped learning. But by their late 20s, they had
each cemented a few pillars into their education; and as those pillars were
honed and polished by experience, they structured their future learning.
Among the pillars in Dorothy's education was socialism without hierarchy, which in her case was anarchy. The movement she later founded
remained a loose affiliation of small, democratic, direct-action agencies
with no status differences between those who ran them and those for
whom they were run. A second of Dorothy's pillars was journalism,
which she had been practicing since childhood, which sustained her and
provided her with a means of communicating her message. The third
pillar was Catholicism, which connected her to God, to that Church's
world body, and which gave her models, such as the lives of St. Francis
and St. Therese (1994), to emulate. Years of study and experience had
gone into each pillar, and by Dorothy's late 20s, she was ready to translate what she knew into action.

There was a final period of journeying about. On the basis of her
novel, she was invited to write for movies and moved with her daughter
to California. Finding the role of studio writer unsatisfying, she lived in
Mexico for a time, then returned to New York to live with her sister's
family. She stayed again on the lower East Side, close to a favored church
and sympathetic priests. Centering her life on her daughter and on free-
lance writing for mostly Catholic publications, she established a reputation
as a principled person. But she needed some spark and it showed up at
her apartment in December 1932 in the form of a "stocky, shabbily-
dressed, elderly man with a knobby, granite-like face" (MacDonald, 1957,
p. 44). His name was "Peter Maurin, the French peasant whose spirit and
ideas (would) dominate the rest . . . of my life" (Day, 1952, p. 189).

"A red-headed Irish Communist in Union Square told me to see
you. He says we think alike," Peter told her, and more formally, he presented a letter of introduction from a mutual friend (Day, 1952, p. 190).
Maurin was an aging French intellectual, eccentric "preaching a purified,
lay, Catholic mission modeled on the example of St. Francis of Assisi"
(C. R. Morris, 1997, p. 143). He was an anarchist, autodidact, and labor

agitator who for 25 years had been wandering around North America working at lumber camps, construction projects, and farms. When out of work, he saw no shame in begging, and when he met Day, he was living just as he pleased, in a 40-cents-a-night Bowery hotel, and passing on his message on street corners and in Union Square.

Peter hated the wage system that made people compete with one another and wanted a world "in which all men would be able to fulfill themselves in the arts . . . to produce what was needed in the way of homes, food, clothing, so that there was enough of these necessities for everyone" (Day, 1952, p. 195). He was not interested in fixing society. He wanted a new society, but unlike Communists, he wanted a society of self, not state, responsibility. He lived what he preached and he embodied Dorothy's ideals: equality, anarchy, poverty, pacifism, community, and Catholicism. And by encouragement and example, he showed her how to put her ideals into action. As she said, Peter "gave clarity and purpose to my life" (C. R. Morris, 1997, p. 143).

Totally unaffected, Peter was often unaware. Once, asked by a prostitute if he wanted to "have a good time," he invited the lady into his hotel room and asked her, "Now what would you say a good time means? Exactly. Let's discuss it" (MacDonald, 1957, p. 54). He was also widely read and a serious student of ideas. He rejected the two major contemporary positions: "The first is liberalism which holds no idealistic promise of history but uses the pragmatic method of keeping the process going . . . The second is Marxism which uses the idea of evolutionary struggle and the inevitable completion of progress in the attainment of an earthly paradise" (W. D. Miller, 1982, p. 240). Like Day and her favorite author, Dostoevsky, Peter distrusted the reason and science that underlay both positions, and he saw both as resulting in specialized societies where status is differentiated, power is accumulated by a few who invariably abuse it, and personal and communitarian ideals are marginalized. He envisioned a society in which people find sustenance, family, and salvation in small, direct-action, modest, and self-sustaining communities. He fancied himself a troubadour of God, found his students in parks and street corners, and preached his combination of anarchy and spirituality inside stylized messages that he called "easy essays."

> The world would be better off
> If people tried to become better
> And people would become better
> if they stopped trying to be better off.
> When everyone tries to become better off
>   nobody is better off. (Day, 1963, p. 26)

Dorothy found Peter "the believable teacher" (W. D. Miller, 1982, p. 243). He "made you feel a sense of his mission as soon as you met him . . . [he] made you feel you and all men had great and generous hearts with which to love God" (Day, 1952, p. 195). He was "as good as bread" (Day, 1963, p. 9), and he gave her the encouragement she needed to initiate the Catholic Worker movement.

It was a timely undertaking. Day and Maurin found each other at the beginning of the 1930s Depression, described briefly in the chapters on Eleanor Roosevelt and Robert Oppenheimer. At the time and in lower Manhattan, the docks were empty, the factories idle: "Bedraggled bread-lines of listless men wound along city streets. On the fringes by the rivers was . . . a collection of jerry-built shanties where the homeless huddled in front of their fires" (Day, 1963, p. 4). There was no welfare, Social Security, or Aid to Dependent Children. With the poor visible and everywhere, there was a lot to do, for Dorothy, Peter, and a host of people, most young, imbued with faith, energy, and with few prospects for gainful employment. Dorothy Day had found Peter Maurin, idealistic men and women found Dorothy Day, and that was the beginning of the Catholic Workers.

Like Lenin, Peter believed that there could be no revolution without a theory of revolution, "Men must think before they act. They must study" (Day, 1963, p. 7), and a newspaper would help to bring about clarification of thought. To Dorothy's question, "Where will we get the money?" Peter replied, "God sends you what you need when you need it" (Day, 1952, p. 197). And maybe God did, for with a few dollars and a borrowed printer, on May 1, 1933, Dorothy and her friends brought out a newspaper, *The Catholic Worker*. The paper was "for the unemployed . . . sitting on park benches . . . huddling in shelters trying to escape the rain . . . walking the streets in the all but futile search for work . . . who think there is no hope" (Day, 2004, p. 1). Dorothy and two friends sold copies for one penny each in New York's Union Square, then a gathering place for the poor and radical. The first edition contained articles about the War Department exploiting Negro labor, women and children working long hours, badly treated migrants, strikes, evictions, and unemployment. The initial press run was 2,500; by 1935, it was 100,000; and by 1940 up to 200,000. At this writing, the press run is 100,000, and it is still sold for one cent a copy.

Peter also wanted houses of hospitality, partly to practice charity, partly to serve as schools where people would study and learn. The houses would be communal, open to all, and run according to Christian principles. The effort began when Peter would bring people to Dorothy and tell her, "They have no place to sleep." Dorothy and her friends were already feeding the poor; it was a short step to sheltering them. Initially, she took them into her own and her brother's lodgings, and when numbers increased, Dorothy found additional rooms and apartments, took over abandoned buildings, and begged or cajoled lodging and support. Modeled after the I.W.W. houses where a worker could find a bed, some stew, and coffee, at Catholic Worker houses there was food, shelter, prayer for those who wished, and a place at Peter's round table where he conducted his worker schools.

As an example of the residents in the early years, at one house, there was a girl just out of prison, another who had been sent by her parents to prostitute herself, a 17-year-old runaway, a college student, an older man who came to die, and a boy with a deformed back. "Some came with their suitcases, intending to stay with us a year, and . . . lingered only for the night. Others came for a weekend and stayed for years" (Day, 1963, p. 35). Day later reflected on the spontaneity with which the charity had begun. "We were sitting there talking when lines of people began to form saying, 'We need bread.' We could not say, 'Go thou be filled.' If there were six small loaves and a few fishes, we had to divide them" (Day, 1952, p. 317). Free meals are to be had at this writing in the 150 Catholic Worker houses all over the world, as well at the two that continue on First and Third streets in lower Manhattan.

The newspaper and the houses gave physical life to Dorothy's ideal of "voluntary poverty, stripping oneself, denying oneself . . . [and practicing] non-participation in those comforts and luxuries which have been manufactured by the exploitation of others" (Day, 2003, p. 1). Catholic Workers have no hierarchy and no bureaucratic specialists who translate intentions into action; they practice direct transfer of charity from one to another. As Day advised: "share with your brothers . . . share with them their sufferings too" (Day, 1952, p. 242).

By her mid-30s, Dorothy was running a newspaper, a series of charitable houses, and a movement where young people came to learn the principles she lived by. And she had found the friendship of her bohemian youth, but without the nihilism and immorality. She had her "community of the poor, who enjoyed being together who felt they had embarked on a great enterprise, who had a mission" (Day, 1983, p. 274). Into the Catholic Worker, she combined "knowledge of the life of poverty she had read about and the life of religious faith as well" (Elie, 2003, p. 438). And she found herself "the joyful mother of children" and so solved the problem of what she called her "long loneliness" (Day, 1983, p. 317).

Peter also wanted to start farming communities or, as he called them, "agronomic universities." Worker farms, modeled after France's peasant communes, would embody democratic ideals and become the foundation of a Christian world order. The enterprise began with characteristically little planning. "We were just sitting there when Peter Maurin came in. We were just sitting there talking and someone said, 'Let's all go live on a farm.' . . . It just came about, it just happened" (Day, 1952, p. 317). And with a little money, the Workers bought a house with an acre of land outside the city where they lived and tried their hand at growing their food. Later they acquired a real farm where they exercised communal and prayerful lives, grew what food they could, opened their doors to whoever came by, and provided—for visitors—some respite from urban life. Over the years, there were more farms, where the Workers and residents lived "in the spirit of Peter Maurin's gentle personalism . . . where we can care for each other more directly" (Cornell, 2003, p. 3), and where the Workers practiced "communal living, charity, humility, pacifism . . . [and] a radical anger at the exploitation of the poor and a joyful embrace of poverty" (C. R. Morris, 1997, p. 143).

Dorothy Day and her Workers were pacifists, but they were also militant, living apart from but in a constant battle with what they considered an invasive state, war-preparing industries, and consumerism. As she explained, "This world is God's world and we have no right to consign it to the devil. We should be fighting like mad against the perverse will of men, and the fight is for the love of God and for the love of men" (Day, 1996, p. 3). In the 1930s, Day and the Workers opposed the Spanish Civil War in general, but, of the two sides, they considered the socialists to be more righteous. In the 1940s, the Workers preached pacifism, refused military service, and opposed paying taxes for war-related efforts or even working in defense industries. Several earned prison terms as a result. In the 1950s, when the government was removing Robert Oppenheimer's security clearance, Dorothy and several co-Workers went to jail for refusing to take part in a practice air raid. "We wanted to act against war and getting ready for war, nerve gas, germ warfare, guided missiles, testing and stockpiling of nuclear bombs, conscription, income tax, against the entire militarism of the state" (Day, 1963, p. 169).

In the 1960s, the first man to burn his draft card in protest against the Vietnam War was a Catholic Worker. And Catholic Worker Michael Harrington (1963) authored *The Other America*, a book that stimulated President John Kennedy's interest in poverty. Other Workers, along with Dorothy, were marching in the South with Martin Luther King Jr. and later in California with Cesar Chavez and his farm workers. For that latter activity, she (and others) were arrested. So Day was in prison again and making her points, "one brick at a time, one step at a time . . . one action in the present moment" (Day, 1963, p. 142). For "truth, justice, life, and peace . . . we make our choice, that personal responsibility which we exercise is what matters" (p. 169). And with her characteristic combination of detachment and involvement, she used this last incarceration to further educate herself. "I learned something as I sat in courts, overheated and stifling and saw the crowded dockets, the masses of documents relating to a million minor offences. I saw that the system is all too big, too ponderous, too unwieldy" (Day, 1963, p. 184). Released from jail, she commented that "the whole experience was good for my soul . . . [because in its absence] I realized again how much good ordinary kindness can do" (Day, 1963, p. 172).

In the 1970s, when her houses were visited by young people who used drugs and talked of free love, she found it troubling, and she disliked their talk of sex. No doubt they found Day an anachronism —in her own words, "an ancient old fogey"—and uncharacteristically, she threw some of them out. But as she said, "I know the bitter aftermath of sin. I knew what a disordered life was" (W. D. Miller, 1982, p. 197). "I know too much of sin from personal experience to feel romantically inclined to talk about it" (p. 467).

Along with the state, she sometimes came into conflict with the Church. In the 1930s, she took the side of the men who dug graves in Catholic cemeteries and who were striking for a wage increase. Also in the 1930s, her advocacy of the socialist side of the Spanish Civil War earned her a rebuke from the Church that supported General Franco. In the 1940s, she castigated the Church's militarism: "What confusion have we gotten into when Christian prelates sprinkle holy water on scrap metal to be used for obliteration bombing and name bombers for the Holy Innocents, for Our Lady of Mercy" (W. D. Miller, 1982, p. 437). In the 1950s, she was accused by many Catholics of Communism, but she found that ideology "impossible for a reasonable person to believe" (Day, 1938/1978, p. 150).

However much they sometimes irritated each other, she and the Church authorities—even New York's Cardinal Spellman—treated one another with respect. And although committed to poverty, direct action, and principled anarchy, Dorothy never wavered from her support of the Church. She had solved the conflict between faith and reason, and had— like Fyodor Dostoevsky and Peter Maurin—decided in favor of faith. On the few occasions when Church authorities gave her correcting advice, she heeded it. In turn, the hierarchy respected her devoutness, emulation of Saints Francis and Therese, and the actions that earned her the acclaim of the pope, as well as Catholic intellectuals such as Jacques Maritain,

Hilaire Belloc, and Thomas Merton. She died at the Worker's Mary-house on Manhattan's Third Street in 1980. New York's then-Cardinal, Terrance Cooke, sang the funeral mass.

CONCLUSION

Dorothy Day's education began with encouraging parents, serious books, writing, thinking about ethical and spiritual matters, and a desire to take part in the issues of the age. Dorothy disparaged her formal schooling, but she made the most of what institutions offered and used her university time to broaden her interests. And because we all need to see ideals in action in order to understand that they are possible, she found mentors—spiritual like St. Francis, temporal like Peter Maurin—who taught her how to put her ideals and her life together. She also used her youth to experiment with alternatives, some that she would later abjure, but those experiences too were an important part of her education. Saintliness is hard to achieve, but in the completeness of experience, Dorothy comes close. She combined her ascetic habits—modest living, meager food, scant quarters, and donated clothes—with an unabating dedication to social justice; and she took on the police, the Communists, the government, the military-industrial complex, and bourgeois respectability, the latter of which she most despised. Like Jane Addams and W. E. B. Du Bois, inwardly and outwardly, she became the person she wanted to be.

CHAPTER 9

Conclusion: Lives of Learning

Contrary to the view of education as an institutional undertaking, this book argues that education is a personal matter, an interior affair, something one does for oneself. Stepladdering its way through American history, the book begins in 1709 with the birth of Benjamin Franklin and ends in 1980 with the death of Dorothy Day, and it describes how a set of men and women created their educations, themselves, their lives, and the events for which they became famous. Even while describing education as more a private than an institutional undertaking, the stories show that the paths these subjects followed were more alike than they were different, and although personally constructed, those paths were not idiosyncratic. The intent of this final chapter is to identify the common elements of those educational paths, a task that provides an opening into the question as to how much of what they did is being done, or could be done, in today's educational institutions.

The common elements, those pillars upon which the subjects established their education, can be stated directly. To begin, each subject, independent of circumstances, read early, well, and widely. From Benjamin Franklin reading his minister's sermons, the Bible, and Plutarch's *Lives* to Abraham Lincoln reading Plutarch's *Lives*, his schoolbooks, and everything he could find, to Jane Addams reading—again—Plutarch's *Lives* and her father's library, to Dorothy Day reading novels, to W. E. B. Du Bois reading Macaulay's *History of England*, each subject—encouraged by elders—was from his or her early years reading good books.

The surprise is not that the subjects did it; the surprise is the ease with which they accessed books, independent of circumstances. Robert Oppenheimer was born into the most—and Lincoln the least—educationally auspicious environment, but in addition to his literate and supportive mother and stepmother, Lincoln, like Franklin before him, availed himself of a host of literate people anxious to share their learning and their books with interested youth. Using Bailyn's (1960) definition of *education* as "the entire process by which a culture transmits itself across generations" (p. 14), one can see that even in early and frontier America, there was an informal but active educational system.

So our subjects read, and within lives that were no less prosaic than our own—indeed, what could be more prosaic than Lincoln clearing brush or Eleanor Roosevelt living in Grandmother's austere house—they expanded their language, increased their stock of referential information, and awoke to the world of ideas. They read, they reflected, and they wrote, "personally [and] subjectively" as Dorothy Day put it (Day, 1938/1978, p. 34), and advanced their understanding of events and of themselves relative to events. They wrote in diaries, letters, commonplace books, school assignments, and some distinctive ways: in the case of Dorothy Day, a family newspaper; in the case of Benjamin Franklin, his own versions of journal articles; in the case of W. E. B. Du Bois, a valedictory speech on the life of Wendell Phillips; in the case of J. Robert Oppenheimer, a learned disquisition at New York's Museum of Natural History; and in the case of Abraham Lincoln, practicing letters by firelight, reading his essays to his stepmother, and putting his elders' "dark sayings" into words that "any boy I knew [could] comprehend" (Luthin, 1960, p. 11). Each understood that words connect to ideas and ideas connect to events, and each wanted to take part in the events of the time. So they came to understand, early on, the power of intelligence and the power of intelligent expression.

Attending their eagerness to learn was an element of seriousness. In their lifetimes, adolescence and life-saving drugs had not been invented, children went to work early, death was a frequent visitor, and none of the subjects had much in the way of childhood. Franklin and Lincoln worked from their early years; Roosevelt was orphaned and passed around; Day raised her baby brother, before going off to college at 16 and professional work at 18. Addams as a child became acquainted with death, heroism, and fate's random injustice; and young Du Bois helped support himself and his mother. Life was serious, understanding life was serious, and the way to understand and even improve life was through learning. Among the things the subjects studied and reflected upon was their own behavior. They understood that important undertakings require cooperation, and cooperation requires socially appropriate behavior.

Assisting their self-study was an element of Judeo/Christian morality, which in the eighteenth through mid-twentieth centuries was in America's air, and the subjects breathed it from their earliest days. Franklin was born in still-Puritan Boston and moved to Quaker Philadelphia;

Addams's father was a member of the Quakers' more fundamental wing, while her stepmother was an evangelical Christian. The Lincolns and Roosevelts were descended from New England Puritans whose Congregational descendants set the tone in Du Bois's Great Barrington. Oppenheimer came from Jewish traditions that, like Puritanism, provide a sense of autonomy and purpose, and a vision of truth, beauty, and good. Those doctrines teach that although one cannot understand God, one can understand his works and words, and learning the works and words will make one better, not merely better off. Day came to morality from her early charitable inclinations, and she too believed that being better off, unanchored to any higher purpose, was at the least suspect, and more likely sinful. Ethical lessons were part of the subjects' interior lives. They understood that the goal was responsibility, not riches; none suffered from or even entertained notions of unenlightened self-interest. Doing the right thing was a social and utilitarian as well as a personal and moral duty. They took for granted that one's self and the world would be better if one did the right, the ethical and moral, thing.

Instrumental to their interest in language and ideas were the subjects' methods of knowing, which were channeled from the beginning into Western empiricism. They accepted without question that, as Berlin (1997) puts it, "the world can be described and explained by the use of rational methods . . . [and] if life is to be organized and not left to chaos . . . then it can be organized only in the light of such principles and laws" (p. 327). Franklin studying electricity; Lincoln, legislation; Du Bois, the lives of Philadelphia blacks; Addams, child labor; Roosevelt, political processes; Oppenheimer, nuclear physics; Day, radical politics: All pursued their work with rational and empirical—Western—methods. Each was aware of other ways of knowing. Jane Addams (1910/1998) sensed the world's "relentless and elemental forces" (p. 18); Lincoln dreamed of his impending death; Oppenheimer used Eastern mysticism to explain what physics could not; Eleanor Roosevelt found church attendance comforting; and Dorothy Day was drawn to the mystical writings of Catherine of Siena. Franklin expressed a loose form of deism, and Du Bois admired the work of black churches. But when faced with the world and with the necessity of getting things done, and with the sometimes exception of Day who prayed to St. Joseph when the bills came due, there was no talk of deism, dreams, literal or loose interpretation of scripture, or mysticism. There were observations to be made, aggregated, and organized; there were resulting inferences and rational conclusions, all tempered by reflection and self-criticism. For all, including Day, the world was an empirical and knowable place and one was ethically obligated to know it and to improve it through the knowing.

In addition to their early immersion in language, ideas, worlds beyond their own, and Western ways of knowing, the subjects took intu-
itively to formal instruction. With the exception of anarchist Dorothy
Day who belittled institutional forms of anything, and despite the fact
that the book's subjects were inveterate autodidacts, each respected and
benefited from institutional schooling. Oppenheimer and Du Bois were
teachers; Franklin, Roosevelt, and Addams started schools. By her own
account, Day did little at university, but her high school record earned
her a scholarship. And both his teacher and his fellow students spoke of
Lincoln's dedication to his schoolbooks.

These subjects understood that schooling was an unmitigated good
and that the instructional situation was designed for their benefit, that
they were the net gainers in the classroom exchange. They never criticized or looked behind the lessons into the teachers' foibles or the
schools' shortcomings. Schooling was a personal and personally enrich-
ing experience, and each found one or more teachers to admire. Roosevelt had Mlle. Souvestre, and Day her Latin teacher; Franklin found his
writing instructor a "skillful master," and Du Bois so impressed his principal that the man arranged his college financing. In addition to embrac-
ing instruction and personally connecting to one or more teachers, the
subjects exhibited just those qualities that schools try to teach: logic,
analytical skill, respect for facts, and carefulness of expression. In turn,
the subjects received their schools' and their teachers' best efforts.

As well as learning from instructors, the subjects sought out like-
minded friends and colleagues with whom they shared knowledge and
ideas (without such sharing, autodidacticism can deteriorate into quack-
ery). Franklin had his Junto Club, and Lincoln his debate society or
whomever he could find. Maybe cousin John Hanks understood everything that young Abraham was telling him; maybe he did not. But that
he listened while Abraham put the ideas into words was important to
Abraham, as was the attention of his scientific colleagues to Oppenheimer. Addams was a debater and Day had her socialist friends. Du Bois
wore the race issue everywhere he went, Oppenheimer's associates were
scientists like himself, and Roosevelt carried on her work with a host of
like-minded and forward-thinking women. Serious learning was not limited to institutions; it permeated all levels of our subjects' associations.

During their 20s, each was presented with the necessity of finding
work that would satisfy larger ideals and private ambitions. For some,
the transition to adulthood was fairly smooth. Even as a young man,
Franklin had his print shop and involved himself in a widening range of
communal activities. Oppenheimer discovered physics as a sophomore at
Harvard, and Du Bois, a life of letters in his first year at Fisk. But Jane

Addams was stalled by restrictions on women, particularly the role of the family's unmarried female member, and Eleanor Roosevelt had to marry, bear children, and be the political helpmate her ambitious husband needed. Lincoln had to do his soldiering, flat-boating, storekeeping, and surveying before he found law and politics, and Dorothy Day had to live out her radical and bohemian youth. For all, their 20s was a time of continued study, sorting themselves out, and leaving off earlier limits and former friends who were perhaps more willing to accept the world as presented. But our subjects did not accept the world as presented, nor did they imagine that things must always be the way they are now. They did not allow the past to lock them in or the present to limit their horizons. They wanted to create better selves and a better world, and they used their 20s to find out how to go about doing it.

So they found mentors who escorted them into work. Arnold Toynbee presented Jane Addams with a way to combine her religious and charitable inclinations. Louis Howe discovered Eleanor Roosevelt and presented politics to her and her to politics. Benjamin Franklin not only found wise elders on the lookout for promising youth, he corresponded regularly with European scientists. Several learned elders found Abraham Lincoln and encouraged him to take up law, then politics. Alexander Crummell presented W. E. B. Du Bois with the idea of a "talented tenth," and the latter took that notion into who he would be and how he would pursue his work. Robert Oppenheimer found Cavendish and Bohr exploring atoms, and at the end of her 20s, Dorothy Day found Peter Maurin who taught her how to combine anarchy, religion, and activism. In their early adulthood, our subjects remained open to learning, expanded their knowledge, and found encouragement from experienced elders.

And like Ishmael for whom "a whaling ship was my Yale College and my Harvard" (Melville, 1851/1996, p. 118), the subjects continued their education in work where they actualized earlier ideals. The veil between him and the white world became a life career for Du Bois. Lincoln's modest beginnings, common touch, and interest in ideas became focused on local and state politics, then onto the great issues of the time. Addams carried her childhood concerns for salvation and her Quaker morality into running a settlement house and from there into early Progressivism. Roosevelt's early ethics and charitable leanings gave her a sense of social justice, and her domineering mother-in-law and self-indulging husband impelled her into democratic politics, which she learned from the bottom up. Day applied her anarchy and spirituality to the events and issues of the age. Lincoln may have given up general reading, but he was an avid student of politics and, during the war, of military tactics. Franklin gave up business and spent his time studying science and nation building; Oppenheimer did nuclear physics 16 hours a day; and Du Bois centered his scholarship on the evolving nature of inequality. Onto their work, these subjects focused their earlier and transcendental ideals, tempered their autodidacticism with experience and, as Henry Adams (1918) advised, "allowed the forces of the age to educate" (p. 416).

And the forces did. So Franklin went from English loyalist to American revolutionary, and Lincoln from the Wilmot Proviso to the Emancipation Proclamation. Moving with the forces of her age, Addams went from washing babies to leading an international peace movement, and Day from youthful journalist to radical organizer and founder of a newspaper and a social movement. It took many years and openness to the forces of the age for Roosevelt to go from bored debutante to chairing the United Nations Human Rights Charter, and almost as many for Oppenheimer to move from physics student to father of the atomic bomb. For Du Bois, it was a long journey from teacher of Greek at Wilberforce to leader of the Niagara Movement and advocate-propagandist for the NAACP. Joining themselves with the forces of their age, participating fully in the attendant conflicts and strife, the subjects found practical outlets for earlier ideals. In work, they continued their habits of study, reflection, intellectual openness, willingness to learn from others, discussion, and critique.

Further, as each identified with a large endeavor and became a respected member of multiple associations, so each was called on to articulate overlapping and common efforts. Because Robert Oppenheimer could make sense of diverse ideas about nuclear fission, he was chosen to lead Los Alamos. Because Benjamin Franklin was identified with Pennsylvania's communal and military efforts, he was selected to take the colony's concerns to Parliament, and in time he became America's spokesman to England, later France. Abraham Lincoln's status as a moderate, contributing, and loyal party man lead to his assignment to debate Stephen Douglas, and from there he orated his way into the presidency. In addition to being a respected teacher and researcher, W. E. B. Du Bois was an active participant in the larger movement for racial equality, so he was asked to edit the NAACP's *Crisis* and became equality's national spokesman. Jane Addams's work with overlapping social causes led to her recognition as a leader of American Progressivism; and that most articulate anarchist, Dorothy Day, was and remains the quintessential Catholic Worker. As our subjects submersed themselves in large endeavors and worked across associations and with those similarly inclined, they were recognized for their commitment, mastery of ideas, and ability to articulate, and so were selected to represent, then lead, those endeavors.

There is also among our subjects evidence of strong—self-reflective, balanced, critical—interior lives that steadied them in the face of adversity. In 1862, after the battle of Antietam, Lincoln was the most vilified man in America. Early in World War I, Theodore Roosevelt, whose nomination for president she had seconded, publicly ridiculed Jane Addams's pacifism and referred to her as "poor bleeding Jane" and "Bull Mouse" (Elshtain, 2002, p. 232). W. E. B. Du Bois, born and living on the other side of the veil, was cursed by whites even as he followed his son's funeral carriage. He was arrested and handcuffed at 79 years old, denied a passport, and later hounded out of his country. Robert Oppenheimer, after giving the country the weapon it asked for, was denied a security clearance and for the rest of his life was regularly spied upon by the government. And Dorothy Day, perhaps referring to an early abortion that did not, as she had hoped, help her keep the man she loved, said she "knew the bitter aftermath of sin." Each of the subjects suffered personal and professional setbacks, depression, remorse, feckless or too-soon departing children, unhappy or unfaithful lovers or spouses, and public opprobrium. And so we see that education does not protect from life's vicissitudes, but it enabled our subjects to not be overwhelmed by fate and to stay focused and moving in a thought-out and discernible direction.

For our subjects, then, education began with their early encouragement, early reading and writing, and early interest in, and personal identification with, ethical and moral issues and with large events and transcendental ideals. From there, and almost simultaneously, each inferred the power of intelligence and the power of intelligent expression. Later, there was schooling, a little or a lot, and more important, extrainstitutional and informal associations wherein knowledge about events and ideas were expressed and exchanged. In their 20s, there were times of casting off earlier restrictions, and finding teachers and mentors who guided them into work where they applied the ideas to practice and focused their learning on larger issues with those similarly engaged. In time, the latter, recognizing the subjects' commitment and abilities, selected them to articulate the endeavor to larger publics, so they assumed positions of leadership. And the sum of it all, from the early awareness of language and learning to their final positions of eminence, was their education.

The argument that education, at least for these seven Americans, is a personal undertaking has been made as well as I can make it. Although education has become in the public mind identified with institutions of schooling, for these seven at least, there was little about it that was institutional. Rather, it flowed from a self-created and overlapping set of formal and informal, sometimes institutional but more often ad hoc, public and private associations. As our subjects show us, education depends on being open to learning, open to participating fully, and open to creating the person one becomes.

As an afterthought, one would hope that in a democratic society that has institutionalized and made compulsory some of the model's elements, quality education of the type attained by the subjects would be available to all. And I would argue that to a considerable degree, it is. Despite the unfortunate tendency to label so many schools as "failing," based on their students' averaged test scores, both our society and its schools are information rich, and in them students can find encouraging and interested teachers, and find as well reading, writing, books and ideas, arts and sciences, libraries and the Internet, like-minded companions, and associations where ideas can be explored and careers planned. Admittedly, inequalities of circumstance make it more difficult for some students to chisel out an education, and positive elements may be more accessible in schools with a greater percentage of students who are acclimated to education. But all schools have teachers who watch for and nurture interested youth, and the current practice of judging schools on students' averaged scores can obscure the good things that go on in reputedly failing schools. As Harold Stevenson and his colleagues (Stevenson & Lee, 1990) demonstrated in their studies of high-achieving and later-successful children of poor Asian immigrants, possibilities for serious learning exist in all schools. As for educational disadvantages, one can go on and on about them, but this book's subjects, from Franklin to Oppenheimer, Jane Addams to Dorothy Day, teach us that for the individual who desires an education, the point is not to.

However, it is the nature of institutions to accumulate expectations, and since the late 1960s, the expectation is that schools are more responsible for education than the individual. It is not enough for schools to offer equality of opportunity; they are expected to assure something resembling equality of outcomes. So having presented a model of education predicated on the lives of seven individuals, one may ask, is it reasonable to expect institutionalized schools to take responsibility for a similar and quality education for all?

The answer—based only upon the lives of these seven—is "no, it is not reasonable." Schools were only one of several of our subjects' overlapping educational associations. Their families encouraged their reading, writing, and their penchant for serious study; their religion introduced them to transcendental ideals; their associates assisted with discussions and critiques; and their work stimulated further learning. Schools open some of the possibilities of an education to all, but by themselves, they are only bureaucratic institutions. Even free, universal, comprehensive, and filled with requirements, electives, events, and activities, they offer only part of an education; and their diplomas and degrees offer only a bureaucratic illusion of completeness. However structured—or endlessly restructured—schools offer only a beginning, an outline, some basic information, friendly encouragement, and the hope of continued learning.

The educational elements demonstrated by this book's subjects— intellectual curiosity and the accompanying autodidacticism, ethical striving, identification with and involvement in larger issues—may be encouraged in schools, but they are the responsibility of the individual. It is not in school but in life where the knowledge one learns in youth is turned into action, and knowledge and action combine into the person one is. Our seven subjects show us that education requires a choice of learning as a way of living, and requires as well what Ortega y Gasset (1932/1960) calls "a life of effort, ever set on excelling oneself" (p. 65).

References

Adams, H. (1918). *The education of Henry Adams.* Oxford: Oxford University Press.

Addams, J. (1902). *Democracy and social ethics.* New York: Macmillan.

Addams, J. (1998). *Twenty years at Hull House.* New York: Penguin. (Original work published 1910)

Adler, F. (1892). *The moral instruction of children.* New York: Appleton.

Adler, F. (1927). *An ethical philosophy of life presented in its main outlines.* New York: Appleton.

Anderson, D. D. (1970). *Abraham Lincoln.* New York: Twayne.

Anderson, F. (2000). *Crucible of war: The Seven Years War and the fate of empire in British North America, 1754–1766.* New York: Knopf.

Arendt, H. (2000). *The portable Hannah Arendt* (P. Baehr, Ed.). New York: Penguin.

Bailey, G. (1988). *Galileo's children: Science, Sakharov, and the power of the state.* New York: Little Brown.

Bailyn, B. (1960). *Education and the forming of American society: Needs and opportunities for study.* New York: Vintage.

Banfield, E. C. (1970). *The unheavenly city: The nature and future of our urban crisis.* Boston: Little Brown.

Bentham, J. (1879). *An introduction to the principles of morals and legislation.* Oxford: Clarendon Press.

Berger, M. (2002, January 14). Obituary of Cyrus Vance. *New York Times,* p. A20.

Berlin, I. (1997). *The proper study of mankind: An anthology of essays* (H. Hardy & R. Hausheer, Eds.). London: Chatto and Windus.

Bernstein, B. (1982, March 18). Personal history: Family matters. *The New Yorker,* pp. 53–112.

Bhagavad Gita. (1979). Berkeley: University of California Press.

Bloom, H. (1994). *The western canon: The books and school of the ages.* New York: Harcourt Brace.

Brands, H. W. (2000). *The first American: The life and times of Benjamin Franklin.* New York: Doubleday.

Brookhiser, R. (2000). *Alexander Hamilton, American.* New York: Simon and Schuster.

Brown, V. (1999). Advocate for democracy: Jane Addams and the Pulllman Strike. In R. Schneirov, S. Stromquist, & N. Salvatore (Eds.), *The Pullman*

Strike and the crisis of the 1890s (pp. 130–158). Urbana: University of Illinois Press.

Bunyan, J. (1932). *The pilgrim's progress.* London: Oxford University Press. (Original work published 1678)

Canetti, E. (1999). *The memoirs of Elias Canetti.* New York: Farrar, Straus and Giroux.

Carlyle, T. (1984). *A Carlyle reader: Selections from the writings of Thomas Carlyle* (G. B. Tennyson, Ed.). Cambridge, England: Cambridge University Press.

Clark, R. W. (1971). *Einstein: The life and times.* New York: World Publishing.

Cohen, I. B. (1990). *Benjamin Franklin's science.* Cambridge, MA: Harvard University Press.

Cook, B. W. (1992). *Eleanor Roosevelt: 1884–1933* (Vol. 1). New York: Viking Penguin.

Copley, F. B. (1923). *Frederick W. Taylor: Father of scientific management.* London: Harper and Brothers.

Cornell, T. C. (2003, May). Peter Maurin's farm. *The Catholic Worker,* p. 3.

Darnton, R. (2000, December 21). Extraordinary commonplaces: The politics of reading in early modern England. *New York Review of Books,* p. 82.

Davis, N. P. (1968). *Lawrence and Oppenheimer.* New York: Simon and Schuster.

Day, D. (1952). *The long loneliness: The autobiography of Dorothy Day.* New York: Curtis Books.

Day, D. (1963). *Loaves and fishes.* New York: Harper and Row.

Day, D. (1978). *From Union Square to Rome.* New York: Arno Press. (Original work published in 1938)

Day, D. (1983). *By little and by little: The selected writings of Dorothy Day* (R. Ellsberg, Ed.). New York: Knopf.

Day, D. (1996, October-November). November is the month of the dead. *The Catholic Worker,* p. 3

Day, D. (2003, May). Editorial. *The Catholic Worker,* p. 1.

Day, D. (2004, May). To our readers. *The Catholic Worker,* p. 1.

de Tocqueville, A. (1946). *Democracy in America.* London: Oxford University Press.

Dewey, J. (1891). *Psychology* (3rd ed.). New York: American Book Company.

Diggins, J. P. (1973). *The American left in the twentieth century.* New York: Harcourt Brace Jovanovich.

Diliberto, G. (1999). *A useful woman: The early life of Jane Addams.* New York: Scribner.

Du Bois, W. E. B. (1961). *The souls of black folk: Essays and sketches.* Greenwich, CT: Fawcett. (Original work published 1903)

Du Bois, W. E. B. (1967). *The Philadelphia Negro: A social study.* New York: Schocken Books. (Original work published 1899)

Du Bois, W. E. B. (1968a). *The autobiography of W. E. B. Du Bois: A soliloquy on viewing my life from the last decade of its first century.* New York: International Publishers.

Du Bois, W. E. B. (1968b). *Dusk of dawn: An essay toward an autobiography of a race concept.* New York: Schocken Books. (Original work published 1940)

Du Bois, W. E. B. (1969). *Darkwater: Voices from within the veil.* New York: AMS Press. (Original work published 1920)

Du Bois, W. E. B. (1971). *The seventh son: The thought and writings of W. E. B. Du Bois* (J. Lester, Ed.). New York: Random House.

Elie, P. (2003). *The life you save may be your own: An American pilgrimage.* New York: Farrar, Straus and Giroux.

Elliot, H. (1917). *Herbert Spencer.* New York: Henry Holt.

Elshtain, J. B. (2002). *Jane Addams and the dream of American democracy.* New York: Basic Books.

Emerson, R. W. (1965). *Selected prose and poetry.* New York: Holt, Rinehart and Winston.

Euclid. (1908). *The contents of the fifth and sixth books of Euclid (with a note on irrational numbers)* (M. J. M. Hill, Ed.). Cambridge, England: The University Press.

Everitt, A. (2003). *Cicero: The life and times of Rome's greatest politician.* New York: Random House.

Faderman, L. (1999). *To believe in women.* Boston: Houghton Mifflin.

Farrell, J. C. (1967). *Beloved lady: A history of Jane Addams' ideas on reform and peace.* Baltimore: Johns Hopkins Press.

Fichte, J. G. (1970). *Science of knowledge* (*Wissenschaftslehre*) (P. Heath & J. Lachs, Eds. & trans.). New York: Appleton-Century-Crofts.

Fifty years of the H-bomb. (2002, November 2–8). *The Economist,* p. 79.

Fogel, R. W. (2000). *The fourth great awakening and the future of egalitarianism.* Chicago: University of Chicago Press.

Foucault, M. (1994). *Critique and power: Recasting the Foucault/Habermas debate* (M. Kelly, Ed.). Cambridge, MA: MIT Press.

Franklin, B. (1904). *The works of Benjamin Franklin, including the private as well as the official and scientific correspondence together with the unmutilated and correct version of the autobiography* (J. Bigelow, Ed.). New York: Putnam's and Sons.

Franklin, B. (1958). *Autobiography and other writings* (R. B. Nye, Ed.). Boston: Houghton Mifflin. (Original work published 1793)

Freidel, F. (1952). *Franklin D. Roosevelt.* Boston: Little Brown.

Freud, S. (1935). *Autobiography* (J. Strachey, Trans.). New York: Norton.

Garland, H. (1899). *Main traveled roads.* New York: Harper.

Gladwell, M. (2002, December 2). Group think: What does "Saturday Night Live" have in common with German philosophy? *The New Yorker,* pp. 102–107.

Goodman, J. (2002, May 26). Peculiar institution: A Review of *At the hands of persons unknown* by Philip Dray. *New York Times Book Review,* p. 21.

Grant, U. S. (1885). *The personal memoirs of U. S. Grant.* New York: Webster.

Graves, R. (1957). *Good-bye to all that.* Garden City, NY: Doubleday.

A great yarn. (2003, December 20). *The Economist,* p. 73.

Greenberg, C. (1939). Avant-garde and kitsch. *Partisan Review, 6*(5), 34–49.

Greer, T. (1958). *What Roosevelt thought: The social and political ideas of Franklin D. Roosevelt.* East Lansing: Michigan State University Press.

Halberstam, D. (1993). *The fifties.* New York: Villard.

Hareven, T. K. (1968). *Eleanor Roosevelt: An American conscience.* Chicago: Quadrangle Books.

Harrington, M. (1963). *The other America: Poverty in the United States.* Baltimore: Penguin.

Heckscher, A. (1980). *St. Paul's: The life of a New England school.* New York: Scribner.

Hegel, G. W. F. (1974). Dialectic and human experience. In F. G. Weiss (Ed.), *Hegel: The essential writings* (pp. 37–79). New York: Harper and Row.

Heidegger, M. (1976). *Existence and being.* South Bend, IN: Gateway Editions. (Original work published in 1949)

Herndon, W. H., & Weik, J. W. (1930). *Herndon's life of Lincoln, the history and personal recollections of Abraham Lincoln as originally written by William H. Herndon and Jesse W. Weik.* Cleveland, OH: World Publishing Company. (Original work published in 1889)

Himmelfarb, G. (1991). *Poverty and compassion: The moral imagination of the late Victorians.* New York: Knopf.

Hodges, A. (1983). *Alan Turing: The enigma.* New York: Simon and Schuster.

Hoodbhoy, P. (1991). *Islam and science: Religious orthodoxy and the battle for rationality.* London: Zed Books.

Houser, M. L. (1957). *Lincoln's education and other essays.* New York: Bookman.

Howe, I. (1976). *World of our fathers.* New York: Harcourt, Brace, Jovanovich.

Johnson, O. (1968). *Stover at Yale.* New York: Collier Books.

Johnson, P. (1987). *A history of the Jews.* New York: Harper and Row.

Jorgenson, C. E., & Mott, F. L. (1962). *Benjamin Franklin: Representative selections, with introduction, bibliography, and notes.* New York: Hill and Wang.

Klingaman, W. K. (2001). *Abraham Lincoln and the road to emancipation, 1861–1865.* New York: Viking.

Kraut, B. (1979). *From Reform Judaism to ethical culture: The religious evolution of Felix Adler.* Cincinnati: Hebrew Union College Press.

Kropotkin, P. (1971). *Memoirs of a revolutionist.* New York: Dover. (Original work published in 1899)

Lao Tsu. (1972). *Tao Te Ching* (Gia-fu Feng & J. English, Trans.). New York: Vintage.

Lash, J. P. (1971). *Eleanor and Franklin: The story of their relationship, based on Eleanor Roosevelt's private papers.* New York: Norton.

Lash, J. P. (1984). *Life was meant to be lived: A centenary portrait of Eleanor Roosevelt.* New York: Norton.

Lawrence-Lightfoot, S. (1983). *The good high school: Portraits of character and culture.* New York: Basic Books.

Leo XIII. (2002). Rerum novarum: On capital and labor. In Catholic Church,

Pope (R. W. Rousseau, Ed.), *Human dignity and the common good: The great papal social encyclicals from Leo XIII to John Paul II* (pp. 9–54). Westport, CT: Greenwood Press.

Lewis, D. L. (1993). *W. E. B. Du Bois: Biography of a race* (Vol. 1). New York: Henry Holt.

Lewis, D. L. (2000). *W. E. B. Du Bois: The fight for equality and the American century, 1919–1963.* New York: Henry Holt.

Lincoln, A. (1940a). Autobiographical sketch written for use in preparing a campaign biography [1860]. In P. V. D. Stern (Ed.), *Life and writings of Abraham Lincoln* (pp. 599–608). New York: Modern Library.

Lincoln, A. (1940b). Second inaugural address [1865]. In P. V. D. Stern (Ed.), *Life and writings of Abraham Lincoln* (pp. 839–842). New York: Modern Library.

Lincoln, A. (1940c). Speech at New Haven, Connecticut [1860]. In P. V. D. Stern (Ed.), *Life and writings of Abraham Lincoln* (pp. 591–592). New York: Modern Library.

Lincoln, A. (1940d). Speech at Peoria, Illinois, in reply to Senator Douglas [1854]. In P. V. D. Stern (Ed.), *Life and writings of Abraham Lincoln* (pp. 338–385). New York: Modern Library.

Lincoln on-line: New treasures. (2002, February 16). *New York Times*, p. B9.

Locke, J. (1975). *An essay concerning human understanding* (P. H. Nidditch, Ed.). Oxford: Clarendon. (Original work published 1690)

London, J. (1931). *Martin Eden.* New York: Macmillan. (Original work published 1909)

Luthin, R. H. (1960). *The real Abraham Lincoln: One complete volume history of his life and times.* Englewood Cliffs, NJ: Prentice-Hall.

MacDonald, D. (1957, October 4). The foolish things of the world (Vol. 1). *The New Yorker*, pp. 37–56.

Martin, J. (2002). *The education of John Dewey: A biography.* New York: Columbia University Press.

Mather, C. (1808). *Essays to do good: Addressed to all Christians, whether in public or private capacities.* Boston: Lincoln and Edmands. (Original work published 1710)

McGuinness, B. (1988). *Wittgenstein: A life, young Ludwig, 1889–1921.* London: Duckworth.

McMaster, J. B. (1970). *Benjamin Franklin as a man of letters.* New York: Arno. (Original work published 1887)

Melville, H. (1996). *Moby Dick.* New York: Tom Doherty Associates. (Original work published 1851)

Menand, L. (2001). *The metaphysical club.* New York: Farrar, Straus and Giroux.

Menes, A. (1960). Patterns of Jewish scholarship in Eastern Europe. In L. Finkelstein (Ed.), *The Jews: Their history, culture, and religion* (Vol. 1, pp. 376–426). New York: Harper.

Michelmore, P. (1969). *The swift years: The Robert Oppenheimer story.* New York: Dodd, Mead.

Miller, P. (1953). *The New England mind: From colony to province.* Cambridge, MA: Harvard University Press.

Miller, W. D. (1982). *Dorothy Day: A biography.* New York: Harper and Row.

Moore, J. B. (1981). *W. E. B. Du Bois.* Boston: Twayne Publishers.

Morgan, T. (2003). *Reds: McCarthyism in twentieth century America.* New York: Random House.

Morris, C. R. (1997). *American Catholic: The saints and sinners who built America's most powerful church.* New York: Times Books.

Morris, E. (2002). *Theodore Rex.* New York: Modern Library.

Morse, J. T. (1917). *Benjamin Franklin.* New York: Houghton Mifflin.

Nagel, T. (2002, April 11). In the stream of consciousness. *New York Review of Books,* pp. 74–76.

Nicolay, J. G., & Hay, J. (1917). *Abraham Lincoln: A history.* New York: The Century Company.

Olmsted, F. L. (1861). *The cotton kingdom: A traveller's observations on cotton and slavery in the American slave states. Based upon three former volumes of journeys and investigations by the same author.* New York: Mason Brothers.

Oppenheimer, J. R. (1956). Introduction. In H. Cohen (Ed.), *Jews in the world of science* (pp. v–vi). New York: Monde.

Oppenheimer, J. R. (1989). *Atom and void: Essays on science and community.* Princeton, NJ: Princeton University Press.

Ortega y Gasset, J. (1960). *The revolt of the masses.* New York: Norton. (Original work published 1932)

Orwell, G. (1956). Such, such were the joys. In *The Orwell reader: Fiction, essays, and reportage* (pp. 419–456). New York: Harcourt Brace.

Pauen, M. (2004). Does free will arise freely? *Scientific American Mind, 14*(1), 41–47.

Piaget, J. (1929). *The child's conception of the world.* New York: Harcourt Brace.

Pius IX. (2002). Quadragersimo anno: On the reconstruction of the social order. In Catholic Church, Pope (R. W. Rousseau, Ed.), *Human dignity and the common good: The great papal social encyclicals from Leo XIII to John Paul II* (pp. 55–116). Westport, CT: Greenwood Press.

Plutarch. (1891). *Plutarch's lives, translated from the original Greek, with notes critical and historical, and a new life of Plutarch* (J. Langhorne & W. Langhorne, Eds. and Trans.). New York: Harper Brothers.

Popper, K. R. (1965). *Conjectures and refutations: The growth of scientific knowledge.* New York: Harper and Row.

Powers, T. (2002, December 1). Deciding Germany's fate: A review of *The conquerors: Roosevelt, Truman and the destruction of Hitler's Germany, 1941–1945,* by Michael Beschloss. *New York Times Book Review,* p. 11.

Powers, T. (2004, February 12). Spy fever. *New York Review of Books,* pp. 21–23.

Raban, J. (2002, February 4). My holy war. *The New Yorker,* pp. 29–36.

Raistrick, A. (1950). *Quakers in science and industry: Being an account of the Quaker contributions to science and industry during the seventeenth and eighteenth centuries.* New York: Philosophical Library.

Rankin, H. B. (1924). *Intimate character sketches of Abraham Lincoln.* London: Lippincott.

Ravitch, D. (2000). *Left back: A century of failed school reforms.* New York: Simon and Schuster.

Redding, S. (1918). The forethought. In W. E. B. Du Bois, *Souls of black folks* (pp. viii–xi). New York: Fawcett.

Rhodes, R. (1986). *The making of the atomic bomb.* New York: Simon and Schuster.

Roosevelt, E. (1937). *This is my story.* New York: Harper and Brothers.

Roosevelt, E. (1949). *This I remember.* New York: Harper.

Roosevelt, E. (1992). *The autobiography of Eleanor Roosevelt: My life.* New York: Da Capo. (Original work published 1961)

Roosevelt, S. D. (Mrs. J.). (1933). *My boy Franklin, as told by Mrs. James Roosevelt to Isabel Leighton and Gabrielle Forbush.* New York: R. Long and R. R. Smith.

Roth, G. (2004). The quest to find consciousness. *Scientific American Mind, 14*(1), 32–39.

Rouzé, M. (1964). *Robert Oppenheimer: The man and his theories* (P. Evans, Trans.). London: Souvenir Press.

Royal, D. (1969). *The J. Robert Oppenheimer story.* New York: St. Martin's Press.

Rudwick, E. M. (1969). *W. E. B. Du Bois: Propogandist of the Negro protest.* New York: Atheneum.

Scaturro, F. J. (2000). *The Supreme Court's retreat from reconstruction.* London: Greenwood Press.

Sheaffer, L. (1968). *O'Neill: Son and playwright.* Boston: Little Brown.

Sinclair, U. (1985). *The jungle.* New York: Penguin Books. (Original work published 1906)

Sizer, T. (1984). *Horace's compromise: The dilemma of the American high school.* New York: Houghton Mifflin.

Sloan, A. P. (1964). *My years at General Motors* (J. McDonald & C. Stevens, Eds.). Garden City, NY: Doubleday.

Stern, P. V. D. (Ed.). (1940). *Life and writings of Abraham Lincoln.* New York: Modern Library.

Stevenson, H. W., & Lee, S. Y. (1990). *Contexts of achievement: A study of American, Chinese, and Japanese children.* Chicago: University of Chicago Press.

Stowe, H. B. (1852). *Uncle Tom's cabin; or, Life among the lowly.* Boston: J. P. Jewett.

Strauss, L. (1978). *The city and man.* Chicago: University of Chicago Press. (Original work published 1964)

Strout, C. (Ed.). (1963). *Conscience, science, and security: The case of Dr. J. Robert Oppenheimer.* Chicago: Rand McNally.

Tarbell, I. M. (1900). *The life of Abraham Lincoln.* New York: Doubleday and McClure.

Therese de Lisieux. (1994). *The autobiography of Therese of Lisieux* (R. Blackstone, Ed.). London: Hodder and Stoughton.

Thomas, B. P. (1993). *Abraham Lincoln: A biography.* New York: Barnes and Noble. (Original work published 1952)

Tims, M. (1961). *Jane Addams of Hull House.* New York: Macmillan.

Tolstoy, L. N. (1899). (I. F. Hapgood, Trans.) *What is to be done? Life.* New York: Dumont.

Toynbee, A. (1920). *Lectures on the Industrial Revolution of the eighteenth century in England: Popular addresses, notes and other fragments.* New York: Longmans, Green. (Original work published 1884)

Uglow, J. (2002). *The lunar men: The friends who made the future.* New York: Farrar, Straus and Giroux.

Van Doren, C. (1938). *Benjamin Franklin.* New York: Viking Press.

Vidal, G. (1984). *Lincoln.* New York: Random House.

Washington, B. T. (1901). *Up from slavery.* New York: A. L. Burt Company.

Weber, M. (1946). The protestant sects and the spirit of capitalism. In H. Gerth & C. W. Mills (Eds.), *Max Weber* (pp. 302–322). New York: Oxford University Press.

Weiss, F. G. (Ed.). (1974). *Hegel: The essential writings.* New York: Harper and Row.

Welch, J. (2001). *Jack: Straight from the gut.* New York: Warner Books.

Wendell, B. (1882). *Cotton Mather: A biography.* New York: Barnes and Noble.

Wharton, E. (1920). *The age of innocence.* New York: Merideth Press.

Wharton, E. (1964). *The age of mirth.* New York: New American Library. (Original work published 1905)

Wharton, M. (1955). *A nation's security: The case of Dr. J. Robert Oppenheimer.* London: Secker and Warburg.

Wilson, S. M. (2003). *California dreaming: Reforming mathematics education.* New Haven, CT: Yale University Press.

Wilson, T. W., Jr. (1970). *The great weapons heresy.* Boston: Houghton Mifflin.

Woodward, C. V. (1974). *The strange career of Jim Crow.* New York: Oxford University Press. (Original work published 1957)

World Almanac Books. (2003). *The World Almanac and book of facts.* New York: Author.

Wright, E. (1986). *Franklin of Philadelphia.* Cambridge, MA: Belkap Press.

Yarrow, A. L. (2001, November 15). Nathan Pusey, Harvard president through growth and turmoil alike, dies at 94. *New York Times*, p. D11.

Index

About the Author

Philip A. Cusick is Professor and Chair in the Department of Educational Administration at Michigan State University. He is the author of *Inside High School: The Student's World* (Holt, Rinehart & Winston, 1973), *The Egalitarian Ideal and The American High School* (Longman, 1983), *The Educational System: Its Nature and Logic* (McGraw Hill, 1993) and co-author of *Selling Students Short* (Teachers College Press, 1987).